COMPACT HISTORY OF WELSH HEROES
THE REVOLT OF MADOG AP LLYWELYN

COMPACT HISTORY OF WELSH HEROES

the revolt of madog ap llywelyn

Craig Owen Jones

ISBN: 978-1-84524-075-2

Cover design: Sian Parri

First published in 2008
Llygad Gwalch, Ysgubor Plas, Llwyndyrys, Pwllheli, Gwynedd
Wales LL53 6NG.
Phone: 01758 750432
e-mail: gai@llygadgwalch.com
Website: www.llygadgwalch.com

CONTENTS

ACKNOWLEDGEMENTS

I would like to thank a number of people for helping me with my research, particularly the staff of Llyfrgell Genedlaethol Cymru, Aberystwyth; the library staff of Prifysgol Bangor; and Michael Prestwich. Hefyd, buaswn yn hoffi diolch i'r bobl ganlynol: Myrddin ap Dafydd am ei gefnogaeth; Ken Lloyd Gruffudd; Mr. Clive Jones; Mr. Glyn Jones; Mrs. Laura Richards; David Williams; a Kate Olson, a oedd yn ddigon caredig i gynnig nifer o sylwadau helpgar iawn.

Lastly, I would like to thank my family for their support, and my sister Sonia, to whom this book is dedicated.

Craig Owen Jones, August 2007

FOREWORD

Every account of the revolt that broke out on 30th September 1294 has related that it caught the English authorities in Wales completely off-guard; and indeed, there were a number of surprising elements to it. Unlike the localised revolts of 1287-8, 1314, or 1316, or the Shaldeford crisis of 1344-5, the 1294-5 rising was a national concern. The most Anglicised area of Wales, Glamorgan (Morgannwg), which hitherto had been notable for the steadfast refusal of its inhabitants to revolt against the English, supplied some of the revolt's most tenacious military acts, particularly the storming of several castles and the siege of Abergavenny. Furthermore, the revolt's leader, Madog ap Llywelyn, was a former adherent of the king of England, Edward I, who had, it seemed, maintained a low profile in the years after Edward's invasion – a most unlikely figurehead for the Welsh people.

Given the increasingly rude health of Welsh historiography today, it is perhaps surprising to note that a book has yet to be written about Madog ap Llywelyn, or more specifically, the revolt that he led; yet it merits further consideration. Madog's revolt attracted widespread support at all levels of Welsh society, lasted for almost a year, and was so serious that it caused Edward to postpone his plans for an expedition to Gascony in order to suppress it. In the ten years that had passed since the death of the last prince of independent Wales, Dafydd III ap Gruffudd, there had been no revolt of such scope and magnitude; for the remainder of the medieval era, only the revolt of Owain Glyndŵr in the 1400s would surpass it in terms of longevity and significance. In spite of this, Madog's name is known today only to Wales' historians. It is hoped that this book, which was written with a popular readership in mind, will address that omission, and that it will soon be supplanted by an academic study of Madog's life, and his revolt.

Craig Owen Jones, July 2007

A NOTE ON PERSONAL NAMES

The issue of how best to refer to Wales' princes created some peculiar problems. Previous historians, particularly those of the Victorian and Edwardian eras – writers such as John Rhys and David Brynmore-Jones – often adopted the ordinal system when referring to Welsh rulers. With the notable exceptions of T. Jones-Pierce and Glanville Jones, post-war historians have not employed this system.* Its usefulness in popular history texts has, however, been underestimated. Its chief advantage is that it allows the uninitiated reader to easily differentiate between the numbers of different Dafydds and Llywelyns who ruled in Wales from the late twelfth century onwards. It is therefore applied here. Some works in which the system is used accord Llywelyn ap Seisyll (r. 1018-23) the title of 'Llywelyn I', such as the Everyman *Dictionary of Dates* (sixth edition, 1971). This is exceptional, however, and the numbering adopted by Rhys and Brynmore-Jones is preferred. Below, the name given on the left is that given on the ruler's first appearance in the text; the one on the right is that by which he is referred thereafter.

Dafydd I ab Owain (d. 1203) = Dafydd I
Llywelyn I ab Iorwerth (d. 1240) = Llywelyn I
Dafydd II ap Llywelyn (d. 1246) = Dafydd II
Llywelyn II ap Gruffudd (d. 1282) = Llywelyn II
Dafydd III ap Gruffudd (d. 1283) = Dafydd III

* Interestingly, J. E. Lloyd used a version of it – with reference to Dafydd II – on at l one occasion during the inter-war years. See 'Ewloe', pp. 1-3 of *Y Cymmrodor* Vol. XXXIX (1928).

ERRATA

p. 19 line 24 – for '*concilium* regis' read *'concilium regis'*

p. 20 line 22 – for 'distain' read *'distain'*

p. 33 line 4 – for 'on the level ground to the eastern' read 'on the level ground to the east'

p. 78 note – read 'and R. R. Davies'

p. 83 line 4 for 'beforehand not' read 'beforehand or not'

p. 106 line 27 – for 'less that' read 'less than'

p. 129 line 3 – for 'England' read 'Ireland'

p. 131 note 18 – for 'Glydŵr' read Glyndŵr'

p. 146 footnote 16 – for 'Provicke' read 'Powicke'

p. 173 line 15 – for 'a common' read 'common'

p. 222 – for 'Llywelyn I' read 'Llywelyn II'

p. 227 – for 'denotes affair' read 'denotes birth out of wedlock'

1 – INTRODUCTION

> Item ante guerram Madoc ap Lywelyn, quondam Principis Wallie, dicti Burgenses habebant Molendina & Hanoteria Regis ad firmam, & alia officia que optabant, de quibus butiri, caseor', & carnium copiam habuerunt; mediantibus quibus, Castrum de Hardelege tempore dce guerre viriliter conservarunt, & sine quibus omnes tam Burgenses quam Castellani fame perire potuissent post dcam guerram, cum p'dca officia ad firmam habere nequiverunt, quamcumque p' eis vellens offerre ac prestare.[1]
>
> *Rotuli Parliamentorum, Tempore Edwardi R. I,* Vol. 1, p.276

R. R. Davies called the uprising of 1294-5 'a classic anti-colonial revolt',[2] and the most conclusive proof of this statement is the fact that its leader, Madog ap Llywelyn, accorded himself the title of prince of Wales. In the ten months between the onset of revolt and Madog's surrender, he behaved in many ways like the illustrious princes of Wales who were his ancestors and relatives. He is known to have issued grants of land, and one contemporary historian has spoken of the 'entourage' which he gathered around him during his few brief months of supremacy in Gwynedd. He is accorded the title of 'prince' or 'prince of Wales' in almost a dozen contemporary or near-contemporary English and French administrative records or chronicles.[3] Moreover, it is largely through the existence and make-up of this body of men that he can be shown to have begun, or at least to have contemplated, the process of re-assembling the constitutional bodies on which the governance of Wales had rested until Edward I's invasion put paid to Welsh independence in 1282-3.

The scope of Madog's vision was imprinted on the consciousness of the Welsh people for some time afterwards, as is demonstrated by a representation of the burgesses of Harlech to Edward II's Parliament in 1308, quoted above. In it, they note how they defended Harlech castle against Madog, who is described not as a rebel or a traitor, but as 'quondam Principis Wallie' – the 'sometime Prince of Wales'. It is difficult to fathom the significance of the note of qualification sounded here. Inclusion of the word 'quondam' may be an indication of an equivocal view of the revolt on the part of the burgesses, or the English administration to whom the petition was addressed, or both. After all, Madog's principate, like that of Dafydd III ap Gruffudd in 1282-3, was never recognised in English eyes, and sensitivity to that fact may have produced this guarded description of Madog's status. Be that as it may, the document clearly demonstrates that the position of Madog as prince during the revolt was understood both by Edward's men and the burgesses, however loathe they may have been to concede the point. The report provides crucial evidence that Madog's claim to princely status was not viewed in Wales in the early fourteenth century as a mere product of charlatanism.

In instigating the revolt, Madog was expressing his belief in the concept of an independent Wales. He therefore stood in sharp contrast to the last leader of a Welsh revolt, Rhys ap Maredudd, whose ill-conceived insurrection of 1287-8 seemed to have no broader political aim other than (perhaps) his own restoration as leader of a rejuvenated Deheubarth in the south-west, or to Llywelyn Bren, whose revolt of 1316 was largely confined to Morgannwg and Gwent. Unlike these men, Madog's policy was rooted in the ideology of Welsh politics before 1283; and to understand his revolt, it is necessary to look at the nature of that ideology in greater detail.

The concept of a Welsh princeship: its advent and development

Over seven hundred years have passed since the successful conclusion of Edward's invasion of Wales, and subsequent events have largely resulted in the exclusion of that year and those preceding it from the memory and consciousness of the Welsh public. In the three and a half centuries before Edward's invasion, there were long periods in which Wales enjoyed the status and fruits of independence. Its border with England alternately shifted east and west, as did the borders between the lands of the four main kingdoms of Gwynedd, Powys, Deheubarth and Morgannwg in times of disunity, and the extent to which Welsh rulers could exercise their powers free of English interference varied accordingly, but their will to rule was indisputable.

Some historians of the eighteenth and nineteenth centuries interpreted the internecine quarrels between the Welsh rulers as evidence that the Welsh never united, and that as a consequence, they never established governmental traditions of their own. It is true that several flukes of geography and history made the creation of a Welsh polity difficult:

> Wales was [small] and [poor], with a physical geography... inimical to centralised rule; it had been deeply penetrated by the Normans...; and its proximity to England made any

> concentration of hostile strength... likely to provoke retaliation by the Crown.[4]

However, the problems of internal organisation and external political pressures, though they complicated the tasks of Welsh kings and princes from the ninth century onwards, did not prohibit the growth of a Welsh polity. In fact, the leaders of the house of Gwynedd were persistent (if not always successful) nation-builders; and on several occasions, and in spite of a relative dearth of source material, it is possible to discern the functioning of Welsh royal government. In the thirteenth century in particular, that government, in its dealings with its neighbours, the people under its rule, and its concerns and intrigues, was comparable to that of any small nation in western Europe, though perhaps on a somewhat smaller scale.

By the beginning of that century, the Welsh model of royal government was based on the authority of the prince of Wales, who ruled directly over Gwynedd and indirectly over the rest of his lands. He also presided over his council, the Welsh version of the executive body of the kings of England which was to be the forerunner there of the English parliamentary tradition. This mode of royal government was largely developed during the reigns of the two Llywelyns (1194-1240; 1246-1282), but its roots went back to the reign of Owain Gwynedd (1137-70). If the stance that Madog was to adopt is to be accounted for, we must begin our examination of Welsh political ideology with the reign of Owain, ruler of Gwynedd and, in turn, prince of Wales.

It was only in the final years of his life that Owain came to exercise authority over parts of Wales beyond Gwynedd. For more than a century until the 1160s, Gwynedd, Deheubarth,

Powys, and the remaining semi-independent Welsh commotal lordships in Morgannwg had existed independently of one another, only forming temporary, regional alliances in order to repel Norman incursions into Wales. Such an alliance was to form the basis of Owain's power. In 1165, the English king Henry II led an army into northern Wales with the intention of conquering Gwynedd and bringing the region firmly under English rule. Owain conferred with the leaders of the other Welsh kingdoms, who agreed to unite to repel the incursion. In August, Henry decided to take his army into Wales through the Berwyn mountains; but after a few inconclusive skirmishes between isolated detachments in the Ceiriog valley, the weather turned, and Henry's army found the mountainous and difficult terrain unsuited to their style of warfare. He retreated, and never again led an expedition into Wales, instead opting for a policy of containment, strengthening castles on the Wales-England border. While he still exercised considerable influence over Welsh affairs, he declined to directly intervene in those affairs after his failure in 1165.

Owain lost no time in exploiting the possibilities afforded him by the king of England's new stance. His creation of the concept of a Welsh princeship was heralded by his adoption of a new style. In two of three surviving letters written in the 1160s to Louis VII, king of France, Owain styles himself 'king of Wales', or 'rex Walie' in the Latin original. In the third letter, the phrase 'Waliarum princeps' ('prince of the Welsh') is used to describe Owain's standing. By the end of the decade, Owain was being referred to in English correspondence as 'princeps Wallie' ('prince of Wales'), strongly suggesting that this form was also used by Owain in letters which are now lost.[5]

Two of these forms of address refer not simply to Owain's territory of Gwynedd, but to Wales as a whole. As such, we can take them as an indication of Owain's higher standing in this period as a national leader. He began his rise to power as king of Gwynedd; now he called himself (and was acknowledged as) prince of Wales. The precise nature of the overlordship on which Owain's position rested is, however, less than clear. There is, for example, no evidence indicating that any type of body such as a prince's council existed at this time. Similarly, Owain certainly had not brought Wales directly under his control by conquest, in the way that leaders such as Gruffudd ap Llywelyn (d. 1063/4) had in earlier times. What existed during the latter years of his rule was rather a loose conglomerate of kingdoms, united by awareness of their shared culture and language, and linked more by bonds of kinship, trade, and transient military needs than by means of formalised constitutional agreements. The fact that Owain could and did use such terminology as 'princeps Wallie' in his letters, however, meant that the other native rulers recognised his overarching authority, that they were in agreement with Owain's policies, and that they felt he was able to protect their interests in dealings with other leaders and speak for them on the wider political stage.*

After Owain's death in 1170, there was no significant development of his concept of a Welsh polity. Indeed, Wales promptly split in two, with Rhys ap Gruffudd ruling over the south, and Dafydd I ab Owain over the north. The next step

* Though it may be argued that a later reference in an English record to the presence of envoys of the 'kings of Wales' at the Anglo-French peace negotiations of July 1168 can be interpreted as suggesting that the ruler of the kingdom of Deheubarth, Rhys ap Gruffudd ('the Lord Rhys'; d. 1197), sent his own representatives independently of Owain. See Huw Pryce, 'Owain Gwynedd and Louis VII: The Franco-Welsh Diplomacy of the first Prince of Wales', *Welsh History Review*, Vol. 19 No. 1 (June 1998), pp. 1-28, esp. pp. 1-2, and references therein.

forward occurred during the reign of Llywelyn I ab Iorwerth, Owain's grandson, who acceded to the crown of Gwynedd in 1194.

After consolidating his power in the north, by 1212 Llywelyn had achieved a position of pre-eminence among the native Welsh rulers of Wales, as is demonstrated by his signing of a treaty with the king of France, Philip Augustus, that was designed to establish an alliance between the two men against King John of England. Though Llywelyn is referred to only as 'princeps Norwallie' ('prince of northern Wales') in the document, the fact that the French king appears to have made the initial overtures to Llywelyn alone of all the Welsh rulers is itself a tacit acknowledgement of Llywelyn's position as the *de facto* ruler of Wales during this period. Indeed, by this time Llywelyn had already done much to build on Owain Gwynedd's foundations for a Welsh polity.

Llywelyn was almost certainly responsible for creating the executive body known as the prince's council. The earliest direct evidence for the existence of the council dates from the Franco-Welsh treaty of 1212, though its appearance is probably a more solid manifestation of the long-established tradition of Welsh sovereigns taking leading members of their society into counsel. In England there were two such bodies, the *magnum concilium* or 'great council' and the *concilium* regis or 'privy council'. The former provided a basis for England's leading men to have a say in the governance of the nation, while the latter formed the principal instrument of rule for the monarch, and debate over the manner in which the two should co-operate informs much of English history in the thirteenth century.[6] At this time, however, it seems that both functions were absorbed in the same council in Wales, for Llywelyn's letter of 1212 to the king of France mentions only one such body. It informs Philip that Llywelyn had 'summoned the council of his leading men' to ratify the agreement, which was done 'with the consent of all the rulers *(principum)* of Wales'.[7]

The council's members had clearly delineated roles. Its principal member after the prince, the *distain* or 'steward', functioned as the chief official in the prince's royal government. For much of Llywelyn's reign the post was filled by Ednyfed Fychan (d. 1246), whose progeny would later found the Tudor dynasty. The *distain* was responsible for (among other things) leading diplomatic missions to other countries; indeed, it is possible that Ednyfed was the senior official in the Welsh delegations sent by Dafydd II ap Llywelyn (r. 1240-6) to entreaty with the king of France in Paris in 1241, and with the Pope in Genoa in 1244. Ednyfed also had a judicial role, representing the prince in court cases – he is recorded as having done so for Dafydd some time in the early 1240s in a case against his brother Gruffudd – and also hearing the pleas of minor rulers elsewhere in Wales. Other members of the council included prominent ecclesiastics and members of the prince's dynasty. Aided by the distain and these other members, Llywelyn would debate and decide on policy matters pertaining to the governance of Wales.

There is evidence, too, to suggest that an element of Llywelyn's royal government was engaged in overhauling the law books of Wales, the texts traditionally held to have been composed in assemblies convoked by Hywel Dda in the early tenth century. The Iorwerth redaction of the law books, probably drawn up in Gwynedd during Llywelyn's reign, contains subtle differences in interpretation of the role of the queen in Welsh society that can only have come about as a result of the central role Llywelyn's consort Joan came to play in Welsh politics in the early thirteenth century. Similarly, another version of the lawbooks believed to have been drawn up in the latter years of Llywelyn's reign places emphasis on the heir of the king as the person to whom obedience must be sworn in the future. This revision of the law was undoubtedly made in response to Llywelyn's decision to go against tradition and name his youngest son Dafydd as his successor. That Llywelyn had the facilities to make these changes to the laws is a clear demonstration of both his increasing administrative resources and also his authority during this period of his principate.[8]

In other ways, too, Llywelyn seems to have innovated in order to further bolster his, and Wales', standing. The balance of evidence suggests that he was responsible for the production of the first native Welsh coinage since the days of Hywel Dda at a mint in Rhuddlan;* and if this act did not quite establish a monetary system that encompassed all of Wales – the coins in question seem not to have been in widespread circulation outside Gwynedd – the imitative issues it produced based on the English 'Short Cross' pennies are at least indicative of the increasing importance to the Welsh economy of money.[9]

However, Llywelyn's principate still lacked a greater cohesion. As has been observed, 'he had neither the administrative means nor the political resources to create a unitary principality'.[10] The council members were at this time drawn from Gwynedd only; Llywelyn thus imposed his will on the minor rulers of Wales in Powys and Deheubarth via a different mechanism, that of homage. In 1216 these rulers met

* Though his predecessor Dafydd I ab Owain (d. 1203) may also have minted coins; see footnote 9.

Llywelyn at an assembly held at Aberdyfi, at which legislation was passed dividing the disputed kingdom of Deheubarth between the descendants of Rhys ap Gruffudd, and it is highly likely that the rulers swore homage to Llywelyn. While it would be going too far to say that this was the first Welsh parliament, it is clear evidence of Llywelyn's ability to unite the minor rulers as his vassals (see map on page 221). Powys and Deheubarth were now under his overlordship as vassal states or protectorates of Gwynedd, and forming part of independent Wales; but it was only in Gwynedd that Llywelyn ruled directly. His authority elsewhere rested not on institutional foundations, but upon his personal relationships with the minor rulers, an arrangement that could often lead to bitter feeling. For example, in 1220 Llywelyn coerced one of Deheubarth's rulers, Rhys Gryg, to cede the Gower peninsula and other adjacent territories to English landowners to maintain good Anglo-Welsh relations, a move that angered Rhys and which seems to have caused lasting resentment.[11]

After the difficult reign of Llywelyn's successor, Dafydd II ap Llywelyn (1240-46), Llywelyn II succeeded to the Welsh throne, at first ruling in Gwynedd only in conjunction with his brother, Owain. Having inherited a country impoverished by two years of war and weakened by English trade embargoes, the pair were forced to accede to the terms of the Treaty of Woodstock (1247), which pushed the boundaries of Gwynedd back to the river Conwy. Yet Llywelyn showed remarkable tenacity. Within ten years, he had assumed the sole princeship of Gwynedd and conducted successful military campaigns in southern Wales; and on 3rd June 1257 Welsh forces under the command of his brother Dafydd routed an English army in the battle of

Cymerau near Llandeilo. Later that year, the king of England, Henry III, accompanied an expedition into Wales, but was repulsed.

Llywelyn's prowess in the field of politics was no less impressive, though limited by the difficult political climate of the times. In March 1258, styling himself 'prince of Wales', he concluded an alliance with Scotland, pledging not to attack one another or to aid the English in their campaigns, and guaranteeing trade links. Though the alliance was short-lived, it was a signal of intent. In the spring of 1258, possibly at the time of the signing of the Cambro-Scottish treaty, an assembly was convened at which the lesser rulers of Wales pledged their loyalty to Llywelyn. The differences between this manifestation of the prince's council and that of Llywelyn's grandfather's time have recently been delineated.[12] Whereas only the men of Gwynedd were members of Llywelyn I's council, under Llywelyn II the body counted among its number men from across Wales. Though there was probably a 'working council' that met to discuss day-to-day matters of governance, the institutional framework was now in place to bind the rulers of Wales together more closely than ever before. The Treaty of Montgomery (1267), in which Henry III recognised Llywelyn's claim to be the leader of a Wales that included all of the nation we know today, with the exception of Gwent, Morgannwg, southern Pembrokeshire, and Hawarden in the north (see map on page 222), was not merely made by Llywelyn alone, but by his council also. After 1267, the institution of the council would continue until the imposition of English rule in 1283.

In examining the various manifestations of royal governance that emerged in Wales between the 1160s and the 1280s, it is important to recognise the distinct lack of continuity in models of government. While the position and status of the king of England – if not his councils – had long since been established, the fact that Wales was home to several rival royal houses and kingdoms, some of which were riven by internal divisions, meant that it was exceedingly difficult for one man to exert authority over the nation as a whole. As has been noted in previous studies, Gwynedd became the focal point of Welsh politics as time went on; but it did not follow that the leader of that kingdom automatically qualified as leader of Wales. All three of the leaders of Gwynedd whose careers have been described above ruled over large swathes of modern-day Wales, but not one succeeded in establishing ineffable traditions of leadership and governance that were beyond dispute.

Each leader developed his own concept of Welsh royal government. Records pertaining to Owain Gwynedd's rule in the 1160s are meagre compared with those of his successors, but those that survive demonstrate that he had clerics under his wing who were called upon to draw up official documents of the sort produced by royal governments throughout Europe. Owain also believed in the idea of an independent Welsh church, as is attested to by his firm stance in an 1165 letter to Thomas Becket, archbishop of Canterbury, in which he puts forward a case to have his own candidate appointed as bishop of Bangor. The precise nature of his political aspirations is more uncertain, but usage of the term 'prince' to describe his standing at a time when the term 'king' was beginning to lose its potency as an indication of power clearly points to a belief in his own pre-eminence.

Llywelyn I pursued a far closer bond between the Welsh

kingdoms, securing the support of the lesser rulers as early as 1212. It is during his reign that we see the first indisputable glimpse of the political ideology that served as the backbone of attempts to maintain a unified Wales for the remainder of the century. In the 1230s, Llywelyn began using the form of address 'Lewelinus princeps de Aberfrau, dominus Snowdon' ('Llywelyn, prince of Aberffraw, lord of Snowdon') in his correspondence.[13] This change arose from a need to more effectively communicate the nature of his claim to be leader of Wales, and it helped to clarify his position both to the lesser native rulers and to the English authorities. The court at Aberffraw on Ynys Môn was the ancient seat of the princes of Gwynedd, and according to a long-standing tradition, it was held that the prince of Aberffraw paid gold to the king of London, while the rulers of Wales paid gold to Aberffraw. Llywelyn justified his overlordship by invoking this tradition in his title. As Huw Pryce notes, 'the new style drew a new distinction between, on the one hand, Llywelyn's aspirations to Wales-wide authority as prince of Aberffraw and, on the other, his position as territorial lord of Gwynedd or Snowdon'.[14] Coming at a time when the fortunes of Powys and Deheubarth were in decline, the style's emergence did much to promote the idea that Gwynedd was the wellspring of Welsh independence, and that its ruler had a claim to the overlordship of Wales – an idea that retained its potency in the time of Madog's revolt.

Llywelyn II, meanwhile, made strides of his own. Under Llywelyn I's leadership, the royal council was responsible for the effective functioning of government, but the lesser rulers of Wales were not admitted to its ranks. Llywelyn II, however, did include lesser rulers from outside Gwynedd in his council, and together they debated issues of foreign policy and possibly jurisprudence. He also differed from his namesake in title: 'princeps Waalie et dominus Snowdonia' ('prince of Wales and lord of Snowdon') is the style employed after 1262,[15] placing emphasis not on overlordship, but rule of two joined but distinct territories.

Each man, therefore, had his own idea of what the position of prince entailed. Given the difficult geographical and political circumstances of a country with poor internal communications and deeply penetrated in some areas by Anglo-Norman lords, a leader's policy could only be one of pragmatism, seizing opportunities for consolidation when they appeared, and attempting to impose certain procedures and ideologies on royal governance with as much forcefulness as he could muster in the hope that they would endure the test of time. Consequently, although we see gestures towards the creation of an immutable and permanent structure for a Welsh royal government particularly during the reigns of the two Llywelyns, the thrust to create a fully functioning and robust medieval Welsh polity was destined to end in failure.

Many aspects of these attempts at creating a Welsh polity endured after 1283. However, perhaps the most important survival in respect of Madog's revolt of 1294-5 was the continued existence of Welsh independence as an ideal. By 1294, a mere ten years had passed since the imposition of English authority in Wales had been codified in the Statute of Rhuddlan (1284), and one may reasonably assume that the abruptness of the disappearance of the Welsh polity had given rise to real political aspirations among native Welsh society, particularly the *uchelwyr* or nobles. (Indeed, and as the revolt of Owain

Glyndŵr (1400-15) so amply demonstrates, recovery of the native polity still seemed achievable in Wales for generations after 1283.) Madog's revolt was to be a manifestation of these aspirations.

An English perspective: the view from Y Bere

There is no monument in Wales to Madog ap Llywelyn's memory, but it is a testament to the ubiquity of his forces during the revolt of 1294-5 that if one had to decide on a location for such a memorial, one would not suffer from a lack of choice. There is an abundance of places associated with him and his revolt. Rebel forces acting under his aegis struck at dozens of locations across Wales: at Cricieth, Harlech, Llanfaes and Caernarfon in the north-west; at Flint, Hawarden, Denbigh and Rhuthun in the north-east; at Aberystwyth, Cefnllys, Rhaeadr and Builth in the midlands; at Cardigan and Carmarthen in the south-west; and at Resolven, Caerffili, Abergavenny and Newport in the south-east.

Yet on any list of possible sites for a memorial in memory of Madog, one might justifiably place Castell Y Bere in mid-Wales near the top. Like that of Owain Glyndŵr a century later, Madog's revolt was one primarily composed of sieges, and the reduction of Y Bere after a protracted siege was one of Madog's most impressive military accomplishments. Yet it is not merely from a Welsh perspective that the story of Y Bere in 1294-5 is typical. For the English, too, the revolt was one long struggle to maintain garrisons in castles throughout Wales, many of which spent weeks or months under siege in territory controlled by the rebels. An overview of the situation in Wales immediately prior to the revolt might usefully proceed from this starting-point at the foot of the Cader Idris range.

In September 1294 Y Bere was under the control of Robert Staundon.[16] Staundon's career had followed a slow but steady progression upwards, from humble beginnings in the king of England's service to a position of moderate standing in one of the king's newest possessions, Wales. Holding the various titles of sheriff, mayor, constable, and judge, he was the most powerful man in his community, and presided over two of the grandest castles in the country. Little is known about Staundon's earlier career in Wales, but he seems to have attained a position of authority with relative ease. He was appointed the first sheriff of Meirionydd after Edward I's invasion of Wales in 1282-3, and by 1288, he had also assumed the title of deputy-justice of northern Wales. Edward ruled Wales according to the same principles of administration that he had used in Aquitaine in France and the English-occupied parts of Ireland. The country was separated into variously-sized administrative units, the largest of which were 'Northern Wales' and 'Southern Wales', and the smallest of which were the *cymydau* or commotes, the ancient units of land by which the Welsh princes had demarcated their territory, and which were well suited to Edward's purpose.

There were four such commotes in Meirionydd, one of the poorest and most thinly populated regions in Wales. As its sheriff, Staundon occupied a position of considerable power. He held a monthly court for the dispensing of justice, and was at the head of an impressive array of bureaucrats and officials. Prominent among them was the *rhingyll* or ringild, who presided over the levying of fines against tenants and oversaw the collection of taxes. Whenever Staundon received orders from the exchequer at Caernarfon requesting the levying of money from the county in order to finance Edward's military campaigns overseas, he delegated the responsibility for its collection to these officials. Taxes in the early 1290s had risen sharply, and were much heavier even than those imposed by the last great prince of Wales, Llywelyn II, during the final years of his reign. Indeed, a new type of tax had recently been introduced, the lay subsidy, which was levied on the movable goods – that is, animals such as cows and sheep, grain, crops, and even boats and fishing nets – of the laymen in each community. The amount raised by the lay subsidy in Wales in 1292-3 has been estimated at £9,500-£10,000, a huge figure by previous thirteenth-century standards. (By comparison, Llywelyn II's annual income in his triumphal years as prince of Wales was no more (and probably less) than £5,000.)[17] Several months before the revolt began, there were reports of refusals to pay the subsidy, and a royal agent, John de Godelegh, was sent to Wales in late 1293 to investigate the matter for himself. Discontent arising from this state of affairs was to be a major factor in sowing dissension among the Welsh.

Castell Y Bere, of which Staundon had been constable since December 1293, was built by Llywelyn I in 1221, and was (with the possible exception of Cricieth) the strongest native Welsh castle ever built, so strong that historians of a later age mistakenly assumed it to be an English construction. Unlike Edward's great castles of Harlech, Caernarfon, Conwy and Flint, Y Bere was situated in the Dysynni valley inland, around seven miles south-west of Dolgellau, and in a position of immense natural strength. The outcropping of rock on which it sat rose steeply from the valley floor on three sides, while the one remaining approach – from the south-west – was so narrow that assault from that direction would be a risky proposition for any would-be assailants.

By Welsh standards, the castle was an expensive undertaking. The keystones above the doorways were made of specially imported sandstone, and these and other decorative features that were uncommon in native Welsh castles, such as ornate stonework and mouldings, were testaments to its strategic and symbolic importance as a stronghold on Gwynedd's southern frontier. Inside the ward were several store-houses and barns for the substantial supplies that would be necessary for the garrison in the event of a siege, for although Y Bere was superbly situated to withstand an attack, that same remoteness also meant that it could be easily blockaded.

In an era when English castle designers placed their faith in circular towers, the Welsh were making increasing use of the aspidal or D-shaped tower. As did the castles at Ewloe, Cricieth and Carndochan, Y Bere boasted examples of these towers, which afforded defenders a wide field of fire. The South Tower was of such a design, probably added as an afterthought by Llywelyn II in the late 1250s, as was the castle's barbican and drawbridge. The North Tower was also aspidal, and, judging by the carved stone found in the ruins in later times, probably housed the castle's chapel.

Though the castle's early history was uneventful, by April 1283, Y Bere was being besieged by the English in the last months of the conflict that would extinguish Welsh independence. Dafydd III ap Gruffudd had been prince of Wales for four months. Llywelyn II had been killed the previous December, and Dafydd and his advisors decided to fight on; but the loss of Ynys Môn and much of Eryri (including Dolwyddelan castle) to Edward I's forces undoubtedly demoralised his men. He had despairingly fallen back on Meirionydd in the spring, but as the English advanced from the east and the south, Dafydd left a small garrison at the castle and went to ground, along with his wife Elizabeth and a group of noblemen including Rhys Wyndod and Hywel ap Rhys. William de Valance, who had spent the last few months fighting his way through Ceredigion, encamped outside Y Bere with 1,000 men on 15th April. Any hopes the garrison might have had of holding out were surely dampened by the arrival on 21st April by Roger Lestrange of Montgomery, with a further 2,000 infantry and a scattering of horsemen. One of this substantial siege party was an engineer by the name of Master Bertram, who was presumably present in case it was necessary to undermine the castle walls; siege equipment was on hand; and most ominously of all, shortly after the commencement of the siege the defenders were offered the sum of £80 if they surrendered the castle to the English immediately – with the implicit assurance that the garrison would suffer if the offer was refused. The custodian of the castle, Cynfrig ap Madog, capitulated accordingly on 25th April 1283.[18]

Such was Y Bere's involvement in war; and at his newly-built castle at Harlech, Robert Staundon would have had ample time to reflect on the satisfactory conclusion to the English invasion of Wales that followed its surrender. Dafydd spent a few weeks at large before being caught at Cader Idris, probably on 22nd June; on 3rd October 1283, he was dragged by horse through the streets of Shrewsbury, hanged, drawn and quartered, one of the first men of status in history to meet his death in this manner.[19]

Since then things had been quiet in Wales. By the following year, preparations for the English administration of Wales were well in hand, the Statute of Rhuddlan was drawn up to provide for the administration of Edward I's new possession, castles were being built at several locations in the north, and most satisfyingly of all, Llywelyn's crown and seal had both come into the king's possession (he is recorded as having ordered the latter to be melted down to make a chalice). There was also the matter of the *Croes Naid,* allegedly a piece of the True Cross, which was handed over to Edward by the clerk Huw ab Ithel (probably one of the foremost officials in the now defunct royal government of Dafydd) and other prominent Welshmen in a ceremony at Aberconwy. It was a final act of submission from a subjugated people.[20]

Staundon's area of jurisdiction, Meirionydd, had long had a reputation for being the last bastion of Welsh resistance, but although Castell Y Bere had been hurriedly reinforced during the revolt of Rhys ap Maredudd in 1287-8, the county had remained at peace. Construction work on the castle at Harlech had proceeded at a leisurely pace in the mid-1280s, and in 1284 Staundon was lucky enough to play host to the king himself. Edward visited the county twice, stopping at Harlech and Y Bere in late autumn – his week-long stay at the latter castle prompted the procurement of ten barrels of wine, and may well have caused the construction of a new chamber in one of the towers in preparation for the royal visit.[21]

Edward had also used the opportunity to confer upon Y Bere the status of a borough, with the castle's constable as its mayor. The English drive to create new towns in Wales was a powerful one, and it was common policy to found settlements alongside castles, whose garrisons could provide vital trade for the inhabitants. At Y Bere, the first buildings were constructed in the mid- to late 1280s, perhaps inside the castle walls or on the level ground to the eastern. However, the borough did not develop with the same speed as that at Flint or Caerffili, or even nearby Harlech. By 1293, there were only sixteen taxpayers (around two-thirds of them English) in the community, and it was found that the entire administration of the borough could be handled with a staff of just three. However, in difficult times there was always the castle's garrison to maintain trade; and to a traveller passing through the district, it might well have seemed as though the future was bright for the fledgling settlement. At the same time, the English carried out some minor alterations on the castle itself, repairing siege damage and strengthening existing defences. The works also eliminated the castle's one weak spot – the relatively flimsy curtain linking the South Tower with the main courtyard – by means of a substantial stone wall.[22]

Before the autumn of 1294, Staundon would likely have asserted that the chances of Y Bere's defences being tested was remote; but that year a cloud appeared on the horizon. Edward had spent much of 1294 preparing for a campaign in Gascony, a territory in south-western France that had been a bone of contention between England and France for decades. Edward's latest attempt to capture it once and for all was to be no mean effort; but the preparations were expensive, and the royal coffers were already feeling the strain. The king resorted to somewhat unconventional methods to find troops for the campaign, even offering pardons to convicted criminals in return for service in the infantry (three hundred are recorded as having taken him up on the offer). He also called upon his officials in Wales to press the native Welshmen into service. Reginald de Grey, a prominent landowner in north-eastern Wales, was to raise men in Flintshire and the Denbigh area, while Walter de Pederton and Geoffrey Clement were made responsible for the south and the borderlands or 'marches'.[23]

Staundon had had a hand in raising men in Meirionydd, Caernarfonshire and Ynys Môn, but none of them had as yet joined the royal forces at their embarkation point at Portsmouth. At the end of August, mere weeks before Edward was due to set sail for France, a large section of the Welsh contingent had refused to serve in the king's army. This was a serious matter, far more so than was appreciated at the time, and by the end of September, the destiny of the Welsh soldiers in the king's pay was still uncertain.[24]

The imminent expedition to Gascony had one other crucial repercussion: it resulted in the removal of a great many of the Englishmen who controlled Wales to France to serve with the king. These men included Fulk Fitzwarin; the justice of west Wales, Robert Tibetot; and even the man Staundon had replaced as constable of Castell Y Bere, Robert Fitzwalter. Garrison numbers in castles across Wales were also dangerously small, and had been for much of the previous decade. Y Bere was no exception. Immediately after its fall in 1283, Y Bere was held by almost sixty soldiers, including horsemen and crossbowmen; but only a year later, the same castle was home to a mere fifteen crossbowmen and a single artilleryman – indeed, there were more civilians living in the castle than military men. In 1294, the number of soldiers quartered in Y Bere cannot have been very much higher than this figure.

It was also the case that construction work on a number of castles in the north, including Caernarfon, had been proceeding at a snail's pace in recent years as money earmarked for Edward's castle-building programme was siphoned off to finance his military campaigns overseas. Moreover, the men of the English border counties such as Shropshire – the very counties whose populations would be called on to serve in Wales in an emergency – were all already assembling at Portsmouth.

One need not, therefore, look very far for either the motive or the opportunity for Madog's revolt of 1294-5. From a Welsh perspective, English positions in Wales were vulnerable as they had not been since 1282, and the population were fitful and disgruntled due to the tax burden placed upon them and the overbearing behaviour of some of the English officials engaged in running the country. We can only speculate as to whether Staundon had any insight into what was about to happen; but the lack of preparedness of his castles suggests that he, like the vast majority of English officials in Wales, had no conception of the disaster that was about to befall him. In all probability, he could hardly have known that by the end of 1294, one of his castles would be under close siege, the other would be lying in ruins, the communities under his authority would be under the influence of a full-blown revolt, and his power and prestige would be hanging by the slenderest of threads.

[1] *Rotula Parliamentorum Edward I*, Vol. 1, p. 276; the report is noticed in W. W. E. Wynne, 'Harlech Castle', pp. 21-31 of *Archaeologia Cambrensis* (1875), p. 23; G. T. O. Bridgeman, *History of The Princes of South Wales* (1876), p. 207, note 3, and E. A. Lewis, *The Medieval Boroughs of Snowdonia* (London, 1912), p. 54.

[2] R. R. Davies, *The Age of Conquest: Wales 1063-1415* (Oxford, 1987), p. 383.
[3] David Stephenson, *The Governance of Gwynedd* (Cardiff, 1984), p. 113. For contemporary references to Madog as prince, see appendix 1.
[4] Robin Frame, *The Political Development of the British Isles 1100-1400* (Clarendon, 1995), p. 115.
[5] Huw Pryce (ed.), *The Acts of Welsh Rulers 1120-1283* (Cardiff, 2005), pp. 328-9.
[6] For a discussion of the operation of these councils, see B. Wilkinson, *The Constitutional History of England 1216-1399* (Longmans, 1948), pp. 11-14.
[7] Huw Pryce (ed.), *The Acts of Welsh Rulers 1120-1283*, p. 392.
[8] For a fuller discussion of these issues, see Robin Chapman Stacey, 'King, Queen, and *Edling* in the Laws of Court', pp. 29-62 of T. M. Charles-Edwards, Morfydd E. Owen and Paul Russell (eds.), *The Welsh King and his Court* (Cardiff, 2000).
[9] Until recently, the only report of coinage issued under Llywelyn I was provided by seventeenth-century scholar Edward Llwyd (see Roger Turvey, *Llywelyn the Great* (Gomer, 2007), p. 109 and note); but E. Besly, 'Short Cross and other medieval coins from Llanfaes, Anglesey', pp. 46-82 of *British Numismatic Journal* Vol. 65 (1995) provides further evidence in support of this report. Besly notes that 'there is incontrovertible evidence that two Rhuddlan moneyers were active before 1200' (p. 55) – that is, at a time when Rhuddlan was in the hands of the rulers of Gwynedd. Besly also notes that the very first coins from Rhuddlan 'appear to lie during the time of Dafydd ap Owain' (ibid.). This presents a problem, as Dafydd's position in the 1180s was being assailed by several rivals for leadership of the house of Gwynedd, and it is by no means certain that his power and authority were such that he could issue coinage.

A possible solution to this apparent quandary is to suggest that coinage was issued at this time not merely for economic reasons, but also to bolster one's standing and in so doing strengthen one's claim to pre-eminence in Gwynedd. In this connection it is worth recounting the ideas of William Parker. In 'Gwynedd, Ceredigion and the Political Geography of the Mabinogi' (pp. 365-396 of *Cylchgrawn Llyfrgell Genedlaethol Cymru/The National Library of Wales Journal* Vol. 23 (2002)), he proposed the idea that the *Four Branches of the Mabinogi* may have been written in Gwynedd in the late 1180s as an allegorical work designed to boost Llywelyn I's standing during his challenge for Dafydd's title: '... a specific and identifiable dynastic interest may have been involved in the composition and sponsorship of the Mabinogi, i.e. a court community sympathetic to the ambitions of the emergent Llywelyn ap Iorwerth' (p. 382). If correct (and it ought to be noted that Parker's dating of the *Mabinogi* is at odds with that favoured by T. M. Charles-Edwards among others), it becomes conceivable that that same court community – and perhaps those of other would-be princes – sought to promote their candidate for the princeship in other ways such as coining money. After all, and as E. A. Lewis has noted, the right to do so was included among the traditional powers of the ruler of Wales ('Industry and Commerce in Medieval Wales', pp. 121-73 of *Transactions of the Royal Historical Society* Vol. XVII (1903); p. 134). In short, therefore, it seems certain that coinage was issued at Rhuddlan under Llywelyn I, and perhaps under Dafydd I before him. As Besly notes, definitive answers may be forthcoming if further specimens are discovered.
[10] R. R. Davies, *The Age of Conquest: Wales 1063-1415*, p. 245.
[11] R. R. Davies, *The Age of Conquest: Wales 1063-1415*, p. 244.
[12] See J. Beverley Smith, *Llywelyn ap Gruffudd: Prince of Wales* (Cardiff, 1998), pp. 309-319 for a fuller discussion of Llywelyn's council and its functions.
[13] For an assessment of the significance of this change, see J. B. Smith, *Llywelyn ap Gruffudd: Prince of Wales*, pp. 283-5.
[14] Huw Pryce (ed.), *The Acts of Welsh Rulers* 1120-1283, p. 76.
[15] The first document Llywelyn issued using this title – a letter to Henry III – was probably

drawn up in February 1262 or February 1263. See Huw Pryce (ed.), *The Acts of Welsh Rulers 1120-1283*, p. 525.

[16] Many of the particulars of Castell Y Bere's history can be found in E. D. Evans, 'Castell Y Bere', pp.31-44 of *The Journal of the Merioneth Historical and Record Society* Vol. 3 (1957-60).

[17] Keith Williams-Jones, *The Merioneth Lay Subsidy Roll 1292-3* (Cardiff, 1976), pp. xxv, xviii.

[18] See Edward Owen, 'The Croes Nawdd', pp. 1-18 of *Y Cymmrodor*, Vol. XLIII (1932).

[19] The *Brut Y Tywysogyon* (Pen. Ms. 20 version) erroneously gives the date of Dafydd's capture as autumn 1283. See Thomas Jones (ed.), *Brut Y Tywysogyon* (Peniarth Ms. 20 version) (Cardiff, 1952), p. 121.

[20] J. B. Smith, *Llywelyn ap Gruffudd: Prince of Wales*, pp. 580-81.

[21] See L. A. S. Butler, 'Medieval Finds From Castell-Y-Bere, Merioneth', pp. 78-112 of *Archaeologia Cambrensis* Vol. CXXIII (1974); p. 80.

[22] L. A. S. Butler, in 'Medieval Finds From Castell-Y-Bere, Merioneth', speculates (p. 80) that these walls may have been built in 1286-7.

[23] J. E. Morris, *The Welsh Wars of Edward I* (Oxford, 1901), pp. 240-1.

[24] J. E. Morris, *The Welsh Wars of Edward I*, p. 241 notes that the first fleet of ships destined for France set sail at the end of September without taking any Welsh soldiers on board.

2 – THE CAUSES OF MADOG'S REVOLT

A people does not unite and take up arms on a whim. There are always powerful motives, aspirations, and sources of resentment which are usually present at many different levels within society. They vary from place to place, and are seldom uniform in their effects on the different elements of a population, as is demonstrated by the differences in the longevity of Madog's revolt in different areas: for example, rebel activity in Flintshire appears to have diminished to almost nothing even before the end of 1294, while reports of rebel skirmishes in Carmarthenshire can be found as late as June 1295. Yet regardless of the patchy nature of support for Madog, the fact remains that the vast majority of the country rebelled against English rule, and this invites the historian to search for explanations that similarly encompass all of Wales. Such an approach militates against that of many early historians (and some contemporary ones) who view the events of 1294-5 as the un-coordinated protests of a disgruntled but essentially apolitical people; but it must nevertheless be admitted. Within a few days of the attack on Ynys Môn and Caernarfon that heralded the beginning of the revolt, several other attacks and raids had taken place throughout the country. Outside Madog's immediate of sphere of influence in northern Wales, these attacks were led by Morgan ap Maredudd, Maelgwn ap Rhys Fychan, and Cynan ap Maredudd. Regardless of one's assessment of the personal ambitions that drove these men, it stretches credulity to believe that they chose the same moment to launch their assaults by accident, still less to imply that such a grievous outbreak of violence should have occurred in a multitude of locations across Wales by chance on the sole initiative of the Welsh people. Local causes must be taken into account, and their significance weighed when assessing the contributions made to the revolt by its leaders; but given Madog's clearly stated aspiration to restore the line of Gwynedd and reconstitute a system of native Welsh governance, they cannot be allowed to form the whole affair. Just what was it that caused people throughout Wales to bind their grievances together under the leadership of a scion of the house of Gwynedd whose legitimist claims to the Welsh princeship gave the revolt its political hue?

In the case of the 1294-5 revolt, one may begin the search for answers to this question with the ending of Edward's campaign in Wales in 1283. This was the pivotal moment, the ultimate cause of Welsh grievances. After 1283, and the Statute of Rhuddlan that was composed the following year to provide an administrative framework for English rule, the Welsh people had to adjust to life under a new order that in many respects was not favourable to them.

Wales, 1283-94: the English administration

Though the situation before 1283 was rarely stable, it is possible to sketch a rough outline of the Welsh and English spheres of influence within Wales. The odd English incursion aside, the native Welsh in Gwynedd had remained largely undisturbed; but in Gwent, Morgannwg, and southern Pembrokeshire, Welsh rule had been a far shakier matter for many decades. The Welsh communities of the lowlands of the south-east had been uprooted and the land colonised by Anglo-Normans after the fall of the local rulers from power in the 1090s, leaving only the uplands in Welsh control. Further west and with only very brief exceptions, the Gower peninsula and the lands around Carmarthen and St. David's had lain beyond the grasp of the two Llywelyns, and consequently were highly Anglicised by 1283. With the blessing of the local Anglo-Norman administration, large numbers of Flemish colonists had settled in the south-west, with the result that no less than five languages – Welsh, Anglo-Norman, Flemish, English, and (in written form) Latin – were in common usage in parts of Wales for a period of over a century in the later Middle Ages.[1] Meanwhile, the borderlands – or the 'Marches' as they are sometimes termed – were in a state of perpetual turmoil, as Marcher families such as the Mortimers, and the princes and kings of Powys, Elfael and Maelienydd, and Arwystli all sought to stamp their authority on the region.

With all Wales under his control by 1283, Edward set about advancing the process of colonisation begun in the time of William the Conqueror over two hundred years earlier. Colonising Gwynedd west of the mountains would be a tricky business, and consolidating military strength was the priority. Edward thus began erecting the 'Ring of Steel', a network of castles that included Caernarfon, Harlech and Conwy, each of which was complemented by a new borough town. To give these towns the best possible chance of developing, in Arfon on the Llŷn peninsula laws were passed prohibiting the sale of goods outside the borough in order to stimulate trade. However, Edward's need to secure sites for towns and castles led to what must have been some unpleasant scenes between Welsh inhabitants occupying the sites and the English officials sent to remove them. Caernarfon provides one example. By July

1283 work was already beginning there on the new borough, but not before the fledgling Welsh settlement that had previously existed on the site was destroyed and its inhabitants evicted. The work of clearing away the timbers of the settlement's buildings took twenty men five days to complete, suggesting that this was no mere hamlet, and compensation was not paid to those evicted for some years.[2]

Further east, in the Vale of Clwyd other Welsh communities were ejected from their homes in order to make available large tracts of land for English settlers. Though the native inhabitants had little (if any) say in the matter, Edward was at least fastidious in ensuring that those forcibly moved from their dwellings would be provided with land (albeit sometimes poorer land) elsewhere in recompense, unlike at Caernarfon. Relative to the native population, numbers of English settlers remained small in the north, but in some areas this influx would transform the cultural landscape for centuries to come: in north-eastern Gwent, settlers accounted for one in five of the population.[3]

Meanwhile, north-eastern Wales had been the subject of a tug-of-war between the two countries for centuries. By the 1280s the region's population was largely Welsh, but Edward's policy of giving borough status to the towns of the area and thereby encouraging English settlers to move there doubtless caused resentment. After Dafydd III's capture in 1283, his lands in this area were given to Edward's wife, Eleanor, but the men she appointed to administer the lands did so in an aggressive and heavy-handed manner, so much so that an enquiry was held in 1291-2 concerning abuses of privilege on the part of these royal officials.[4] Among those with grievances were the descendants of the princes of Powys. Though they had fought on the Welsh side in the conflict of 1282-3, Edward had looked kindly upon them after their surrender, and granted them status akin to that of English barons, so that they were given back some of their former ancestral lands. Their right to use Welsh law instead of English law in these territories remained ill-defined, however, and the name of Madog ap Gruffydd Fychan occurs again and again in the records relating to the 1291-2 enquiry, suggesting that he in particular fought his corner with persistence. The outcome of Madog ap Gruffydd Fychan's protestations is not recorded, but a decision in favour of the Crown would have undoubtedly fostered even more discord.

There were other, more general grievances. It was found that royal officials had schemed to appropriate lands under the guise of a plan to build a new road in the area; that money had been withheld from the Welsh communities of Hope and Estun for the sale of wood; that the livestock of the Welshmen of Maelor Saesneg had been impounded with no reason given; that the fishing rights of the community of Bangor-on-Dee were in dispute; and that rents had risen across the region. Even some Englishmen presented grievances to the enquiry, and it was noted that although Edward had introduced a policy giving ten years' tax relief to any English settler moving into the towns in north-eastern Wales, settlers were still being charged rent.

Though this enquiry appears to have been surprisingly even-handed, the outcome did little to assuage Welsh disgruntlement. The Welsh received no compensation, and even more gallingly, the English official at the centre of the controversy, Robert Bures, remained in his post. As the attack on Bures' home district of Overton during the revolt suggests, this episode was probably a contributing factor to the high incidence of rebel activity in north-eastern Wales two years later.

Across Wales, other grievances arising from the English administration of Wales served to unsettle the native population. One major problem was the aforementioned lay subsidy, employed in Wales for the first time by Edward I in 1291 in order to meet the bill for a recent military expedition to Gascony. It was not the first time the concept of taxing movable goods had been introduced in Wales. Such measures had been employed by Llywelyn II in 1275, who imposed on the Welsh people a tax of threepence in order to raise the money needed to meet his financial obligations to the English Crown under the Treaty of Montgomery. On that occasion, however, the tax had been restricted to cattle only; for the Welsh, the idea of extending the tax to encompass all of an individual's movable goods was wholly unprecedented.[5] The regulations with which the assessors were supposed to decide which goods were taxable and which were not seem to have been somewhat woolly, a situation which cannot have helped them in their task. As one modern historian ruefully notes, 'angry protestations must have choked the air as the assessors went about their business'.[6]

The way in which the lay subsidy was assessed resulted in massive disparities and unfairness. For example, the thinly-populated county of Meirionydd, one of the poorest in either England or Wales, was required to raise the massive sum of £566, fully one-third of that required of the wealthy and numerous people of Essex. The outrage such assessments must have generated was exacerbated by various other sources of dissension such as the improper behaviour of the English officials, particularly in the north-east and on Ynys Môn, where the county sheriff, Roger de Puleston, was a figure of hate for many of the Welsh inhabitants.[7] Reports of corruption among English officials given the task of collecting the tax, if true, may also have been a factor in heightening tensions in some parts of northern Wales. Over months and years, such injustices must have had their effect on Welsh opinion.

The planning of Madog's revolt

As time went on, it seems that certain sections of the population began to covertly explore the possibilities of staging an attempt to reinstate native Welsh rule. How thorough these preparations were is a question that may never be satisfactorily answered. Quite simply, there is not enough evidence to allow us to ascertain even the most basic facts – who established communication between the local leaders of revolt, and to what end; what form that communication took; to what extent the revolt was co-ordinated between the various regions of Wales. One of the few indisputable indications that the revolt had been several months in the planning can be found in a contemporary document relating the testimony of one 'Iorwerth ap Kenewric [Cynwrig] ap Ririt [Rhirid]', who appeared before a court at Llanerch in Denbighshire in June 1294. He is recorded as having declared that 'before the middle of the month the constable and other English will hear such rumours that they will not wish to come again to Wales'.[8] This outburst seems not to have aroused suspicion among the local English authorities, for the evidence pertaining to the revolt in Denbighshire shows that the nobles were caught cold by the Welsh attack. Nevertheless, it invites speculation that the Welsh had harboured thoughts of revolt for some time before the autumn.

One tantalising aspect of the run-up to the revolt is the part played by the weather. During 1294, England was in the grip of a famine. 'There was a... great want throughout England,' observed the chronicler of Bury St. Edmunds under the entry for 1294. Furthermore, torrential rain in August and September ruined the crops: '... there was a continuous drenching downpour... so that very little or none of the new crop could be harvested before Michaelmas.'[9] Such famines were by no means unknown. A failure of the harvest two years running could have a devastating effect on a rural population, as it did in England during the famine of 1257-8.[10] The famines that ravaged England in 1272, 1277 and 1283 were also alarming in their scale.[11] By the close of the thirteenth century, however, grain production was beginning to increase in England, to the point where the idea of making occasional exports of the (admittedly small) surplus to other countries could be entertained.[12] The fact that there had been no serious famine for a decade meant that the peasantry undoubtedly felt its effects in 1294 all the more strongly. Whether or not the famine extended to Wales is unclear. None of the contemporary accounts of the revolt make much of the famine's contribution to the mood in Wales, and native Welsh sources such as *Brut y Tywysogyon* do not mention it. Still, if the failure of the harvest in England attested to in English records such as the Bury St. Edmunds chronicle and *Historia Anglicana* did indeed extend to adjacent parts of Wales, we ought perhaps to consider the notion that calamities such as famines, 'descend[ing] frequently upon a humanity ill-equipped to combat them', gave rise to 'the emotional instability so characteristic of the feudal era'.[13] It is not too hard to envisage many a Welsh peasant faced with a poor harvest choosing to throw in his lot with the rebels during the first days of the revolt, especially as something of the sort may well have occurred twenty years later during the revolt of Llywelyn Bren in 1316. To some, a life in the service of a Welshman attempting to claim a princely patrimony, in spite of the violent death in battle that might come with it, may have seemed preferable to facing the hardships brought on by scarcity of food.

Events outside Wales soon provided the Welsh with an opportunity to strike. In 1294 England and France went to war over the territory of Gascony in south-western France. The raising of large levies in Wales and Scotland was a desperate move by Edward, who found himself hard pressed to raise the forces for a sustained military campaign. Indeed, he was again to rely on men from outside England during his unsuccessful foray into Flanders in 1297 (including a few native Welsh leaders who had been imprisoned in England since the early 1280s).[14]

It is clear that many Welshmen resented this call to serve what must have been regarded by the overwhelming majority of the *gwerin* or peasantry as a foreign power. As 1294 wore on, it became clear that English attention was firmly focused on the war with the French. Even the lowliest of tenants could not but have been struck by the change that came about at this time. Work on the massive castles of the north gradually ground to a halt as the money was earmarked for the English army, and one by one, the constables of the castles and other English worthies were entrusting their possessions to subordinates and leaving for England, and military duty. The first contingent of troops, which was supposed to include Welsh soldiers, was due to leave for France at the end of September 1294, coinciding with a collection of the lay subsidy. It is hard to believe that the revolt – which began on 30th September – was not deliberately engineered to take advantage of these events.

One pivotal question, therefore, remains to be answered: who took the initiative in organising the revolt, which, after all, was co-ordinated in its early stages with a high degree of precision? This issue has plagued successive generations of historians, and any number of theories have been advanced to answer what appears at first glance to be a deceptively simple question. Some scholars have held that Wales was in the grip of a number of revolts in 1294-5, of which Madog's was merely the most serious. An eighteenth-century historian contended that there were 'three insurrections', 'though it does not appear that they were directed by any common principle of union'.[15] However, even the more zealous advocates of this theory tend to admit that the timing of the revolt, which began in the north, the middle March, the south-west and almost certainly Morgannwg virtually simultaneously, suggests the likelihood that there was at least some element of co-ordination to the Welsh actions. This was the opinion of Edwardian historian O. Morien Morgan, who inferred from the timing of the attacks in the autumn of 1294 that Madog, Morgan and Maelgwn held a 'conference' beforehand to plan their assaults.[16] The one modern historian who studied the revolt in detail, John Griffiths, substantially agrees with this view, writing in 1955: 'Plans must have been carefully prearranged, secret meetings held, and messengers dispatched to the different areas of operations to inform all those who were ready to fight for the national cause.'[17]

Evidence of contact between the rebels in different parts of Wales is not evidence of shared motives, however. It has been recently suggested that the other revolt leaders 'were lesser men with purely local aims'.[18] This view has been shared by many historians, who augment their claims by citing isolated passages in the chronicles which may be read as evidence that some of the leaders placed themselves at the head of the revolt in their area after its outbreak. In 1854, Thomas Owen Morgan wrote of Maelgwn ap Rhys Fychan that 'the people [of south-western Wales] had already risen when they chose him for their leader', going on to theorise that he was happy to play the role of leader at first, 'as an assenting party' to the revolt; the implication is that he became embroiled in the revolt by degrees, and was unable to extricate himself.[19]

Another theory contends that the real impetus for the revolt came not from the remnants of the Welsh aristocracy who came to assume its leadership, but from those *uchelwyr* who had attained positions within the English bureaucracy.[20] They were witnesses to the extortion and abuse of privilege that defined the English administration of Wales in the early 1290s, but, knowing that they themselves carried little weight with the *gwerin*, determined to persuade the most prominent members of the fallen royal houses that the only way the situation could be addressed was by force. This theory is certainly an attractive one, as it offers an explanation as to why four men whose standing in actuality was insignificant but whose reputation as descendants of some of the greatest men and women in Welsh history was well-known could rise to be the leaders of a nation-wide revolt. The truth, however, probably lies somewhere in between. It may be that Madog had envisaged being at the head

Cymer Abbey near Dolgellau, of which Madog's great-great-grandfather, Maredudd ap Cynan, was a patron

Llanfaes church. The original building was burnt by Madog's men

Eagle's tower, Caernarfon castle

The west wall of Caernarfon castle. In 1294, this side was protected by a wooden palisade; it was here that the rebels likely gained access

The interior of Caernarfon castle

Flint castle, besieged by Madog probably in October 1294

Denbigh castle, captured by Madog after a siege in late 1294

Rhuthun castle, captured in 1294

Mold castle may have been assaulted by the rebels

Hawarden castle was recaptured by Edward in December 1294

Builth castle was besieged by the men of Cynan

Castell y Bere was besieged in 1294, before being captured and burnt by the Welsh

Harlech castle, besieged by Madog

Aberystwyth castle, besieged in 1294-5. According to one source, the garrison ran so short of food that they were reduced to eating horseflesh

Cricieth castle was besieged throughout the winter of 1294

The effigy of Ieuaf ab Adda in Valle Crucis abbey, Llangollen. Ieuaf apparently fought on the rebel side, as he killed an English soldier during the revolt.

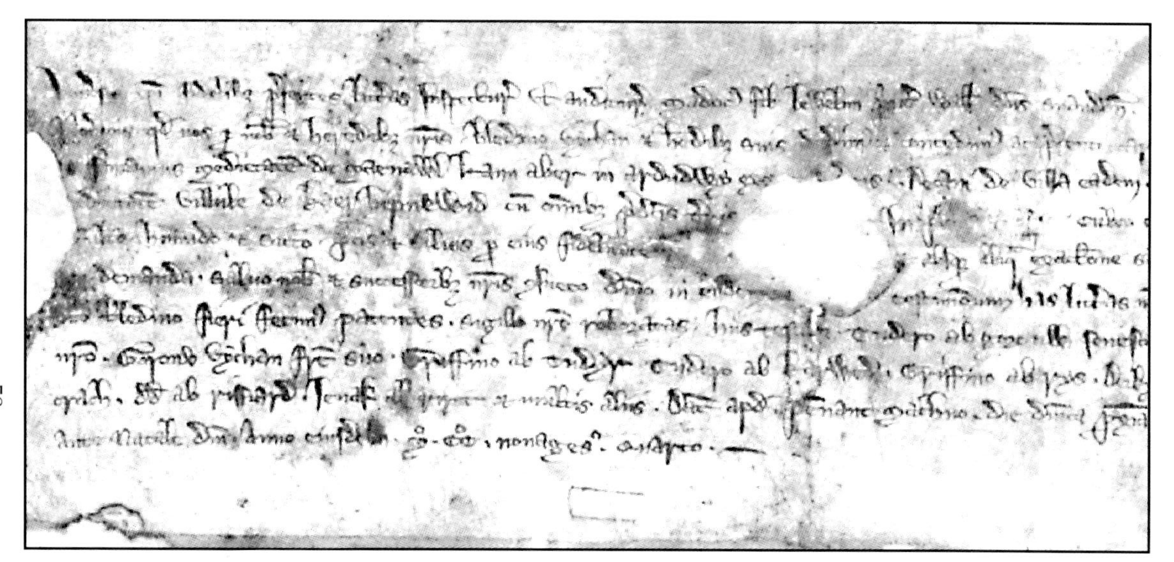

The Penmachno document, in which Madog styled himself 'prince of Wales'

Llantrisant castle, sacked by Morgan ap Maredudd in 1295

Caerffili castle may have been assaulted by Morgan's men

Caerffili castle

Conwy castle was besieged in January 1295; the town was burnt by the rebels.

Kenfig castle, captured by Morgan ap Maredudd in 1295

The site of the battle of Maes Moydog, Powys

This tomb in Gresford church was for centuries thought to be Madog's; he died in prison, and his burial place is unkown

Beaumaris, built by Edward I after the revolt to ensure the security of Ynys Môn

Beaumaris castle

of a restored Welsh royal government for years, perhaps as a result of a feeling that his rightful status had been denied him; equally, he may have been a reluctant rebel who had the role of prince of Wales foisted upon him. Yet it is also entirely feasible that, if indeed, the thought of re-establishing Welsh rule was a long-cherished one, it took the discreet counsel of another *uchelwr* to point out to him that he had a rightful claim to the Welsh princeship, and that much of Welsh society felt the same way.

[1] See *Languages in Britain and Ireland*, ed. Glanville Price (Blackwell, 2000), particularly 'Welsh' by Janet Davies (pp. 78-108) and 'Flemish in Wales' by Lauran Toorians (pp. 184-6).
[2] R. Allen Brown, H. M. Colvin and A. J. Taylor (eds.), *The History of the King's Works Vol. 1: The Middle Ages* (HMSO, 1969), pp. 371-2; for the lack of renumeration for the Welsh inhabitants of Caernarfon, see Keith Williams-Jones, 'Caernarvon', pp. 72-101 of R. A. Griffiths (ed.), *Boroughs of Medieval Wales* (Cardiff, 1978); p. 72.
[3] John Davies, *A History of Wales* (Penguin, 1993), pp. 172-3.
[4] Much of what follows is derived from Natalie M. Fryde, 'A Royal Enquiry into Abuses: Queen Eleanor's Ministers in north-eastern Wales, 1291-2', pp. 366-76 of *Welsh History Review* Vol. 6 (1970-1).
[5] Keith Williams-Jones, *The Merioneth Lay Subsidy Roll 1292-3*, p. xx.
[6] Keith Williams-Jones, *The Merioneth Lay Subsidy Roll 1292-3*, p. xv.
[7] Keith Williams-Jones, *The Merioneth Lay Subsidy Roll 1292-3*, p. xxv; p. xxxv.
[8] Richard Arthur Roberts, *The Court Rolls of the Lordship of Ruthin or Dyffryn-Clwyd* (Cymmrodorion Society, 1893), pp. 2-3.
[9] Antonia Gransden (ed.), *The Chronicle of Bury St. Edmunds* 1242-1307 (Nelson, 1964), p. 123.
[10] R. F. Treharne, *Essays On Thirteenth-Century England* (The Historical Association, 1971), p. 44 notes that this famine was so grievous that it 'drove men forth into distant shires to seek work and food, till they died in such numbers, of hunger and disease, that the administration had to allow their bodies to be buried without waiting for the coroners to view them.'
[11] Philip Ziegler, *The Black Death* (Collins, 1969), p. 32.
[12] R. F. Treharne, *Essays On Thirteenth-Century England*, p. 44.
[13] Marc Bloch, *Feudal Society Vol. 1: The Growth of Ties of Dependence* (Routledge and Kegan Paul, 1962), p. 73.
[14] J. Beverley Smith, 'Edward II and the Allegiance of Wales', pp.139-71 of *Welsh History Review* Vol. 8 (1976-7); p. 142 and note 14.
[15] William Warrington, *A History of Wales in Nine Books* (1823), p. 331 (Book IX).
[16] O. Morien Morgan, *A History of Wales* (Howell, 1911), p. 406.
[17] John Griffiths, 'The Revolt of Madog ap Llywelyn, 1294-5', pp. 12-24 of *Transactions of the Caernarvonshire Historical Society* Vol. 16 (1955); p. 12.
[18] David Walker, *Medieval Wales* (Cambridge, 1990), p. 54.
[19] Thomas Owen Morgan, 'On the Subjugation of Wales by Edward I', pp. 290-300 of *Archaeologia Cambrensis* Vol. 5 (New Series) (1854); p. 298. Morgan's comments seem to have taken their inspiration from Powel, who wrote in 1584 that the men of west Wales 'chose' Maelgwn (p. 380).
[20] See A. D. Carr, *Medieval Wales* (Macmillan, 1995), particularly pp. 87-8 and pp. 93-4, and also 'An aristocracy in decline: the native Welsh lords after the Edwardian Conquest', pp. 103-29 of *Welsh History Review* Vol. 5 (1970-1).

3 – MADOG AND THE LOCAL LEADERS OF REVOLT

Madog ap Llywelyn

In writing his landmark analysis of Owain Glyndŵr's revolt, R. R. Davies admitted that his work had to concern itself primarily with the revolt rather than the leader behind it, 'since the sources do not exist to compose an individual portrait of the man'.[1]

Unfortunately for historians, what is true of Glyndŵr is doubly true of Madog ap Llywelyn. There are few more important figures in medieval Welsh history about whom so little is known. Scholars of the Victorian and Edwardian periods both struggled to pin down his origins – his lineage, previous military experience, and even his name were sources of controversy and confusion. With the aid of previously overlooked sources, contemporary historians have been able to solve some of these conundrums, but assembling a coherent picture of Madog's life remains a task that forces one to resort to educated guesswork.

The first obstacle to be overcome is that of Madog's ancestry. The medieval writers Trivet and Hemingburgh both agreed that Madog was related somehow to Llywelyn II. On this basis historians have repeatedly attempted to establish the precise nature of this relationship, but even this minor task presented huge difficulties until relatively recently because of the inconsistencies in the historical record. John of Everisden calls the Welshman 'Maredudd ap Llywelyn', while an unnamed monk writing in Chester calls him 'Madog ap Maredudd'; and this is to say nothing of the inevitable variations in spelling in other sources.[2] The Welsh usage of the patronymic (taking one's father's name as a surname) was sometimes a source of confusion to English chroniclers, and the fact that these writers were often separated from the emotional and cultural climate in which the revolt took place by great distance – John of Everisden lived near Bury St. Edmunds, over one hundred and fifty miles from the action – meant that there was often no local source to confirm or deny the evidence that reached them. Under such circumstances, mistakes and inaccuracies were bound to creep into the accounts of English chroniclers.

By the late nineteenth century, scholarly opinion leaned towards the identification of Madog as an illegitimate son of Llywelyn II. This was based on circumstantial evidence contained within his name, seemingly confirmed in the chronicle of Lanercost. But as was later pointed out, it is most unlikely that Edward, who had made a point of tracking down and capturing Llywelyn's brother Dafydd, along with his wife and children, would have allowed a possible direct heir to the title of prince of Wales to slip through his net and perhaps foster discontent at a later period.* Accordingly, later historians discarded this theory in favour of another, more plausible one. The historical references to Madog being part of the royal house of Gwynedd may be explained by his having come from the line of Meirionydd, a minor branch of the royal family whose leader had been dispossessed of his lands by Llywelyn II in 1256. That man's name was Llywelyn ap Maredudd, which gives credence

* Of Llywelyn II's three brothers, Dafydd had been executed in 1283 and Owain Goch died at around the same time. Only Llywelyn's other brother, Rhodri, had a claim to the throne superior to that of Madog; but by 1294 he had been living on a private estate in southern England for some time, supported the English in the wars of 1276-7 and 1282-3, and was clearly not considered to be a viable prince by dint of his evident lack of interest in his patrimony. He died around 1315.

to the notion that the English writers at Bury St. Edmunds and Chester correctly identified Madog's lineage, but confused the order in which the names ran. This theory confirms Madog's status as a member of the house of Gwynedd, and would mean that Madog and Llywelyn II were indeed related. Their closest common ancestor was Owain Gwynedd (d. 1170), making them fifth cousins (see page 227).

This at least allows us to place Madog within the tradition of a line of lords of Meirionydd, but brings us little closer to the man himself, for we know tantalisingly little about his forebears. There seems to have been a history of rivalry between the leaders of the line of Meirionydd and the leaders of the house of Gwynedd, for again and again we see attempts by the two Llywelyns to claim Meirionydd as their own. Madog's great-great-grandfather, Maredudd ap Cynan ab Owain (d. 1212), ruled Meirionydd and the Llŷn peninsula in part during the early reign of Llywelyn I. As lord of Meirionydd, he was of sufficient standing to act as patron of Cymer Abbey near Dolgellau.[3] He is on record as having been expelled from his lands in Llŷn by Llywelyn in 1201 in the opening broadside of what would turn out to be a long-running feud.[4] The following year he was dispossessed of Meirionydd as well, and Llywelyn's construction of Castell Y Bere in the heart of that territory in the 1220s may be viewed as an expression in stone of his desire to stamp Gwynedd's authority on the disputed area.[5]

However, Maredudd's son, Llywelyn (also known as 'Llywelyn Fawr', a somewhat confusing happenstance for today's readers, as Llywelyn I was also known by the same epithet), recovered the land in September 1241, when the then prince of Wales, Dafydd II, was forced to yield to Henry III's demands. Thus began the close relationship between the line of Meirionydd and the English throne, which lasted until the outbreak of hostilities precipitated by the failure of the peace between England and Wales in the early 1260s.

It was under Madog's father, Llywelyn ap Maredudd, that the line of Meirionydd was to be dispossessed for good from its ancestral territory. He wrote a letter to Henry III some time in 1256 or 1257 complaining of his plight under Llywelyn II, who had gained sole control over Gwynedd after his victory against the forces of his brothers Owain and Dafydd at the battle of Bryn Derwin in 1255, and who would shortly assume the title of prince of Wales. In his letter, Llywelyn ap Maredudd expressed his hope to 'recover his land soon through the favour of God and the king'.[6] By 1259, he was living on a yearly pension of forty marks from Henry's coffers in recognition of his opposition to Llywelyn II. However, it would seem that by June 1262, Llywelyn ap Maredudd had resolved his differences with his distant relative. When he died in an unnamed battle (possibly in the Marcher area) on 27th April 1263, he appears to have been fighting not with Henry's forces, but on the side of the prince.[7]

It is at this point that Madog makes his first appearance in the historical record. A later English inquiry established that it was upon the occasion of his father's death that Llywelyn II bestowed upon Madog and his brother Dafydd lands on Ynys Môn, almost certainly in the commote of Malltraeth, where Madog is known to have had holdings in later years. There is, however, no evidence that Llywelyn returned Meirionydd to Madog's family at this time. He was doubtless young, probably only in his teenage years, in the early 1260s, and there is no further record of him until the war of 1277, when he is recorded as having been in the service of Edward I. On 12th November that year, a payment of ten marks was made to him; his name is recorded in the accounts as 'Madoco f'[ilio] L'[eulini]' (Madog son of Llywelyn). Of far more importance for our purposes is a second payment made a week later. In this document, created at Chester, 'Madocio fil' Leulini' is styled 'domino de Meroneth' ('lord of Meirionydd').[8]

Two snippets of information can be gleaned from this. Firstly, it is clear that Madog believed that his lands had been wrongfully taken from him, and that his allegiance to the English king was therefore probably motivated by self-interest. As the English armies swept through Wales in the spring, he likely saw which way the wind was blowing, and decided to align himself with the victors in the hope of having his grievances properly addressed. Secondly, the fact that the document confers upon Madog a title which he aspired to but did not yet possess suggests that Edward did not oppose – and may, perhaps, have supported – Madog's bid to reclaim the lordship of Meirionydd.

He stopped short, however, of taking pity on the young Welshman and giving him his ancestral lands outright. There were greater issues to be dealt with, such as the nature of the peace in Wales; and in that respect, Meirionydd was of far more worth to Edward as a concession to the defeated Llywelyn. The Treaty of Aberconwy signed by Edward and Llywelyn after the conclusion of the war in 1276-7 accordingly granted the area to the prince rather than Madog. Lying behind the Eryri massif, it was a large territory, yet poor enough and sufficiently distant from the seats of English power for Llywelyn to hold it without posing a threat. As for Madog, Edward allowed him to pursue a legal remedy for his predicament, and in 1278 he brought a court case against Llywelyn at the earliest opportunity, citing his rightful claim to Meirionydd.[9] Whatever the circumstances and details of this action, it was clearly unsuccessful, for the case was adjourned on account of Llywelyn's failure to attend the proceedings; a record of 1280 shows that Llywelyn remained in possession of the area. By 1284, a presumably chastened Madog was apparently living on his townships in Ynys Môn.[10] That is the last we hear of him until his spectacular re-appearance in 1294.

The paltriness of the evidence on which Madog's biography rests thus far is plain enough, and it forces the historian into the realms of guesswork. What shape did Madog's life take after the dispossession of his family, and what happened to Madog after his father's death in 1263? Some historians have speculated that Madog was exiled in England after 1256, but if that was the case, it makes no sense for his father to have been recorded as fighting with the Welsh in 1263. Still less does it make sense that Madog should then have acquired land in what remained territory under Welsh control. If he did spend time in England, as Owain Glyndŵr did during his formative years, the period seems likely to have been a short one. Two plausible scenarios are that he was in England during the late 1250s or early 1260s with his father, or possibly for a time in the mid-1270s before returning to Wales to claim his birthright with the triumphant Edward and his army. Edward was certainly well disposed to Welshmen seeking refuge in England: he had given asylum to a group of Welshmen who had plotted to assassinate Llywelyn in

1274. That Madog abandoned the Welsh cause at this critical moment is certainly another possibility, though it seems odd that no mention of such a defection survives, even for a character of Madog's elusiveness. As has been mentioned, it is also possible that Madog was granted land by Llywelyn II in the early 1260s.[11]

Madog's family life is obscure. He had three brothers, Dafydd, Llywelyn, and Maredudd, and of the two sons he is known to have sired, we may conjecture that one at least went on to establish himself in society, for one 'Hywel ap Madog ap Llywelyn' is recorded as having been in possession of the vill of Lledwigan Llan in Ynys Môn in 1352.[12] This would seem to suggest that Madog married, though there is no other evidence for such a union. His interests remain a mystery, and unlike in Glyndŵr's case, there is nothing in the way of records of service on campaigns with the English king in Scotland or elsewhere to suggest that he had any military experience in English forces. The only possible exceptions are the aforementioned documents relating to the war of 1277, but even here, the records of payments mentioned above need not necessarily have been reward for military service. Recent research, however, may bolster the argument that Madog had some military prowess and experience (see below).

Finally, we turn to Madog's character. This, too, was a complete mystery for many years, but an examination of the Hagnaby chronicle in the 1970s led to an interesting discovery. According to the chronicler, in December 1294 – that is, three months after the beginning of the revolt – a large group of Madog's men went to submit to Edward, who agreed to pardon them if they would serve in France. They agreed, and also promised to capture Madog for the king. After going to their leader, however, he made a rousing speech – its wording has, alas, not survived – and the Welshmen were persuaded once again to back Madog's cause.[13] Though the date and location of these events are somewhat vague, it provides an intriguing insight into the personality of this rebel leader. If the source is reliable, we may infer that Madog was an eloquent orator, as well as a sound judge of the mood of his men. What he may have lacked in military experience was at least partially compensated for by an ability to raise patriotic fervour and command the loyalty of this band of uncertain rebels.

Morgan, Maelgwn and Cynan

Though Madog led the revolt in the north, responsibility in the south fell to three men, Morgan ap Maredudd, Maelgwn ap Rhys Fychan, and Cynan ap Maredudd. The first two (and perhaps the latter as well) were descended from the Lord Rhys, ruler of Deheubarth in the late twelfth century, but their subsequent dispossession from their lands meant that this fact was no guarantee of a lofty position within society. Here too, the historian faces the problem of scarce source material, but despite the frustrating dearth of evidence, a few facts can be established about two of these nobles.

Of the three, we know most about Morgan ap Maredudd, the leader of the revolt in the south-east. He was of the house of Gwynllŵg, a minor royal family in Morgannwg whose territories had previously been fairly extensive. Since the loss of Caerleon in 1217, however, the family's territories had been limited to the commotes of Machen, Edeligion and Llebenydd in modern-day Gwent; his home may have been at Castell

Maredudd in Lower Machen.[14]

Morgan's father, Maredudd ap Gruffudd (d. 1270), saw an opportunity to enhance his position during the power struggle between Llywelyn II and the local English lord, Gilbert de Clare, in the late 1260s, but in the end he was unable to turn events to his advantage. The Treaty of Montgomery had just been signed, and Llywelyn was in a belligerent mood. In 1269, at a hearing in Montgomery, he insisted that he had a right to Maredudd's homage, even though Maredudd's lands had lain within the sphere of influence of the Clare family for decades. With a certain deftness, Llywelyn had also previously bestowed upon Maredudd the commote of Hirfryn, in which the castle of Llanymddyfri stood. This he had done in order to be able to claim that Maredudd was a Welsh baron, and that he was therefore entitled to claim his lands under the Welsh system of ownership, thus extending Llywelyn's influence southwards to the Bristol Channel.[15] The arbiter of this dispute was Edward, then still a prince. He sided with Llywelyn, and when de Clare discovered the outcome had gone against him, he was incensed. A few days after Llywelyn's attack on the half-built castle at Caerffili, de Clare invaded Maredudd's lands and dispossessed him and his family for good.

Maredudd died shortly after the attack, probably on 19th October,[16] leaving Morgan at the head of the family. In 1278 he followed in Madog's footsteps by fighting a legal battle to have his ancestral lands returned to him, and like Madog, he was unsuccessful. His possible later involvement in the conflict of 1282-3 on the Welsh side seems to have had little effect on Morgan's social status.[17]

Morgan's actions during the 1294-5 revolt were just as

spectacular as those in the north. He captured several castles and besieged others, including Abergavenny, and his military prowess was such that, after a period of imprisonment, he later served with Edward on his military expedition to Flanders in 1297.[18] Though a number of historians have questioned his commitment to the Welsh cause in 1294-5 in the light of his behaviour towards the end of the conflict, and his later decision not to support the revolt of Llywelyn Bren in 1316, the sheer range and scope of his campaign in the autumn and winter suggests his determination to give Madog his fullest backing.

The second leader of the revolt in the south, Maelgwn ap Rhys Fychan, was a great-great-great-grandson of the Lord Rhys. His father, Rhys Fychan, fought with Llywelyn II in 1282, but surrendered in January 1283. After the end of the conflict, he apparently endured a long period of imprisonment at Bamborough castle, interspersed with military service in the pay of the English, dying in 1302. By 1294, Rhys' son Maelgwn owned a single commote in northern Cardiganshire, and it is reasonable to assume that frustration with his lot led him to revolt in south-western Wales, where he captured Cardigan castle and raided the lordships of Pembroke and Carmarthen.[19]

Finally, we come to Cynan ap Maredudd, the leader of the rebels in Brycheiniog and the central and southern Marches. Virtually nothing is known about this man, whose jurisdiction during the revolt was only established quite recently (for many years historians assumed that he helped Maelgwn lead the revolt in the south-west). His ancestry is uncertain, but he is believed to have been of noble descent. A Cynan ap Maredudd, whose father, Maredudd ab Owain, died in 1265, is recorded as having died in 1328. This would make Cynan a great-great-

great-grandson of the Lord Rhys, and such an identification would, in fact, be not so far removed from the description given of him in the Welsh chronicle *Brenhinedd y Saesson*, where he is also described as a descendant of Rhys.[20] However, this date of 1328 contradicts evidence in a number of chronicles concerning the 1294-5 revolt. Some historians have tentatively speculated that he, like Maelgwn, was a minor *uchelwr*; but as with so many other questions, the precise nature of Cynan's background must remain a matter of contention.

[1] R. R. Davies, *The Revolt of Owain Glyndŵr* (Oxford, 1995), p. 325.
[2] This discussion is largely informed by J. G. Edwards, 'Madog ap Llywelyn, the Welsh leader in 1294-5', pp. 207-10 of the *Bulletin of the Board of Celtic Studies* Vol. XIII Part 4 (May 1950), particularly p. 208.
[3] Maredudd is known to have issued a grant of lands to Cymer around the turn of the thirteenth century. See Huw Pryce (ed.), *The Acts of Welsh Rulers 1120-1283*, p. 341.
[4] *Brut Y Tywysogyon* (Pen. Ms. 20) gives the following description under the entry for 1201 (p. 81): '... Llywelyn ap Iorwerth, being a young man graced with generosity and worthiness, gained possession of the cantref of Llŷn and Eifionydd, after driving out Maredudd ap Cynan because of his treachery.' Quite what Maredudd did to rouse Llywelyn's anger is not recorded.
[5] The seventeenth-century scholar Robert Vaughan theorised that Y Bere was built several decades earlier during the reign of Gruffudd ap Cynan (d. 1137), but this theory is ruled out by the more recent discovery of a document dating from 1221 referring to the construction of a castle by Llywelyn in Meirionydd. See E. D. Evans, 'Castell Y Bere', p. 31; R. R. Davies, *The Age of Conquest: Wales 1063-1415*, p. 251.
[6] Huw Pryce (ed.), *The Acts of Welsh Rulers 1120-1283*, p. 343.
[7] J. B. Smith, *Llywelyn ap Gruffudd: Prince of Wales*, pp. 155-6 discusses this point in detail, and notes that Llywelyn ap Maredudd was receiving payments from the English as late as June 1262.
[8] J. G. Edwards, 'Madog ap Llywelyn, the Welsh leader in 1294-5', p. 209.
[9] James Conway Davies (ed.), *The Welsh Assize Roll 1277-1284* (Cardiff, 1940), pp. 237-8; J. B. Smith, *Llywelyn ap Gruffudd: Prince of Wales*, p. 443, p. 446.
[10] David Stephenson, *The Governance of Gwynedd*, p. 145 notes that grants were made by Edward I in 1284 to Elise ab Iorwerth (of the house of Powys) and Madog ap Llywelyn to hold their lands in Wales by barony.
[11] R. R. Davies, *The Age of Conquest: Wales 1063-1415*, pp. 323-4; J. B. Smith, *Llywelyn ap Gruffudd: Prince of Wales*, pp. 369-74. For the possibility that Madog was granted land by Llywelyn II, see David Stephenson, *The Governance of Gwynedd*, pp. 146-7.
[12] A. D. Carr, 'Madog ap Llywelyn: The Revolt of 1294-5 in Caernarfonshire', pp. 35-46 of *Caernarfonshire Historical Society Transactions* Vol. 58 (1997), especially p. 36; Glyn Roberts,

'Biographical notes: Madog ap Llywelyn', pp. 41-9 of the *Bulletin of the Board of Celtic Studies* Vol. XVII (1956).
[13] Michael Prestwich, 'A New Account of the Welsh Campaign of 1294-5', pp. 89-94 of *Welsh History Review* Vol. 6 (1972-3); p. 90.
[14] See T. B. Pugh (ed.), *Glamorgan County History Vol. 3: The Middle Ages* (Cardiff, 1971), p. 59.
[15] J. B. Smith, *Llywelyn ap Gruffudd: Prince of Wales*, pp. 345-7 discusses Llywelyn's actions at this time, though he ultimately reserves judgement on the question of Llywelyn's intent when he bestowed on Maredudd the commote of Hirfryn (p. 346).
[16] Both the Brut and *Brenhinedd y Saesson* notice Maredudd's death, but one gives 19th October as his death of death, while the other gives 14th December. See Thomas Jones (ed.), *Brut Y Tywysogyon* (Peniarth Ms. 20 version) (Cardiff, 1952), p. 213. According to J. Beverley Smith, the earlier date is preferable; see *Llywelyn ap Gruffudd: Prince of Wales*, p. 352, note 49.
[17] Morgan witnessed one of the two surviving documents issued by Dafydd III during his principate. See Huw Pryce (ed.), *The Acts of Welsh Rulers 1120-1283*, p. 656-7.
[18] J. B. Smith, 'Edward II and the allegiance of Wales', pp. 139-71 of *Welsh History Review* Vol. 8 (1976-7); p. 142.
[19] T. Jones-Pierce, 'Maelgwn ap Rhys', pp. 609-10 of *The Dictionary of Welsh Biography down to 1940* (Society of Cymmrodorion, 1959).
[20] The relevant passage from *Brenhinedd y Saesson* is quoted in Thomas Jones (ed.), *Brut Y Tywysogyon* (Peniarth Ms. 20 version), pp. 218-9.

4 – MURDER AT MICHAELMAS

The revolt's beginnings

It is agreed that Madog's revolt began at Michaelmas 1294 with assaults at various locations on Ynys Môn, followed by an attack on Caernarfon town and castle. Dating the actions that occurred elsewhere in Wales during those first days of the revolt is, however, almost impossible – the dates of most of them were simply not recorded. Nevertheless, it is reasonable to assume that they had all occurred by mid-October at the latest, for no orders of any importance were issued concerning the Welsh situation by Edward until 15th October, when the English administration suddenly sprang into life, and letters were hurriedly dispatched to military men across England to prepare for duty in Wales.[1]

Due to this infuriating lack of dating evidence, the day-to-day co-ordination of the attacks across Wales cannot be examined very closely. Despite this, the wording and construction of the references in chronicles and royal correspondence means there is no reason to doubt that they occurred within a few days of one another. A report was made on 1st October – the second day of the revolt* – noting that Geoffrey Clement and Walter de Pederton had been killed by 'malefactors'.[2] When taken in tandem with the account of the revolt provided in *Brut Y Tywysogyon*, this report provides crucial evidence that Madog's attacks coincided with an action by Cynan in mid-Wales. For the entry under 1294, the *Brut* notes: 'Geoffrey Clement, justice of Deheubarth, was slain at 'Y

* There is debate as to whether the revolt started on 29th or 30th September, and it should be noted that the earlier date is the one given in some sources, including the Annals of Worcester. A date of 30th September is favoured here, following Powicke (*The Thirteenth Century: 1216-1307* (Oxford, 1953) R. R. Davies).

Gwmfriw' in Builth.' Though some sources claim Clement was at Aberystwyth at the time of his death, it has been convincingly argued that 'Y Gwmfriw' is a corrupt form of 'Y Gamriw', a mountain around five miles north-west of Builth Wells, and well within the area known to have been ravaged by Cynan's forces.[3] If correct – and there is no substantial reason to doubt it – this theory proves that Cynan's men were active from the very beginning of the revolt. The fact that Edward was by mid-October preparing not only an invasion army for northern Wales, but also for mid-Wales and southern Wales, likewise suggests that the opening attacks alluded to in the chronicles and other sources had occurred by that time, though the exact dates of a great many of them we will likely never know.

In the south-east, on or very soon after 30th September, Maelgwn ap Rhys Fychan attacked Cardigan castle with a group of men and captured it.[4] At the same time, Madog attacked and burnt the church at Llanfaes on Ynys Môn with his men. Ynys Môn was the natural place to begin the revolt in the north. There were no fortifications to speak of – Beaumaris castle did not, as yet, exist – and as we shall see, most of Madog's fellow rebels were minor land-holders on the island (see chapter 7). The rebels ravaged Ynys Môn in general before crossing the Menai Straits and descending upon the seat of English power in Gwynedd, the town of Caernarfon,* and since the English in the town were caught by surprise in the attack, it follows that news of the violence had not reached Caernarfon by the time of the rebel assault, suggesting that the sacking of Llanfaes, attacks on other parts of the island, the crossing of the straits and the attack on Caernarfon were all accomplished

* Writing in 1823, William Warrington suggested that Madog's men captured Caernarfon before going on to assault Ynys Môn, but his account is unsound in several particulars.

within a relatively short space of time, or perhaps even on the same day by separate detachments of his force. This interpretation – namely, that the main body of rebels came, at first, from Ynys Môn – is arguably lent further credence by the way in which the revolt's beginnings are reported in the chronicle of Bury St. Edmunds. In the entry for 1294, it is asserted that Madog's men 'invaded Snowdonia'. It follows that the rebels began the revolt elsewhere. Ynys Môn – the island from which so many of Madog's leading men hailed – was indisputably the cradle of his revolt.[5]

Caernarfon, which was holding its fair on the day of the attack, was a fairly typical borough town. Its population at the end of the century has been estimated at around 300-400, making it an average-sized settlement, and its population was mostly English. Since building began on the town in mid-1283 it had expanded slowly but consistently – a bakery and store for hay were both in existence by November that year, and the town was granted its charter the following autumn. The exchequer, the administrative centre of northern Wales, stood within the town walls, as did a number of houses owned by the king and a mill. Its burgesses were helped along the road to prosperity by some favourable clauses in the town charter, such as the one requiring every person who lived within an eight-mile radius of Caernarfon to trade only in the borough. Such measures were hardly unique to Caernarfon; Aberystwyth's burgesses were benefiting from a fifteen-mile catchment area by 1303. Moreover, no less than 1,464¼ acres of land surrounding the town were reserved for the burgesses' use.[6]

As for Caernarfon castle itself, much building work remained to be done. Edward had made a point of building his grandest castle at Caernarfon because of the area's importance to Welsh mythology. According to Welsh legend the fort at Segontium, just half a mile from the castle site, had been a seat of power of Macsen Wledig, reputed to have been emperor of Rome, and whose exploits are attested to in the *Mabinogion*. Links with imperial Rome, however tenuous, were worth cultivating for reasons of prestige. In fact, the (supposed) illustrious past of this part of northern Wales had been used for propaganda purposes once before, by the composer of the biography of Gruffudd ap Cynan. The work, probably commissioned in the 1160s by Gruffudd's son Owain Gwynedd, makes much of earl Hugh de Avranches' decision to build an earlier castle at Caernarfon in about 1090 'in the old fort of the [Roman] emperor', thus giving Gruffudd's capture of the castle added lustre.[7]

Now Edward took advantage of the same imperial tinge of Caernarfon's history. In an effort to underline his supremacy, he commanded his architects to build the castle in a style recalling that of the castle at Constantinople, with polygonal towers and dark bands in the masonry. This allusion to these great classical fortifications of the Mediterranean was flattering to the king, and even if none of the locals had seen the originals or were even aware of the similarity, there was no mistaking the grandiosity of the gesture (and, indeed, the arrogance of the comparison!).[8]

Crucially, however, at the time of Madog's attack the castle was still only half-built. Construction had proceeded apace during the 1280s, but because of Edward's expensive military campaigns, money for the works dried up, and work stopped on the castle in 1292. Crucially for Madog's men, much of the northern side was unfinished, protected only by a wooden palisade, and their attack seems to have commenced on this side.[9]

Contemporary reports note the severity of the insurgent attack on the town, during which they engaged in a bout of indiscriminate killing. For early modern historian Humphrey Llwyd, the attack's significance could be found in the fact that Madog's men 'slewe a great number of Englishmen'.[10] It is true that many English settlers were indeed killed. The slaughter was not, however, confined to that segment of the town's community, for Caernarfon's minority of Irish inhabitants and a smattering of settlers from Savoy also died. This act was to permanently change the town's make-up, for few were prepared to come from outside England to re-populate the town after the revolt's suppression. The king's houses were damaged; the mill was destroyed; the town walls were breached; the town's quay, which allowed for provisioning of the town by sea, was burnt; the exchequer was raided and its documents brought out and destroyed, among them the town's charter. Most impressively, the castle fell to the rebels – the only time in its history that it would be successfully stormed by the Welsh.[11]

The particulars of one other act during the assault on Caernarfon survive. The sheriff of Ynys Môn, Roger de Puleston, was captured, hanged and beheaded by two of his tenants, one of whom, Gronw of Twrcelyn, was an underling in the English administration on the island. That Puleston should have been killed by one of the men under his jurisdiction is surely an indication of the depth of feeling against the English authorities in this corner of Wales. One modern historian considered that the official 'had probably taken advantage of the position he held in the Edwardian Settlement after 1284', noting that he was later accused by the Welsh of issuing false extents. Whether or not the rebels knew of his attendance at the town's fair beforehand not we do not know, but given Gronw's position in the English administrative machinery on Ynys Môn, there is at least a chance that he had a foreknowledge of his superior's movements, and that the act was therefore premeditated.[12]

Elsewhere in Wales, the most ominous sign for the English was the determination with which the Welsh were laying siege to castles. Builth in mid-Wales was blockaded by Cynan's men. The castle had been besieged for six weeks by 12th November, which suggests that this action, too, was initiated at the very beginning of October. The timing was good; as at so many other castles, the constable, John Giffard, was away on military duty. Builth's garrison consisted of six cavalry, twenty crossbowmen and forty archers. This force was sufficient to hold off an attack, but in the long term, feeding such a large body of men could cause great problems. It was presumably for this reason that the Welsh siege caused so much distress to the English authorities, who sanctioned no less than five attempts to relieve the stronghold's garrison before Giffard himself finally managed to drive off the Welsh with a force of ten knights, twenty infantry and forty cavalry around 12th November.[13] This small figure allows us to deduce that Cynan's besieging force was of a similar size, probably on the order of a few dozen men. Two of the very few other Welsh actions recorded in this area during the revolt occurred at nearby Rhaeadr, where two mills and several burgages were burnt by the rebels, and Cefnllys, which lay a mere five miles or so to the north of Builth. Despite the fact that this attack is poorly attested in the historical record, the proximity of Cefnllys to Builth allows us to theorise with a fair degree of confidence that the men of Maelienydd were acting under Cynan's orders when they sacked that castle towards the end of 1294. It has been suggested that the English official Brian Brampton, the head of a Marcher family that attained prominence in the twelfth century, was killed in the assault.[14]

To the west, Margery Clement – Geoffrey Clement's widow – sought refuge in Aberystwyth castle after her estates in northern Cardiganshire were attacked. Whether or not the siege of the castle began at this point is open to question. It may have started some time in November, as the man recorded as being in charge of the castle in early 1295, Roger de Molis, was with the earl of Pembroke in south Wales the previous autumn, and it is reasonable to suppose that gaining entry to the castle even by sea would have been difficult after the siege's commencement. Further north, the English garrisons at Y Bere, Cricieth and Harlech all found themselves blockaded by the Welsh. Assaults in the north-east secured the baronial castles of Hawarden (and possibly Mold) in Flintshire, Rhuthun in Dyffryn Clwyd, and Denbigh (see map).[15] It may be possible to date the actions in Flintshire as occurring very shortly after 2nd October, as local landowner Reginald de Grey is recorded as having visited Ewloe manor on this day in his capacity as justice of Chester – hardly the action of a man faced with the tumult of a revolt on his doorstep (see chapter 5). Meanwhile, in Morgannwg Morgan ap Maredudd began his campaign, capturing Morlais castle near Merthyr Tudful and raiding in the Cardiff area.[16]

Edward had not yet reached Portsmouth when he first heard news of the revolt. To some extent, his sluggish response can be explained by the piecemeal nature of the reports he must have received. After all, to hear of 'malefactors' in a small and remote corner of Wales was by no means a harbinger of disaster. The fact was that many of his possessions in Wales and Ireland, and England as well, suffered from sporadic outbreaks of violence from time to time. More often than not, these were the purely local actions of disaffected peasants or petty officers discontented with their lot, and as such, did not merit much attention; and it may therefore be theorised that it was only when news of widespread attacks across Wales reached the king that he began to take the situation seriously. As for the expedition to Gascony, there was no doubt as to where Edward's priorities lay: the revolt in Wales would have to be put down first. In this respect, Edward probably had the experience of Rhys ap Maredudd's revolt in 1287-8 in mind. On that occasion, he had been in Gascony, and (one presumes) endured agonies as he awaited news of the outcome of the campaign to suppress the Welsh.[17] Determined to avoid a repeat this time around, Edward postponed the Gascony expedition, and directed his energies towards planning the Welsh campaign.

It would be no simple matter. As October progressed and reports arrived of attacks on castles in the north and Welsh raids in the south-west, the severity of the plight of the English garrisons in castles such as Cricieth and Harlech became clear. Nevertheless, Edward proceeded with caution. The loss of castles such as Morlais, Hawarden, and Denbigh were embarrassing, but hardly pivotal, for these strongholds were in any case minor castles that had been constructed by local English landowners. The castles in the north that mattered most to the English – specifically, Harlech, Aberystwyth, and Conwy, which together formed the 'Ring of Steel' – were ail formidable structures which could not be assailed by direct attack, except by very large numbers of men equipped with trebuchets and other siege equipment. Even then their fall could only be forced after a considerable period of time. (The strength of these castles is borne out by the prolonged sieges embarked upon by the English after the Welsh took Aberystwyth and Harlech during Owain Glyndŵr's revolt in the 1400s: for example, Aberystwyth withstood a siege from a massive English force, armed with cannons, for over a year. The Welsh eventually surrendered not after an attempt to storm the castle, but due to lack of food.) Therefore, the threat to the English garrisons stemmed less from the attacks of the Welsh rebels, and more from the simple fact that no supplies could get through the rebel-held territory in which they stood. If these large, strong castles could be kept supplied, they would be more or less safe, and could provide a base secure from attack for English forces once the royal army was provisioned and ready to enter Gwynedd. In the meantime, they would have to hold out as best they could, while small bands of soldiers raised by the local English lords sheltered at those castles in the Marches that were not besieged, penetrating into the Welsh hinterlands as far as was deemed safe.

To this end, Edward made arrangements to have the coastal castles supplied by sea. On 25th October, orders were issued to send ships from Bristol to the northern castles. Tenby remained in English hands throughout the revolt, and one of its ships, the *Blithe,* had to be specially fitted to carry corn, while the *Bonadventure* of Carmarthen was engaged in transporting supplies to northern Wales from 1st November onwards. The treasurer of Dublin, William de Estdene, was instructed to ready ships to supply provisions to the garrisons at Cricieth and Harlech, as was John de Havering on 27th October.[18] Caernarfon had of course already fallen, and although Conwy had not yet been attacked by the Welsh, it almost certainly lay within rebel territory. As its garrison swelled with the later arrival of the royal army, it too would be supplied in this way in early 1295.

Meanwhile, Edward was faced with the difficult problem of finding adequate numbers of fighting men. One division of his army had already sailed for Gascony and could not be recalled; and the unstable political situation in Scotland had itself partly been caused by requests for military service. Accordingly, an order was sent to the northern counties of England in mid-October, requesting that the local magnates in counties such as Cumberland, Westmoreland and Yorkshire raise troops.[19] These counties were not normally called upon to provide soldiers for service in Wales, and many of the men who eventually were pressed into fighting were untrained, unruly and ill-disciplined, as can be seen from the behaviour of the 'army' of Carlisle during their stay at Flint in late 1294. Edward could hardly afford to be choosy. With an army in south-western France, unrest in Ireland and Scotland, and now a revolt in Wales to contend with, his forces were stretched thin.

Siege warfare: the strategies of the Welsh and English

As one modern historian has noted, 'fire was the commonest and most terrible characteristic of medieval warfare'.[20] In an age where timber was the cheapest and most popular building material, a flame could be just as effective a weapon as a sword or a longbow. In the early stages of the revolt, fire would play a most important part in advancing the cause of the rebels, and in checking their progress by the burning of sources of supplies and shelter.

Reginald de Grey was alive to the possibilities of the latter strategy. Of all the Englishmen in positions of authority in Wales on the eve of the revolt, he would react quickest to counteract the rebel threat, assembling a force of around 5,000 infantry and fifty cavalry at Rhuddlan by 9th October.[21] Yet even this force was not enough to prevent a rebel attack on Flint castle. Grey, who either had a foreknowledge of this plan or simply anticipated Madog's next move, hurriedly bolstered the garrisons of both strongholds prior to the assault, placing two dozen cavalry, two dozen crossbowmen and a massive one hundred and twenty archers in Flint, and a smaller force in Rhuddlan.[22] Yet he was still sufficiently worried for the security of Flint to authorise the castle's constable, William de la Leye, to evict the townsfolk from their properties and burn the town, so that the advancing Welsh might not find shelter and provisions there.[23]

At this time, Flint was a largely English town, and a fairly new one at that. The construction of the castle had commenced in 1277, and by August that year more than 2,300 people were at work on the castle and the town's impressive defensive ditch, which modern archaeological excavations have revealed was over ten metres wide. After the castle's completion in the mid-1280s, some of the workers stayed on, settling in a town that was rapidly growing into a local trade centre. By 1292, Flint was home to seventy-four burgesses, including William of Podington, who presumably lived in the Bedfordshire village of the same name before coming to work on the castle as a mason, and one Adam, who was the king's 'tailor', a post whose responsibilities included the buying of provisions for royal forces.[24]

Yet neither the former's service as one of the castle's builders nor the latter's status as a royal official could save their goods and houses from the flames. Flint town was burnt to the ground, probably between 13th and 15th October, during which time Grey's force set out to strengthen the garrison at Flint. This suggests that the Welsh attack and siege came later, perhaps towards the end of the month, but it would prove to be unsuccessful. Grey's tactics, though they may appear with hindsight to have been unnecessarily extreme, nevertheless saved the castle from the fate of its near neighbour at Hawarden. The price, however, was high: in 1296, claims for loss of property and goods made by the townsfolk totalled over £500.[25]

The outlook was not so good at Castell Y Bere, which had been besieged by the Welsh from the beginning of October. On the eighteenth of that month an order to assemble an expedition to relieve the castle was issued by Edward to Richard, earl of Arundel. It will be recalled that the castle was under the jurisdiction of Robert Staundon, who had replaced its nominal constable, Robert Fitzwalter, in 1293 when he had been summoned for military duty, and that its garrison was undermanned. Evidence of the castle's precarious position even at this early stage is provided in another directive, probably also issued on or around 18th October, in which the king enquired after the security of Y Bere. Addressed to Roger Lestrange, and directing him to relieve the garrison, one section of the letter reads in translation: '[T]he King understands that his said castle is destitute of suitable munition at present, and he would be greatly displeased if he were to lose it now by invasion of his Welsh rebels.'[26] That Y Bere should be running low of the essential equipment of war only a few weeks into the Welsh siege can only be taken as a sign of its ill-preparedness to withstand an assault.

Neither the earl of Arundel nor Lestrange were successful in their efforts to relieve the beleaguered garrison, for on 27th October another order was issued, directing the two men to combine their forces with those of Fulk Fitzwarin, Bogo de Knoville, Peter Corbet and the newly-returned Robert Fitzwalter to make another attempt. The tone of Edward's letter this time is one of naked concern – the safety of the castle, it reads, 'we desire with all our heart'.[27] Thereafter there is nothing but silence concerning Castell Y Bere, and the question of the success or otherwise of this second relief expedition was the subject of fierce debate among historians in the early decades of the twentieth century.

Fortunately, excavations at the site have provided an answer to this quandary. Successive archaeological expeditions in the 1950s have produced many fascinating finds, including ample evidence of English occupation in the 1280s and 1290s: coins minted in the reign of Edward I, fragments of glazed pottery, and a lead seal. It was during these excavations that incontrovertible evidence of the Welsh intervention in 1294 was discovered, in the form of a thin layer of ash spread across the castle's interior.[28]

As Y Bere was never re-occupied after 1294, this damage must have occurred during the revolt. It thus seems clear that, at some point perhaps in late October, Madog's men gained the castle either by agreement or assault, ejected or killed the garrison, and fired it, along with the settlement that had grown up alongside it. The sight with which the earl of Arundel and his men were confronted when they finally entered the Dysynni valley some time in November must have caused them to quail, for it was ample proof that the revolt was to be no nine days' wonder.

[1] J. E. Morris, *The Welsh Wars of Edward I*, p. 242.
[2] J. E. Morris, *The Welsh Wars of Edward I*, pp. 241-2.
[3] Thomas Jones (ed.), *Brut Y Tywysogyon* (Peniarth Ms. 20 version), p. 218.
[4] William Rees, *An Historical Atlas of Wales* (Cardiff, 1951 (Faber and Faber, 1959)), p. 43.
[5] John Griffiths,'The Revolt of Madog ap Llywelyn, 1294-5', p. 14; Antonia Gransden (ed.), *The Chronicle of Bury St. Edmunds 1242-1307*, p. 125.
[6] For the construction of a bakery and other buildings and the allocation of lands to Caernarfon burgesses, see Keith Williams-Jones, 'Caernarvon', pp. 77-8; the rights of the burgesses of Aberystwyth are noticed in Ralph A. Griffiths, 'Aberystwyth', pp. 19-46; p. 33.
[7] D. Simon-Evans, *A Mediaeval Prince of Wales: The Life of Gruffudd ap Cynan* (Llanerch, 1990), p. 70.
[8] Keith Williams-Jones, 'Caernarvon', p. 75, p. 77 notes that a first draft of Edward's *Statute of Wales* (1284) shows that Edward intended to govern northern Wales from Caernarfon at an early stage: 'The ecclesiastical heart of the province was, of course, firmly set in Bangor. But Caernarvon had legend, if not a lustrous history, on its side and Edward I was quick to exploit it.'
[9] A. J. Taylor, *The King's Works in Wales, 1277-1330* (London (HMSO), 1974), pp. 377-81.
[10] Humphrey Llwyd, *Cronica Walliae* (ed. Ieuan M. Williams, Cardiff, 2002), p. 223.
[11] Keith Williams-Jones, 'Caernarvon', p. 80, p. 83.
[12] John Griffiths,'The Revolt of 1295 and its effects upon the Edwardian Settlement in the Principality of Wales', unpublished BA thesis, University of Liverpool, 1932, p. 46. See also A. D. Carr, 'Madog ap Llywelyn: The Revolt of 1294-5 in Caernarfonshire', pp. 35-46 of *Caernarfonshire Historical Society Transactions* Vol. 58 (1997); p. 37.

A most interesting reference to the precise spot of Puleston's hanging can be found in John Wynne, *Hanes Sir a Thre Caernarfon* (1861). On page 35 it is noted that '[crogwyd] y prif drethwr, Syr Roger de Pulston, uwch ben drws ei dŷ ei hun, sef y Red Lion presennol' ('... the chief tax collector, Sir Roger de Pulesdon, was hanged over the door of his own house, namely, the present-day Red Lion'). This story seems not to have been recorded in any earlier publication, and its provenance is unclear. The Red Lion Inn stood at 2 Palace Street, but the establishment seems to have been taken over at some point in the late nineteenth century; according to the 1913 edition of *Bennett's Business Dictionary*, the address was occupied at that date by a temperance hotel, and today it is the site of the present Market Hall. The story is well known in Caernarfon today, and more than one other building on Palace Street is claimed to have been the site of the hanging.

[13] J. E. Morris, *The Welsh Wars of Edward I*, p. 252.

[14] The attack on Rhaeadr is noticed in *Calendar of Inquisitions Post Mortem Edward I Vol. 4* (HMSO, 1913), p. 161; for the assault on Cefnllys, see *Annales de Wigornia* (Annals of Worcester), p. 529, in which Luard identifies 'Kenles' with Cefnllys. For Brampton's likely death at Cefnllys, see Paul Remfry, *Castles of Radnorshire* (Logaston, 1995), p. 95.

[15] Clement's escape to Aberystwyth is noticed in J. E. Morris, *The Welsh Wars of Edward I*, p. 249, where Morris also infers that the castle was besieged later than other castles in northern Wales. The castles noted as having been attacked in the north-east are listed in Michael Prestwich, 'A New Account of the Welsh Campaign of 1294-5', p. 89; but see Chapter 5, footnote 16.

[16] J. E. Morris, *The Welsh Wars of Edward I*, p. 251.

[17] 'Rhys ap Maredudd', pp. 202-7 of John E. Lloyd (ed.), *A History of Carmarthenshire* Vol. 1 (London Camarthenshire Society, 1935) gives an account of the revolt.

[18] R. F. Walker, 'The Welsh War of 1294-5', pp. xxvi-liii of E. B. Fryde (ed.), *Book of Prests of the King's Wardrobe for 1294-5* (Oxford, 1962); p. xxviii, pp. xxxiv-xxxv.

[19] J. E. Morris, *The Welsh Wars of Edward I*, p. 244.

[20] A. J. Taylor, 'Scorched Earth at Flint in 1294', pp. 89-105 of *The Journal of the Flintshire Historical Society* Vol. 30 (1981-2); p. 89.

[21] J. E. Morris, *The Welsh Wars of Edward I*, p. 244.

[22] J. E. Morris, *The Welsh Wars of Edward I*, p. 244.

[23] A. J. Taylor, 'Scorched Earth at Flint in 1294', p. 100.

[24] For the development of Flint, see Derek Renn and Richard Avent, *Flint Castle and Ewloe Castle* (Cadw, 1995), pp. 9-11; for the inhabitants of Flint, including William of Podington, see A. J. Taylor, 'Scorched Earth at Flint in 1294', p. 102 and elsewhere.

[25] A. J. Taylor, 'Scorched Earth at Flint in 1294', pp. 90-99.

[26] Quoted by E. D. Evans in 'Castell Y Bere', p. 41.

[27] Quoted in translation in A. J. Taylor, *The King's Works in Wales, 1277-1330*, pp. 368-9.

[28] L. A. S. Butler, 'Medieval Finds From Castell-Y-Bere, Merioneth', p. 80 also notes signs of burning on pottery and stones found during excavations.

5 – MADOG AND THE REVOLT IN THE NORTH

'Too slender a force': a battle at Denbigh, 11th November 1294[1]

Until Edward's armies were ready to enter Wales, responsibility for defence of English interests rested in the hands of local English lords and prominent landowners. In the south-east, Morgan ap Maredudd's principal adversary was the earl of Gloucester, who owned Morgannwg and much of Monmouthshire, while in Brecon and Builth the earl of Hereford and John Giffard opposed the forces of Cynan ap Maredudd. In the south-west, meanwhile, a variety of local barons descended from the Anglo-Normans who settled there in the twelfth century were called upon by William de Caumville to help defend Pembroke and Carmarthenshire against the raids carried out by Maelgwn's men. These included the owner of Laugharne castle, Guy de Brienne, Nicholas Carry, Thomas de la Roche, and William Martin.[2]

In Flintshire and Denbighshire, two men were assigned the task of defending the local seats of English power against the rebels. One of them, Reginald de Grey, enjoyed a measure of success in safeguarding the castles at Rhuddlan and Flint, and the presence of his large force on Flintshire's north-eastern coastal strip allowed communications between the two castles to remain open. If it was the rebels' intention to garrison Hawarden castle after its capture, the presence of de Grey's men in this area to the immediate west, isolating Hawarden as it did from the rest of Welsh-held territory, probably led to the castle's early abandonment long before the arrival of Edward at Chester.

De Grey's counterpart in Denbighshire was the earl of Lincoln, Henry de Lacy. By 1294, the earl was in middle age, and could look back on a long and distinguished military career. He had served under Edward in the war of 1277, and besieged Llywelyn II's castle at Dolforwyn in Montgomeryshire with Otto de Grandson that March. After two weeks, the castle fell, effectively securing the middle March for Edward's forces at a crucial moment during his invasion of Wales. It is a sign of the faith Edward placed in the earl that he ordered Lincoln to escort Llywelyn to Aberconwy to sign the peace treaty after Llywelyn's surrender in the autumn of 1277. During the 1282-3 conflict, Lincoln again distinguished himself, pacifying the rebels in the Denbigh area in the autumn of 1282 after apparently meeting with heavy resistance. As a reward, Lincoln was granted Denbigh on 16th October 1282, and was created 'first lord of Denbigh'. He immediately set about erecting a castle, though not on the scale of the ruins that exist today, which belong largely to the 1290s. A town soon appeared to compliment the fortification, and was granted a charter in October 1285, shortly before Lincoln embarked on the king's military expedition to Gascony. Before long Denbigh was home to over sixty burgesses, virtually all of them English.[3]

The earl of Lincoln was a man of ambition. At a time when only the towns of Conwy and Caernarfon had stone walls in Wales, Lincoln determined to enclose his new settlement within walls too. Edward I visited the town while the building work was being carried out, and was so impressed that he gave the earl the considerable sum of £22 to assist him in the endeavour.[4] By the early 1290s, the work was complete, and Denbigh continued to prosper until the outbreak of revolt in 1294.

Many interpretations have been offered regarding the nature of the fighting in the vicinity of Denbigh during the revolt. It is clear that a majority of the Welsh who were living in the area joined Madog's revolt, though some unfortunate locals who remained aloof paid for assuming pro-English or neutral stances. One such individual was Philip Fychan of Llangernyw – the Anglicised version of the name may possibly be significant – who found his property looted by the rebels. Some historians have asserted that the earl of Lincoln's tenants in the area arose of their own accord, a supposition which leads to the natural conclusion that Madog had nothing whatsoever to do with the rebel actions at Denbigh.[5] This, however, seems hard to believe. Gaining control of the lordships of Dyffryn Clwyd and Rhufoniog – that is, the easternmost areas of the region west of the river Conwy known as the Perfeddwlad – seems to have been central to Madog's military planning. Not only did he go to pains to secure the two principal castles within it, Rhuthun and Denbigh, it has been speculated that Madog also made a bid to control at least one (and perhaps more) crossing-points on rivers that ran through the area.[6] Madog is known to have had taken a great interest in securing the help of those Welshmen in the district whose allegiance was uncertain, such as Bleddyn Fychan (see chapter 6). Also, Madog would appear to have been present in the lordship of Dyffryn Clwyd at some point, for an inhabitant of the lordship, one Iorwerth Fychan, was recorded in August 1295 as having obtained his permission to cut down a tree during the revolt.* The presence of the leader of revolt

* This theory was first propounded by J. E. Morris, *The Welsh Wars of Edward I* (Oxford, 1901), p. 309. Iorwerth was fined after the end of the revolt for this act, but his adherence to the writ of Madog seems not to have harmed his standing, as a man of the same name is recorded as having been a witness to a grant of land in Cilcain in August 1307. See Gwysaney MSS: D/GW 1657 [NLW 279]. He may have still been alive in 1324, as a 'Ior'[werth] Vaghan 'Ior[werth] ap Mad'[og]' is recorded as living in the lordship at that time, possibly in the commote of Llannerch; see R. Ian Jack, 'Records of Denbighshire Lordships II: The Lordship of Dyffryn Clwyd in 1324', pp. 7-53 of *Denbighshire Historical Society Transactions* Vol. 17 (1968); p. 34.

doubtless helped to galvanise morale in the area, and while we should refrain from claiming that the region was solidly and staunchly behind Madog – the apparent ease with which the castles in the area were recaptured by Edward in December denies such a conclusion – it is nevertheless clear that the situation in the inland lordships was a grave concern for the English.

Whatever the circumstances under which the locals arose, it is clear that a rebel force launched an attack on the town and castle at Denbigh in the autumn. Securing the town may have been a difficult proposition, and there is some circumstantial evidence suggesting that both town and castle fell only after a siege. A later addition to the town wall was the so-called Goblin Tower, a salient wall which projects beyond the original to enclose a large well. This addition to the wall's fabric has led one modern historian to speculate that the town fell to Madog due to lack of water, and that the tower was subsequently built to ensure that the town had access to a plentiful water supply should it be besieged again in the future.[7] In any case, the settlement was in Welsh hands by the end of October at the very latest.

By October the earl was ready to embark at Portsmouth for the voyage to Gascony, having been appointed a commander of the royal forces. Edward recalled him immediately, along with his own brother, Edmund, earl of Lancester, and instructed the pair to organise an expedition to retake the castle. J. E. Morris describes what happened next: '... the earl apparently had too slender a force. If he relied on his presence and authority to overawe his tenants, he was soon undeceived, for they encountered him near Denbigh on November 11, and drove him out with serious loss.'[8]

This battle, which has gone unnamed, was evidently a very grave affair for the English in northern Wales. Aside from supplying Madog with what would be one of his rare victories in the field, there is ample evidence to suggest that the loss was so severe that Edward modified his plans in the north to deal with the rebels in Denbigh at the earliest opportunity. During his invasion of northern Wales in 1282-3, Edward had been at pains to keep his army within a few miles of the coast, and he was to follow the same logic again after recapturing Denbigh in December 1294.[9] Yet during the first two weeks of the 1294 expedition, Edward's army followed an altogether different route into Wales, moving south to Wrexham and then to Denbigh before turning north once more for the coast. It has therefore been theorised that this diversion was a result of the presence of of a large concentration of rebels in the Denbigh area. To Edward, it may have seemed that after the defeat of Lincoln, the safest route into Wales for his army – along the Flintshire coastal strip which was safely held by de Grey's forces, and thenceforth onward to the English-held castle at Conwy – would have to be altered in favour of a riskier foray inland in order to suppress the revolt in the Denbigh area as quickly as possible. Such an alteration is at least conceivable. Edward was a highly flexible strategist, open not only to *ad hoc* proposals of military initiatives by his men – as his later sanctioning of a sortie by his infantry at Conwy in early 1295 demonstrates (see below) – but also to new technological developments in the field of warfare.[10] It is in keeping with the king's pragmatic attitude to all things military that the notion of his preparedness to choose an inland route for his 1294 expedition after receiving news of Lincoln's defeat may be admitted with a degree of confidence.

The details of the battlefield defeat that precipitated Edward's decision remain unknown. Unlike the English victory at Maes Moydog, no account survives of the battle at Denbigh. Lincoln seems to have proceeded through the vale of Clwyd, and penetrated as far as the town itself when the Welsh appeared and began their attack. The size of the two forces and numbers of casualties are both unknown, although the language that writers down the centuries have used to describe the fate of the English indicates that the Welsh victory assumed the proportions of a rout. Writing in 1584, Powel claims that when the earl's men 'drew near unto the castle…, the Welsh with great fury and courage confronted them, and joining battle, forced them back with a very considerable loss'.[11] Similar sentiments are expressed in the writings of other historians. These accounts are all very vague, however; and even the precise location of the battlefield is uncertain, though frequent references to the earl's force having reached the walls of the castle suggest it was fought very close to the modern-day town. Given the lack of specific placenames and descriptions in contemporary records, it seems unlikely that the particulars of the battle will ever be identified.

The revolt in Flintshire: strategy or opportunism?

The English loss at Denbigh demonstrated the limitations of the English lords in Wales, and made it imperative that Edward put his plans for the reduction of the rebels into practice as quickly as possible. A parliament convened at Westminster in early November levied a tax to pay for the expenses of the Welsh campaign. The move was unpopular, even among those fighting in Wales: the earl of Gloucester, whose forces were ranged against those of Morgan ap Maredudd in Morgannwg, is recorded as having objected to the percentage proposed by the king. The combined weight of other earls and magnates forced Edward to back down slightly, but the tax eventually levied – one penny in six in the towns, and a tenth elsewhere – was still burdensome. Even the clergy were included. The pithy chronicler of Bury St. Edmunds records the event with dismay: 'The town... was assessed by the ordinary tax-assessors of the region... Never before, since our liberties were first granted to us, had any royal official dared exercise any authority in the town. Nor alas! were we able by prayer or price to save our servants from being classed with the townsmen.'[12]

After Edward met with his magnates at Worcester on 21st November, the mustering of his forces began in earnest. The campaign, like those of 1277 and 1282-3, was to be a three-pronged affair. Armies were being amassed at Montgomery, Cardiff, and Chester, with Edward himself preparing to lead the latter into northern Wales. The earl of Warwick was to be in charge of the Montgomery army, which during December 1294 numbered over 10,000 men, the majority from Shropshire, Hereford, and Staffordshire. The contingent based at Cardiff was at least 4,000 strong, and included infantry from as far away as the Forest of Dean, Wiltshire, and Somerset. Edward's own force was drawn mainly from the north of England. By 1st December 1294, his army at Chester was comprised of around 2,500 men from Derbyshire; 2,350 men from Nottinghamshire; 5,000 men from Yorkshire; over 2,500 men from Lancashire; 800 from the city of York; 850 men from Westmoreland; and 1,900 men from Cumberland, making a total of over 16,000 men. For a short period towards the end of the year, Edward had around 35,000 men in the field, giving Madog the curious distinction of having opposed the greatest number of Englishmen ever to invade Wales.[13]

The multiple demands on Edward's manpower meant that many of these soldiers were inexperienced and ill-disciplined, as the unfortunate inhabitants of Flint were soon to discover. Having already been forced to abandon their homes and their property to aid Reginald de Grey's defensive preparations for the town's castle, they subsequently suffered a siege by the Welsh (though probably not a lengthy one given the numbers of English soldiers de Grey had under his command in the area). Now, probably in the first weeks of December 1294, they experienced the depredations of some of Edward's more unruly soldiers first-hand, when the Chester army was beginning its advance into northern Wales. It would seem that the Cumberland contingent were billeted at Flint castle for some days either on their way into Wales or on their way back to England, because in February 1296 an inquisition was held to investigate losses incurred by the townsfolk due to de Grey's burning of the town, and also a number of cases of looting 'by foot-soldiers coming from Carlisle in the army of the lord king'.[14] Most if not all of these men were peasants, and the majority had doubtless been pressed into service against their will. Forced into marching over a hundred miles from their homesteads in England in the middle of a harsh winter to a strange and distant country whose inhabitants spoke no English cannot have put them in good cheer.

The motives behind the theft of goods from the burgesses at

Flint may be more readily understood when one considers the types of goods for which the townsfolk claimed compensation during the inquisition. One 'Simon the butcher' alleged that forty-eight of his sheep were stolen by the soldiers, while Robert of Frankby lost 26s. 8d. worth of grain. Other losses attributed to the 'foot-soldiers from Carlisle' included one chicken worth ten shillings; seventeen pigs and a quantity of woollen cloths, worth 8s. 8d., several oxen; two horses; a cow; several dozen shillings' worth of grain; 'malt, meat and ale... to the value of 69s. 8d.', which was claimed for by Henry Norris; and various household utensils and leather hides. As can be seen, the majority of claims here are for animals and foodstuffs, which leads one to question the state of the rations provided for the soldiers (though one should also be alert to the possibility that some of the claimants may have exaggerated their losses for personal gain). Nor was the looting limited to the Cumberland soldiers, for Roger of Macclesfield accused men from 'the army of Rhuddlan' of stealing his horse and several cows.[15]

Such misbehaviour was the least of Edward's problems. Every moment he spent on Welsh soil gave his French adversaries more time to make preparations for the campaign in Gascony. As soon as he took command of the army at Chester on 5th December 1294 he decided on an immediate advance into northern Wales. Leaving Chester two days later, he arrived at Wrexham on 8th December, meeting with no resistance on the way.

The ease of Edward's progress through Flintshire and eastern Denbighshire in early December poses an interesting question: just how strong a presence were Madog's men in north-eastern Wales? At first glance, the situation in the area in the autumn of 1294 seems nothing short of disastrous. The Hagnaby chronicle notes that the first targets of the rebels in the north-east were the castles – Rhuthun, Hawarden, Denbigh and, possibly, Mold.[16] When taken with the other well-known reports of rebel activity at Flint and the burning of Overton manor – less than two miles from the English border – the overall impression gained is that the rebels were enjoying supremacy in the north-east (see map on page 223).

Yet regardless of their success in capturing several of the area's castles, this statement cannot be true. Close readings of surviving documents show that Madog's grip on the north-east, and Flintshire in particular, was slender even during the heady opening weeks of the revolt. Nor may it have been among his plans to establish a firm presence in the area at this stage. While it seems very likely that Madog visited the lordship of Dyffryn Clwyd at some point during the revolt, there is no direct evidence for his presence further east. The purpose behind the rebel attacks on the castles in north-eastern Wales, therefore, may have been merely to deny Edward's forces forward bases during their inevitable attempt to recapture the country.

There are other, more compelling reasons for assuming that Madog's revolt was not as thoroughgoing in the north-east as it was elsewhere in the north. The burning of Overton manor has long been used to support the idea that Madog's men were active even on the fringes of the border with England.[17] Yet it may be the case that the act was less a prearranged show of support for Madog made with his knowledge, and more an attempt by local Welshmen to express their dissatisfaction with the local English authorities. It will be remembered that the enquiry into the abuses of the English officials of the early 1290s centred its investigations on the north-east; and it is also worth noting that a local uprising had occurred there in the recent past. After Llywelyn II's forces had been driven out of north-eastern Wales during the 1282-3 conflict, the inhabitants of Bromfield rebelled against the lord of Bromfield and Yale, John de Warenne, burning 'Glyn castle'. This little-known fortification has been identified as the motte and bailey castle whose mound can still be seen in the grounds of the Erddig estate near Wrexham. From the context of the document the uprising would seem to have taken place in late 1282, well after fighting between between Llywelyn's men and Edward's forces had moved further west, and demonstrates that the Welsh of the Wrexham area had been prepared to resort to arms in an attempt to better their lot in the decade or so since the extinguishing of native rule.[18]

The ringleaders of those responsible for the destruction of Overton manor in 1294 were Madog Goch and Nynnio, his brother, both of whom were pardoned for the act by Edward on 3rd January 1295. Neither appears in the lists of Welsh hostages taken by Edward after the revolt or in the list of men bound over to keep the peace in the Denbigh area later that year, and it seems likely that they were both local men. Indeed, several men by the name of Madog Goch are known to have been living in the Wrexham area around this time.* Though none are known to have had a brother named Nynnio, one of them is listed in the 1315 extent of Bromfield and Yale as a free man who held land in Eyton just south of Wrexham, and it is conceivable that this Madog Goch is the same man who was pardoned by Edward in

* There is also a Madog Goch recorded as living in the lordship of Dyffryn Clwyd in 1295, but he seems not to have been implicated in the revolt. See *Ruthin Court Rolls* (1893), p. 14, and elsewhere.

1295. If so, it is a demonstration of how easily many former miscreants reintegrated themselves into society; for Edward's response to the rebels in 1295 was, like that of his son to Llywelyn Bren's revolt of 1316, surprisingly lenient.[19]

Aside from this possibility of local men perpetrating acts of violence in Overton under the cloak of rebellion, there are some indications that Flintshire did not experience the ravages that were meted out to other areas in northern Wales by Madog's men. Most importantly, it appears that unlike in many parts of Wales, industry in the county remained largely unaffected during the revolt. Most intriguing is an extent of the manor of Ewloe, one of only a few extents surviving for Flintshire from 1294-5, made before Reginald de Grey on 28th October 1294, barely four weeks after the commencement of the revolt. (Ewloe castle, which did not feature in the conflict of 1282-3, was again uninvolved in the revolt of 1294-5, probably already being ruinous.) The extent notes the presence of two water mills worth sixty shillings a year, and an iron mine worth thirty shillings.[20] The iron mine – one of only two known in Wales at this time – may well have provided iron for the construction of Ewloe castle in the 1250s, and is known to have supplied iron for repairs made to Flint castle in 1303-4.[21] Clearly the manor was untouched by rebel activity at this early stage in the revolt, and there is no evidence to suggest that it was ever assailed by the rebels. Nor do the area's lead or coal mines seem to have been unduly affected by the revolt. It is true that Edward issued an order on 28th December 1295 for all lead miners in the Flintshire area to be transferred to workings in Devon, but this does not necessarily indicate that the mines themselves were rendered unworkable because of damage caused by Madog's men;

indeed, the lead mining industry in the area was active again by 1301. Coal production in Flintshire, meanwhile, totalled a massive 2,428 tons in 1295; and a February 1296 reference to construction work at Conwy castle – which sourced its coal from Flintshire – presupposes that coal miners had been working seams in Flintshire recently.[22] Taken together, these reports suggest that the effect of the revolt on Flintshire's mining industries was minimal. Thus one might reasonably conclude that the situation in Flintshire returned to normal very soon after Edward's passage through north-eastern Wales in late 1294, even as the revolt remained a cause for grave concern elsewhere in the rest of the country. As further evidence of this, one might consider a grant of the manor of Mostyn given to James of St. George, the celebrated architect of Edward's Welsh castles, made in 1295. The manor, which lay adjacent to Flint, was stated at that time to be worth £25 16s a year.[23] If the area was raided by the rebels in 1294, as one might incautiously conclude from reports of attacks on castles elsewhere in Flintshire, this figure seems excessively high. The obvious conclusion to draw is that de Grey's force of 5,000 men, stationed between Rhuddlan and Flint castles as they were, prevented the rebels from attacking the Mostyn area.

This is not to disregard the effects of the revolt in Flintshire. Though the revolt was clearly not comprehensive in its scope in the area, it is nevertheless clear that there was a great deal of unrest in north-eastern Wales in general. An English administrative record of 1299-1300 notes the plight of two Flintshire tax collectors, Patrick Haselwell and James de la Pulle. According to the record, it was impossible for them to complete their duties in 1294 on account of the revolt: 'They levied a part [of the tax] and then the war broke out on the morrow of Michaelmas and they could not levy even a quarter of [the tax] and dared not. After this time they levied nothing because many of those assessed were killed and others had very little left.' Even if one considers that the two men may have exaggerated their plight during the revolt to help account for their inability to collect the tax in full, it seems clear that there was, for a time at least, killings in Flintshire on a fairly broad scale. Of especial interest in this connection are two reports of murders in the area. One appears in a June 1295 entry in the Rhuthun court rolls, which notes that one 'William the Shepherd' was killed on 16th October. The year in which the murder took place is uncertain, but it is very likely that the previous year – 1294 – was the one meant, and that the death 'occurred in the course of the insurrection which occasioned King Edward's personal interference at the close of this year'. The location of the unfortunate William's murder is given as 'Kilkin', clearly a thirteenth-century version of the name Cilcain, a village in Flintshire two miles west of Mold.[24]

The second report is to be found in the *Calendar of Patent Rolls*, and consists of a pardon issued by Edward on 15th December 1294 at Llandegla, four miles south-east of Rhuthun. The pardon is issued to one 'Yevaf ap Adam', who is recorded as having killed Roger de Eyton.[25] There are grounds for linking such a death with the revolt, as it may be that Roger de Eyton was serving with the English in 1294. He had certainly done so less that twenty years previously, in 1277, when Edward had instructed the sheriff of Hereford to recompense him for losses incurred during his service at Rhuddlan in the closing stages of Edward's first war with Llywelyn II.[26] The identity of 'Yevaf ap

Adam' is not entirely certain, but it is very probable that he is the same man as the Ieuaf ap Adda of Trefor recorded in Welsh genealogies as living there around this time.[27] Trefor lies only two miles east of Llangollen, a handful of miles from Llandegla, and it seems reasonable to suggest that de Eyton was killed somewhere in this area, and that this ancestor of the illustrious Mostyn family was a supporter of Madog's revolt. This theory may be lent credence by the fact that Ieuaf's second wife, Generys, was the grand-daughter of Gronw Fychan, a signatory to the one surviving document issued by Madog during the revolt, and himself a grandson of Llywelyn I's famous *distain*, Ednyfed Fychan. To a great extent, medieval Wales viewed itself 'as a collection of great lineages descended from a few ancestral patriarchs and interlinked by bonds of marriage'.[28] If Ieuaf and Generys were married by this time, it is at least conceivable that Ieuaf's wife's close links to a family whose members formed part of Madog's inner circle drew her husband into the web of revolt.

Conclusive proof that these killings were linked to Madog's revolt is, in the final analysis, lacking. In the case of Madog Goch and Nynnio, for example, it could merely be that the two men saw the opportunity to settle a few old scores, or gain revenge for some unrecorded slight in the run-up to Edward's campaign. Nevertheless, it is at least possible that the two murders noted above were committed, if not by Madog's men, then by men claiming to act in Madog's name, and that they occurred as part of a wider spate of unrest and violence in the north-east. It follows, however, that the extent to which such actions were co-ordinated or linked to Madog's wider strategy is highly questionable. Certainly the killing of a shepherd, or a soldier whose appearances in English administrative records, occasional as they are, indicate his small military standing, cannot have done very much to advance the rebel cause.

Early December 1294: Edward's advance into north-eastern Wales

The absence of evidence relating to a siege or surrender of Hawarden castle in December indicates that the fortification had been long abandoned by the rebels, if indeed Madog ever tried to maintain a garrison in it. The way was therefore clear for Edward to advance, and he did so on 8th December. Only around 5,000 of Edward's men accompanied him, the remainder being sent to join de Grey's force at Rhuddlan. This early advance clearly points to Edward's impatience, as does the often overlooked fact that on 7th December twelve boats and a galley with 500 infantry on board set out from Chester under the command of Henry de Lathom, who was under orders to establish a bridgehead on Ynys Môn.[29] The foray was unsuccessful, but the very fact that Edward sanctioned an expedition of this sort, and in mid-winter of all times, says much for his eagerness to bring the Welsh campaign to an end as soon as possible.

For the moment, however, Edward stayed at Wrexham.* Even his presence on Welsh soil may have been enough to plant doubts about Madog's ability to defeat such an opponent in the minds of some of local Welshmen, for it is recorded that during his stay in the fledgling town, men of the lordship of Bromfield joined his army. It also appears that the aforementioned incident recorded in the Hagnaby chronicle took place around this time.

* Derrick Pratt has noted that Edward would almost certainly have chosen to stay at Holt rather than Wrexham during this period, but for the fact that the castle there was unfinished. See 'The Medieval Borough of Holt', pp. 9-74 of *DHST*, 14 (1965), p. 13.

According to the chronicler, 10,000 Welshmen went to Edward and surrendered. He pardoned them on the condition that they joined his army for service in Gascony, and they in turn promised to bring Madog to the king. Accompanied by a detachment of English soldiers, they returned to Madog, but on hearing their story he made a rousing speech extolling the virtues of the Welsh cause. His words had the desired effect, for his men turned on the English who had been sent with them, and in the resulting confrontation there were casualties on both sides.[30]

It is worth noting that this story is attested to only in this one source, and should therefore be treated with due care. There is, for example, no mention of precisely when the incident occurred, although it can fairly be established that it must have taken place after Edward set foot on Welsh soil, but before Christmas. Locating the incident is impossible. Also, the figure of 10,000 Welshmen seems extremely high – from what we know of the battle of Maes Moydog, it seems that Madog was unable to muster more than a few thousand men at the very most in one place – and the thrust of the story, which revolves around the fickle and untrustworthy nature of the Welsh, leads one to believe that its author was pandering somewhat to the racial stereotype that was common currency in England at the time. This said, other details, such as Edward's insistence that the surrendering Welshmen serve in his overseas army, fit very well with what we know about the king's priorities.

Whatever the truth behind the episode, however, it is clear that – until the commencement of Edward's expedition, at any rate – Madog was, in November and December, enjoying a virtually uncontested authority in north-western Wales. With several military successes to his credit, he began to put into effect his plans for the native Welsh polity.

[1] In attempting to understand why the battle at Denbigh with which this section is concerned has never been accorded a name, it is worth recounting the opinion of Philip Morgan. In an article written in 2000, he suggested that battles are named according to the role they play (or come to play) in the narrative discourse of the victors' culture. It therefore follows that 'not all 'events' which comprised the characteristic range of... actions [associated with battles] were accorded battle names.... The process has left modern historians struggling with a range of labels such as 'skirmish' or 'preliminary engagement' to explain violent conflicts which were not accorded the status of events by medieval writers.' See 'The Naming of Battlefields in the Middle Ages', pp. 34-52 of Diana Dunn (ed.), *War and Society in Medieval and Early Modern Britain* (Liverpool, 2000).

[2] Thomas Owen Morgan, 'The Insurrection of Maelgwn Fychan', pp. 290-300 of *Archaeologia Cambrensis* Vol. 5 (New Series) (1854); pp. 298-9.

[3] For Lincoln's service in 1277, see J. B. Smith, *Llywelyn ap Gruffudd: Prince of Wales*, p. 416, p. 444; for his service in 1282, ibid., p. 528-9; for his service in Gascony, J. S. Hamilton, 'Henry de Lacy', pp. 181-3 of the *Oxford Dictionary of National Biography* Vol. 32 (Oxford, 2004).

[4] Julian Pettifer, *Welsh Castles* (Boydell, 2000), p. 62.

[5] J. E. Morris, *The Welsh Wars of Edward I*, p. 253.

[6] Cledwyn Fychan, 'Bleddyn Fychan a Gwrthryfel Madog ap Llywelyn, 1294-5', pp. 15-22 of *Transactions of the Denbighshire Historical Society* Vol. 49 (2000); p. 19.

[7] Julian Pettifer, *Welsh Castles*, p. 66.

[8] J. E. Morris, *The Welsh Wars of Edward I*, p. 253.

[9] R. F. Walker, 'The Welsh War of 1294-5', pp. xxix-xxx.

[10] For example, Michael Prestwich has speculated that Edward's likely use of gunpowder at the siege of Brechin on his Scottish campaign of 1303-4 was the first time the tactic had been employed at a siege in Britain. See *Edward I* (Guild, 1988), p. 499.

[11] David Powel (rev. Richard Llwyd), *The History of Wales* (1832), p. 271.

[12] Antonia Gransden (ed.), *The Chronicle of Bury St. Edmunds 1242-1307*, p. 125.

[13] See J. E. Morris, *The Welsh Wars of Edward I*, pp. 244-8; also J. G. Edwards, 'The Battle of Maes Madog and the Welsh Campaign of 1294-5', particularly pp. 2-3. Edwards refrained from giving an upper estimate for Edward's total forces in the field, but did suggest that 'the main forces [in Wales] on 6 December must have been over – probably well over – 31,000 foot' (p. 3).

[14] See A. J. Taylor, 'Scorched Earth at Flint in 1294', p. 91.

[15] A. J. Taylor, 'Scorched Earth at Flint in 1294', pp. 90-9.

[16] See Michael Prestwich, 'A New Account of the Welsh Campaign on 1294-5', p. 89. The identification of Mold as a target for Madog's men remains problematic. Prestwich notes that 'Ruthin, Hawarden and Denbigh are specified [in the chronicle] as being the [rebels'] initial targets, with the scribe leaving a blank for a fourth castle', but stops short of theorising as to the identity of that castle. R. F. Walker, in 'The Hagnaby Chronicle and the

Battle of Maes Moydog' (pp. 125-38 of *Welsh History Review* Vol. 8 (1972-3)), suggests that the blank space was left for Caernarfon. In *Edward I* (1988) Prestwich names Mold as one of the castles attacked, but does not provide a direct reference. The context of the passage as well as the footnote appended to it suggest that Prestwich had abandoned his earlier caution, and now identified Mold as the castle the scribe intended for the blank space in the Hagnaby chronicle. Presumably this decision is based on the context in which the blank space appears in the chronicle: 'Item post festum sancti Michaelis Wallenses suspicaverunt regem Anglie transisse in Franciam congregati sunt et fecerunt sibi principem nomine Madoch ut expugnarent Angliam primo occidentes in Wallia omnes Anglos et castellas diruentes, ex quibus quatuor ante festum sancte Martini funditus exstirparentur, scilicet castellum domini Reginaldi Gray, Ruffin, et castellum domini Rogeri de Mohaut, Hawardin, et Dynebir, et ______.' ('A New Account of the Welsh Campaign on 1294-5', p. 93).

It can be seen that the blank space occurs after the identification of Roger of Mold's castle at Hawarden as one of those captured. Given that Mold was another of his possessions at the time, it might be argued that that was the place-name the scribe intended to insert. The theory, however, is less than sound; the name 'Dynebir' (Denbigh) is interposed between Hawarden and the blank space. Denbigh was held by the earl of Lincoln, not Roger of Mold; and 'castellum' is in any case singular. On this evidence, it is therefore unsafe to conclude that Mold was the name intended for the blank space, though the fact that the other castles mentioned are all in the north-east may argue in favour of the theory.

The case in favour of identifying Mold as the fourth castle may, however, receive a certain amount of support from the fact that the castle's owner, Roger de Mohaut, was not famous for his fair treatment of the Welsh on his lands. M. Bevan-Evans theorises (*Mold and Moldsdale* (Flint County Library, 1949), p. 46) that 'wholesale evictions [of Welsh tenants] had followed the war [of 1282-3]' in Moldsdale, and that de Mohaut was responsible for them. It is not inconceivable that – as was the case in the Wrexham area in 1282 – the local Welshry were roused to revolt solely through the machinations of the local English administration. Roger de Mohaut died in 1296; 'his short life was not distinguished by any great deed of statesmanship or war' (p. 50).

[17] R. F. Walker makes this inference in 'The Welsh War of 1294-5', p. xxvii, and note 1; see also E. A. Lewis, *Medieval Boroughs of Snowdonia*, p. 226.

[18] This episode is noticed in Derrick Pratt, 'The Medieval Borough of Holt', pp. 9-74 of *Denbighshire Historical Society Transactions* Vol. 14 (1965); p. 11.

[19] J. E. Morris, in *The Welsh Wars of Edward I* (p. 253), offers a different interpretation of the attack at Overton, explicitly linking it with the Welsh soldiers earlier arrayed by the English who had helped to precipitate the revolt. If Madog Goch and Nynnio were among those in the king's service, this theory would certainly gain a boost; but the present writer has been unable to find any evidence to indicate that they were part of the Welsh contingent of soldiers for the Gascony expedition. For the pardon of Madog and Nynnio, see *Calendar of Patent Rolls 1292-1301*, p. 128; for Madog Goch in 1315, see T. P. Ellis, *First Extent of Bromfield and Yale* (Honourable Society of Cymmrodorion, 1924), p. 61.

[20] Noticed in M. Bevan-Evans, *Mold and Moldsdale*, p. 48.

[21] Arthur Jones (ed.), *Flintshire Ministers Accounts 1301-1328* (Flintshire Historical Society, 1913), p. 45.

[22] For Edward's order and recovery of lead mining industry by 1301, see W. J. Lewis, *Lead Mining in Wales* (Cardiff, 1967), p. 29; for figures on Flintshire lead production and February 1296 reference, see Ken Lloyd Gruffudd, 'The Development of the coal industry in Flintshire to 1740', unpublished MA thesis, Prifysgol Cymru Bangor, 1981, pp. 24-5. I am grateful to Mr. Lloyd Gruffudd for his permission to use this reference.

[23] See R. Allen Brown, H. M. Colvin and A. J. Taylor (eds.), *The History of the King's Works Vol. 1: The Middle Ages*, p. 204.

[24] For the non-payment of taxes in Flintshire, see Natalie Fryde, *List of Welsh Entries in the Memoranda Rolls 1282-1343* (Cardiff, 1974), p. 20; for the killing in Cilcain, see Richard Arthur Roberts, *The Court Rolls of the Lordship of Ruthin or Dyffryn-Clwyd* (Cymmrodorion Society, 1893), p. 5.

[25] *Calendar of Patent Rolls 1292-1301*, p. 128.

[26] Edward was in Deganwy at the time; see J. G. Edwards (ed.), *Calendar of Ancient Correspondence concerning Wales* (Cardiff, 1935), p. 262.

[27] P. C. Bartrum, *Welsh Genealogies A.D. 300-1400* (Cardiff, 1974), volume 4; Tudur Trefor 3.

[28] R. R. Davies, *The Revolt of Owain Glyndŵr* (Oxford, 1995), p. 139.

[29] R. F. Walker, 'The Welsh War of 1294-5', p. xxix.

[30] See Michael Prestwich, 'A new account of the Welsh campaign of 1294-5', pp. 89-92 of *Welsh History Review* Vol. 6 (1972-3); p. 90; also R. F. Walker, 'The Hagnaby Chronicle and the Battle of Maes Moydog', pp. 125-38 of *Welsh History Review* Vol. 8 (1972-3), particularly pp. 125-7.

6 – THE NEW PRINCIPATE

Revolt is a fraught business, and the objectives of rebel leaders are not always clear. Owain Glyndŵr, who was styled 'by the grace of God, prince of Wales' in documents issued by his officials during the middle years of his revolt (1400-15), was alleged by the burgesses of Holt to have no greater prize in mind than the lordship of Bromfield and Yale when he began his insurrection. Similarly, the nobleman Llywelyn Bren may have been agitating for nothing more than the return to him of a post in the English administration of the lordship of Morgannwg when he revolted in early 1316.[1] Contemporary records are completely silent on the subject of Rhys ap Maredudd's aims during his revolt in 1287-8.

We are slightly better informed when it comes to Madog ap Llywelyn's intentions, however; for there survives a remarkable document issued in Madog's name when he was at the height of his powers (see plates).[2] The document takes the form of a grant, and resembles in form and tone those issued by the native princes of Wales earlier in the thirteenth century. Like those of his predecessors, the grant accords Madog a princely title. It also includes a witness list headed by an individual referred to as a *distain* – an office that had remained vacant since the termination of Dafydd III's principate. In short, it seems to have been intended as an act issued from the royal government of a head of state.

The document was drawn up at the small settlement of 'Pennant Machno', or modern-day Penmachno, just south of Betws-y-Coed and in the heart of rebel territory, on 19th December 1294. It concerns two grants of land in Maenol

Llanaber and 'Kaer Hepnewid' to one Bleddyn Fychan. Bleddyn's identity has been a matter of speculation, but recent research has revealed a great deal about this enigmatic figure. It is now believed that Bleddyn was a land-holder in Llansannan near Denbigh, and that he was born around 1270, which would put him in his mid-twenties at the time of the Penmachno document's writing.[3]

Bleddyn strikes one as something of an opportunist. Though he had a pedigree of sorts – a distant ancestor named Aser was, it seems, a member of the retinue of Owain Gwynedd – his standing in the world would appear to have owed much to the philosophy of the self-made man. After the collapse of Welsh resistance during the 1282-3 conflict, he appears to have placed himself at the disposal of the newly-installed English authorities, and before long found himself elevated to a position of importance in the administration of the earl of Lincoln's lordship. While actual details of his duties are not known, Bleddyn was in some way responsible for large tracts of land under the earl's control. With this power came other benefits: Bleddyn not only secured lands in Rhufoniog Uwch Aled, but became the fourth richest landowner in the town of Nefyn on the Llŷn peninsula. A record of 1293 lists the property of one Bleddyn Fychan in that town: it included six oxen, three cows, two horses, six shillings' worth of flour, and a boat amongst other items. However, it seems that Bleddyn did not ascend to this position of relative wealth without a certain degree of ruthlessness. If a record of 1650 is to be believed, he helped to evict the Welsh tenants of the district of Archwedlog near Denbigh on the orders of the earl of Lincoln in order to plant a forest there. According to another later record, Bleddyn acquired lands on Ynys Môn at some point, and his sons owned no less than eight mills in Rhufoniog Uwch Aled by 1334. We can, therefore, be reasonably certain that by 1294, Bleddyn was both well-off and also an integral part of the English administration in the earl of Lincoln's lordship. Of the two grants in the Penmachno document, the former concerned a plot of land in Ardudwy in west Wales. The location of the somewhat smaller plot at 'Kaer Hepnewid' has defied historians for years, but may well have been in Rhufoniog Uwch Aled, around ten miles west of Denbigh. In attempting to answer the question of how Bleddyn reacted to this offer, we must first try to comprehend the reasoning behind it, and its broader significance as an indication of Madog's aspirations.[4]

A clue to the prince's intentions can be gleaned from the resemblance of the document to two others issued by Dafydd III at Llanberis in May 1283. It will be recalled that by this time in the 1282-3 conflict, Castell Y Bere had already fallen to the English, and that Edward's forces were converging on Eryri. His options dwindling, on 2nd May Dafydd attempted to gain support for his flagging cause by sending a letter to the men of Builth, Brecon, Maelienydd, Elfael, Gwerthrynion and Ceri, asking them to continue the fight against Edward in his name. On the same day he made a grant of the commote of Penweddig to Rhys Fychan ap Rhys ap Maelgwn, who had recently surrendered, and was now serving with the English. In the hope of persuading Rhys to return to his side, Dafydd made an enticing offer, promising Rhys the land in perpetuity, and excusing him from paying dues. It was the longest of long shots, and neither the men of the south-east nor Rhys responded to Dafydd's exhortations.[5]

In his charter of 19th December, Madog was attempting a similar manoeuvre: clearly he hoped to persuade Bleddyn Fychan to take up arms and support him. In this, he seems to have enjoyed more luck than his predecessor. Though he can hardly have been unaware of the fact that Edward was already on Welsh soil in the north-east with a considerable army, Bleddyn appears to have responded positively to Madog's offer. In seeking an explanation for this surprising decision – after all, as a hitherto loyal member of the English administrative machinery in northern Wales Bleddyn had little to gain and everything to lose by changing allegiance – one should take into account the audacity of Madog's decision to issue the grants.

The existence of the Penmachno document is not by itself so remarkable. It is true that the issuing of charters was on the increase across Britain in the time of Madog. In Scotland, for example, the earls who owned the lordships of Strathearn and Lennox employed clerks to issue documents and correspondence throughout the thirteenth century. It follows that the ability to have such documents produced by clerks was not beyond the means of many a Scottish nobleman or some of the Welsh *uchelwyr*. Cynthia J. Neville writes of the Scottish example:

> The native [Scottish] earls, for their part, came to see in [the issuing of charters] a way of consolidating their authority, not only in relation to the crown but, equally important, within the changing tenurial world of their own territories.[6]

Seen in the context of the relationship between a lord and his prospective tenant, the Penmachno document fits very well into this conceptualisation of the charter's role. Yet its issuing was clearly meant to be far more portentous than that of a mere grant of land. Considering Madog's circumstances at the time, the Penmachno document was a remarkable proclamation. In its usage of a title for Madog last employed by Dafydd III, it was redolent of the times of native Welsh rule. It was drawn up according to proper forms and used accepted terminology. Madog's conceit was to claim the right to issue lands in the territory under his control in the manner of his forebears.* As such, the document was an instrument through which Madog could proclaim his opposition to English rule in writing. The majority of surviving documents issued by leaders of the Welsh royal houses

> were... statements of the ruler's authority, through the inclusion of his style (though outside the major principalities this usually consisted only of a name and patronymic) and also through the attachment of his (usually equestrian) seal.[7]

The provenance of the Penmachno document is given added meaning when seen from this perspective; for Madog's employment of a princely style (discussed below) may have been complemented by use of a seal. The point cannot be conclusively proved, but the existence of two slits in the bottom of the document presupposes that the document originally bore

* Cledwyn Fychan offers a more cautious assessment: 'Fe ddichon mai enghraifft yma o Fadog ap Llywelyn... yn gwobrwyo ei gefnogwyr gyda thiroedd o fewn rhanbarth cnewyllol... etifeddiaeth ei deulu ym Meirionnydd ac Ardudwy, yn yr un modd ag y bu'r ddau Lywelyn yn gwobrwyo eu gweinyddwyr pwysicaf...' (It may be that we have here an example of Madog ap Llywelyn... rewarding his supporters with land within the nucleal area of his family's patrimony in Meirionydd and Ardudwy, in the same manner in which the two Llywelyns rewarded their most important ministers...' 'Bleddyn Fychan a Gwrthryfel Madog ap Llywelyn, 1294-5', p. 19; see Bibliography.

a tag, and, one presumes, a seal as well. Would that we had an impression of that seal today, for its design might reveal a great deal about Madog's determination to emulate his predecessors. Llywelyn I is the first prince known to have had a great seal; his successor Dafydd II used one, and Llywelyn II had one in addition to his privy seal, used for private correspondence.[8] If Madog did indeed choose to create for himself a great seal based on that of one of the native princes, it would be further evidence of his desire to assume their royal status, as well as a further proclamation of his intent to assume control over Wales. In the medieval era the usage of a great seal was 'one of the main symbols of independent sovereignty'.[9] Given his ambition, it would have been strange indeed had Madog not decided to sanction the creation of such a device. Unfortunately, and unless other documents issued by Madog come to light, there can be no resolution to this intriguing point.

Another remarkable feature about the Penmachno document is Madog's title. In it, he is styled 'Madocus filius Lewelin princeps Wallie dominus Snaudon' ('Madog ap Llywelyn, prince of Wales, lord of Snowdon').[10] This is a word-for-word adoption of the style used by Llywelyn II from 1262 onwards, and also by Dafydd in the documents issued in May 1283. Its use sent out the clearest of signals regarding not only Madog's long-term goals, but perhaps also how he sought to present his standing to the Welsh people.

As has been recently noted, the origins of the distinction between the term 'prince of Wales' and 'lord of Snowdon' lay in the need to differentiate between ruling one's immediate territory directly (i.e., 'Snowdonia' or Gwynedd) and ruling a larger territory by means of overlordship.[11] So why did Madog choose the style 'prince of Wales, lord of Snowdon' over another? In theory he could simply have plumped unthinkingly for the title of his predecessors, but it seems likelier that his use of the style was a conscious attempt to demonstrate to native society his determination not only to re-establish a Welsh polity, but to pick up as near as possible where the two Llywelyns left off. The debacle that was the revolt of Rhys ap Maredudd was probably still fresh in the minds of a great many people, some of whom must have been wondering about the nature of Madog's intentions. Madog was doubtless aware of this, because everything we know about his plans for the projected new principate indicates that he did as much as he could to convince the recipient of the Penmachno document of his willingness to reintroduce the trappings of Welsh royal government. His use of the plural of majesty, and the style 'prince of Wales, lord of Snowdon' was simply another declaration of his intention to, in time, re-assert the system of royal governance used by the two Llywelyns. If this is so, the policy raises the important question: how was the rest of Wales to be governed? The vestiges of native rule were still sufficient in Gwynedd to allow for some sort of return to the old administration, but in Powys and Deheubarth, they had been obliterated. The question must remain unanswered, as must that of Madog's installation as leader. Unlike Dafydd II in 1240 or Owain Glyndŵr in 1400, Madog seems not to have been crowned in a formalised ceremony. Llywelyn's coronet or *talaith* was of course in English hands by 1294, and given Madog's aspiration to be the legitimate ruler of Wales combined with an inclination towards protecting the established trappings of that office (see below), it is improbable that he would sanction a coronation with, say, the crown or coronet of some other lesser native ruler,* and the creation of a new crown would have been beyond his means, and in any case would not have served his purpose as well. Though we should not automatically dismiss the possibility of some sort of ceremony having taken place, the absence of evidence relating to such an event, combined with the fact that Madog seems to have struggled to gain the support of the church (see chapter 10), suggests that Madog attained few of the physical trappings that went with the title of prince of Wales.

Madog's 'retinue': a prince's council in waiting?

There are a number of intriguing elements to the Penmachno document. The first is the place at which it was composed. Penmachno's proximity to Dolwyddelan led David Stephenson to speculate that the area was an important base for the rebels. As pointed out by Stephenson, the theory is lent credence by the fact that two of the document's signatories had links with the area – Gruffudd ap Tudur was constable of Dolwyddelan castle during the 1280s, while 'Deikyn Crach' was keeper of Dolwyddelan's vaccaries.[12] These monastic cattle farms were numerous in the area, and housed as many as 552 head of cattle, making the post of keeper one of no small importance. It would be unwise, however, to infer from this that the castle at Dolwyddelan was itself utilised by Madog's forces. There is no record of a visit to the castle by Edward's men in 1294 or 1295,

* Or, indeed, an older coronet of the princes of Gwynedd. In *Llywelyn ap Gruffudd: Prince of Wales* (1998), J. Beverley Smith suggested that the coronet appropriated by Edward in 1283 may have been a different one to that which Dafydd II is known to have worn during his meeting with Henry III in May 1240. The fact that a coronet was found among Llywelyn II's possessions after his death in 1282 leads one to speculate that he was crowned in a formal ceremony, perhaps at some point during the late 1260s when his authority was unquestioned. No documentary evidence exists to support this theory, however, and the earliest likeness showing Llywelyn wearing a crown or coronet dates from the sixteenth century and is of questionable veracity.

and the castle was probably abandoned shortly after 1290 on account of its remoteness.[13]

Another interesting feature of the document is its witness list. In many European societies, such lists functioned not only as guarantees of a document's veracity, but also as a way of allowing the issuers of charters 'to identify publicly the men, whose advice, counsel and friendship they valued most'.[14] As such, the the list of witnesses appended to the Penmachno document provides a fascinating insight into Madog's inner circle. It bears the names of some of the foremost men in native Welsh society in the north (see table 2 on page 227). These included men such as Tudur ab Gronw, Gronw Fychan, Gruffudd ap Rhys ab Ednyfed Fychan, Tudur ap Carwed, and several others – Madog's 'entourage', as they have been described, and, presumably, the men with whom he conferred regarding his military response to Edward's campaign. The list is reminiscent of those enumerating the members of the royal council that were appended to documents in the time of the two Llywelyns. It is not too misleading to suggest that, had the revolt been successful, these men would have formed the nucleus of a rejuvenated prince's council. Whether or not these men actually formed such a body during Madog's revolt we can only speculate; even if they had done so, their writ cannot have run beyond the confines of Gwynedd above the Conwy, and even then only for a period of a few months. But their presence in the witness list is testament to the scope of Madog's vision, as is the tantalising reference to Tudur ap Gronw as 'our steward'.

The aforementioned office of *distain* or steward formed the cornerstone of Welsh royal government. The *distain* likely had jurisdiction in military matters by the middle decades of the thirteenth century, and the post had also absorbed the functions of the *ynad llys*, the court judge, at this time: hence the incumbent was sometimes referred to as a 'justiciar'.[15] Both Llywelyns had appointed men to serve in the role (see table below), and for our purposes, it is worth pointing out that Tudur ap Gronw was a direct descendant of two of the most respected and well-remembered *disteiniaid* during their reigns: Ednyfed Fychan (d.1246), who served Llywelyn I and Dafydd II, and Gronw ap Ednyfed (d. 1268), who served Llywelyn II.

Table 1: *Disteiniaid* of the princes of Wales in the thirteenth century

Prince	Distain	*Period in office*
Llywelyn I ab Iorwerth	Gwyn ab Ednywain	Early 1200s(?)-1216
	Ednyfed Fychan	c. 1216-1240
Dafydd II ap Llywelyn	Ednyfed Fychan	1240-1246
Llywelyn II ap Gruffudd (also (?) Owain ap Gruffudd)	Gruffudd ab Ednyfed	1247(?)-1256 (early 1258?)
Llywelyn II ap Gruffudd	Gronw ab Ednyfed	c. 1258-1268
	Tudur ab Ednyfed	1268-1278
	Dafydd ab Einion	1278-1282
Dafydd III ap Gruffudd	Goronwy ap Heilyn	1282-1283
English rule (1283 onwards)	-	-
Madog ap Llywelyn	Tudur ap Gronw	1294

That Madog should have bestowed the title of *distain* on Tudur ap Gronw was a powerful declaration of intent. It certainly did not indicate that any sort of structured system of governance was in existence – nothing of the sort could possibly be in operation mere weeks after the onset of the revolt, with several castles in Madog's rear still in English possession and an army marching on Gwynedd – but it did reveal Madog's determination to revert to the old native traditions of governance. In the Middle Ages, Wales, like many other European countries, was a place where kinship and family ties bound society together, and the fact that Tudur ap Gronw was a descendent of the noble line of Ednyfed Fychan gave Madog's plans a sheen of legitimacy and continuity. By appointing a *distain* from a family who had supplied several men for the role in the past, Madog could claim that he was restoring Ednyfed Fychan's family in the person of Tudur to its rightful place in the echelons of native Welsh society – namely, as men of influence in the council of a reconstituted royal government. True, Tudur's duties during the winter months of 1294-5 can hardly have been of the nature of his ancestors, and the existence of a royal council was probably never more than theoretical during the revolt. Even so, a reversion to the old ways was in the offing, and to many Welsh people including Bleddyn Fychan, a new native administration must have been a notion of considerable allure, and profound political significance.

Bleddyn knew some of the document's witnesses personally. His name appears alongside those of Tudur ap Carwed and Ieuaf ap Rhiryd in a document dated to 1283 as one of forty-six Welshmen from the areas of Rhos and Rhufoniog who were bound over to keep the peace by none other than Madog's future opponent, the earl of Lincoln, at a meeting at Llanefydd. Also, if Bleddyn was indeed a landowner in Ynys Môn, he would have undoubtedly have been acquainted with Tudur ap Gronw and Gronw Fychan, who owned lands in neighbouring

Penmynydd, and Gruffudd ap Tudur was a native of Penhwnllys on the island.[16]

This familiarity with the document's signatories raises a tantalising question: at what point was Bleddyn approached by Madog and his fellow rebels? Given his later success as an official in the English administration of northern Wales (see chapter 10), it may be tentatively theorised that Bleddyn at first remained aloof from the rebels, but changed his mind on receipt of the Penmachno document and backed Madog, swayed perhaps by news of Madog's early successes and the fact that so many of his friends had thrown in their lot with the rebel prince.

This coup for Madog might also owe something to the emotional atmosphere in northern Wales at the time. Thus far, the revolt had gone more or less to plan. Neither the dismissal of the Welsh siege at Conwy nor the rout at Maes Moydog had yet occurred; indeed, until well after Christmas 1294 Madog enjoyed only success on the battlefield, securing several important castles and winning a substantial victory at Denbigh in November – only in Flintshire had he been thwarted by the quick-thinking de Grey. The mountain fastnesses of Gwynedd were once more under Welsh control, and with the country in the grip of a hard winter, any attempt by an army to flush out the rebels would be tough going. It may also be the case that the rebels were enjoying a degree of success in smuggling vital supplies of food into Wales in spite of the trade restrictions that had been placed on the country. A March 1295 entry in the *Calendar of Patent Rolls* giving a safe-conduct to one John le Cupper of Nottingham to bring 'to the king and his faithful subjects in Wales bread, meat, fish and other victuals' specifically forbade the merchant from selling any of his wares to the Welsh, from which one may reasonably infer that other English traders were doing just that.[17] Though the size of Edward's forces meant that the odds were stacked against the Welsh, to a casual observer there was as yet nothing to suggest that resistance could not be maintained and the English incursion checked or even repulsed, especially given Edward's other troubles in France and Scotland.

This said, one must also consider the fact that there may have been something of the pragmatist in Bleddyn. If his attitude towards the revolt was one of ambivalence – and the very fact that Madog had to entreat with him to secure his support suggests that he had hitherto refrained from backing one side over the other – then his decision to accept Madog's offer may have been motivated by self-interest as much as by patriotic sentiment. Madog's offer of land was no small reward; and if on the other hand Edward proved victorious, he could always argue that he had remained impartial for as long as possible, pointing to the date on which the document was issued. As with so much of what happened during the revolt, Bleddyn's true feelings towards the revolt can only be a matter for speculation.

Madog's revolt: the European context

What little we know about Madog's character points to a man with at least a modicum of skill when it came to dealing with his fellow men. There is no evidence that Madog himself explored any such possibilities (though Morgan ap Maredudd may have done so – see chapter 7). However, it seems unlikely that the thought of enlisting the help of his Celtic or Continental neighbours in his struggle against England did not at least occur to him, as they did less than three years later to the Scottish rebel leader William Wallace, who in October 1297 – mere weeks after his victory over the English at Stirling Bridge – despatched letters to the kings of Norway, France and elsewhere to underscore Scotland's independence.

Probably the most well-known examples of European diplomacy in the Welsh context are the forays which Owain Glyndŵr repeatedly made into European politics, attempting to forge alliances with Ireland and Scotland, establishing diplomatic relations with Castile (Spain), and initiating a correspondence with the king of France which eventually led to the landing of French troops in Wales and a combined Franco-Welsh invasion of England in 1405. There were, however, a number of earlier precedents that doubtless would have been known to Madog. Both Owain Gwynedd and Llywelyn I had carried on diplomacy with the king of France, as did Dafydd II in 1241; and Llywelyn II had signed a treaty (albeit a short-lived one) with Scotland in 1258.[18] Could Madog emulate the example of his princely predecessors?

The closest potential allies to hand were the Irish, a mere few dozen miles to the west. Given that most of Ireland's east coast was in the hands of the English at this time (indeed, several of the ships employed to re-supply Edward's coastal castles set out from Dublin),[19] forging an alliance with one of the native leaders may have been problematic. If the (admittedly somewhat suspect) story that Rhys ap Maredudd managed to escape to Ireland following the collapse of his revolt and returned to Wales three years later with an army numbering in the thousands is true, it might have provided an intriguing precedent.[20] However, a recent development in Irish politics would have made an alliance a political impossibility on this occasion. A local revolt in Kilkenny, which had erupted in 1293, had been suppressed as recently as early 1294, and it is unlikely that the Irish in the south would have seen fit to bear arms so soon after the failure of this initiative.[21] Animosities between the Irish and the Welsh might have outweighed any desire for an alliance in any case. Irishmen fought alongside the English against Dafydd II in the mid-1240s; and a force of Welsh mercenaries in the pay of the English had been fighting in Ireland for some years. Their exploits were hardly likely to induce an Irish ruler to look favourably on any request for help.[22]

Further afield, there was the kingdom of Scotland. The short-lived but significant Cambro-Scottish alliance of 1258 with Scotland was undoubtedly common knowledge among the *uchelwyr* in Wales, if not a diplomatic success fondly remembered by the older nobles in his retinue (such as Tudur ap Gronw, who was an official in Llywelyn II's service during the latter years of his reign). Such men would have been negligent in their newly-assumed duties as princely advisers if they had not pointed out to Madog that relations between England and Scotland were far from cordial. After the failure of the royal line in Scotland during the late 1280s, Edward had stepped in, claiming overlordship over Scotland. His intervention led to the crowning of John Balliol as king of Scotland in 1292, who was required to do homage to Edward, a demand that incensed Balliol's council. Even more promisingly for the Welsh, Edward had insisted on the provision of Scottish troops for service in France in the summer of 1294, and as in Wales, the policy had angered a great many Scotsmen.[23]

The most desirable goal was a military alliance with Philip

IV of France, against whom Edward was preparing to go to war in Gascony. On this front there was a genuine possibility of success, for both sides had much to gain from such an alliance. For Madog, French military aid would be a godsend, especially in the guise of ships, for he had none. From a French standpoint, meanwhile, the idea of attacking England through Wales must have been an attractive one. It was to be a recurring feature of military strategy during the late Middle Ages, and not just on the part of the French – the Bruces considered attempting such a manoeuvre with a combined Scots-Irish army on two occasions in the early fourteenth century.[24] The two countries had already concluded one treaty in the past, and although Madog would have been wholly unknown to Philip before his revolt, one fancies that the Welsh prince could have constructed a compelling case for co-operation.

However, any optimism was tempered by the immense logistical difficulties Madog faced in opening correspondence with foreign rulers in 1294. The easiest way to get a letter to either France or Scotland was via England, southwards and across the Channel in the case of the former, and through the Pennines in the case of the latter. It has been postulated that Owain Gwynedd's messengers travelled to France via a Channel crossing from Kent in the late 1160s. Such a journey would be impossible in Madog's era. England was on a war footing, and any Welshman attempting to send messengers through England could be certain that his charges would have to run the gauntlet, contending with royal agents who had orders to apprehend anyone trying to smuggle messages through to enemies of the king. Even if they succeeded in reaching the south coast of England, surveillance of the Channel ports was undoubtedly far more stringent than in Owain Gwynedd's time. It is worth noting that a messenger of Owain Glyndŵr was captured in England in the early 1400s bearing a letter intended for the king of Scotland.[25]

The only other alternative was a sea voyage direct from Wales to either Scotland or France; but such a voyage would be extremely difficult. Not only was sea travel a far riskier proposition in 1294, but as the Welsh had had no navy since the early years of Llywelyn II's reign,* a voyage could only be accomplished by hiring a merchant vessel. There is some circumstantial evidence to suggest that the rebels were supplied by sea during the revolt,[26] but it would be unwise to infer from this that Madog's access to sea travel was easy or that the option of a sea voyage was viable for the purposes of a diplomatic mission. Doubtless he would have been hard pressed to find a captain who was willing to risk his ship (and his neck!) in such a venture, given the nature of the hostilities between Wales and England.

Thus Madog was faced with the unenviable task of fighting Edward's forces on his own. By a combination of forward-thinking policies and a charismatic (or at least persuasive) personality, he seems to have secured the allegiance of the greater part of the native population of Wales. Yet his political initiative had definite limits in a practical sense, and perhaps in a personal sense as well. He was well-informed, pragmatic and intelligent; but these qualities are only so useful without a

* Evidence for a Welsh navy in Llywelyn's time is fragmentary, and rests primarily on Matthew Paris' report of Llywelyn's sea blockade of Caerfyrddin in the late 1250s (see J. Beverley Smith, *Llywelyn ap Gruffudd: Prince of Wales*, p. 106). The report does not, however, seem to be of the same kind as those of the twelfth century, which describe Welsh rulers as hiring mercenaries to bring ships to Wales for military campaigns, and the possibility that Llywelyn had such ships outfitted on his own initiative must accordingly be admitted.

measure of experience, and the question of whether the outbreak of the revolt was badly timed will be considered below.

Nevertheless, and though the conceit of Madog's assumption of the position of prince is clear enough, it was not so far-fetched as some earlier historians have suggested. History has shown that such statements quickly acquire legitimacy if those who issue them are successful in their ambitions. In not dissimilar circumstances to Madog, Robert Bruce made himself king of Scotland – then under English control – in 1306 by dint of a coronation ceremony at Scone in March of that year. Before long he was being ridiculed in England as 'King Hob', and, like Madog, was excommunicated; yet when he died as ruler of an independent, reinvigorated Scotland in 1329 no-one saw fit to doubt his royal credentials.[27] Even closer to home, the sheer longevity of Owain Glyndŵr's revolt in the 1400s, combined with his determination to establish native Welsh governmental institutions, persuaded many a scornful English chronicler to nevertheless concede the title of prince of Wales to him without qualification. Madog's period of supremacy was very short – a bare six months in Gwynedd, and rather less in north-eastern Wales – and so on issues such as the planned internal workings of a Wales restored to native rule, we can only speculate. Still, the survival of the Penmachno document affords a tantalising glimpse into Madog's wide-ranging plans for a revived native principate, and allows us to deduce that, whatever his failings, a lack of vision was not one of them.

[1] For Owain Glyndŵr, see R. R. Davies, *The Revolt of Owain Glyndŵr*, p. 154; for Llywelyn Bren, see J. Beverley Smith, 'Edward II and the Allegiance of Wales', pp. 146-7.

[2] The early part of this chapter owes a debt to an essay by Cledwyn Fychan, 'Bleddyn Fychan a Gwrthryfel Madog ap Llywelyn, 1294-5', pp.15-22 of *Transactions of the Denbighshire Historical Society* Vol. 49 (2000), in which both the Penmachno document and the life of Bleddyn Fychan are considered in detail. The document was examined in facsimile form only in the course of research for this book; the original is currently held in the National Archives at Kew. The text of the document has, to my knowledge, never been published, though a partial transcription can be found in *The Royal Commission on the Ancient Monuments in Wales and Monmouthshire, Vol. 6: Merioneth* (HMSO, 1921), p. 40. I am grateful to Katharine Olson for her invaluable help in transcribing and translating elements of the document not published in that volume.
[3] Cledwyn Fychan, 'Bleddyn Fychan a Gwrthryfel Madog ap Llywelyn, 1294-5', p. 15.
[4] Cledwyn Fychan, 'Bleddyn Fychan a Gwrthryfel Madog ap Llywelyn, 1294-5', pp. 16-20.
[5] See Huw Pryce (ed.), *The Acts of Welsh Rulers 1120-1283*, pp. 655-7 for amplification of these points.
[6] Cynthia J. Neville, *Native Lordship in Medieval Scotland: The Earldoms of Strathearn and Lennox, c. 1140-1365* (Four Courts Press, 2005), p. 190.
[7] Huw Pryce, 'Welsh Rulers and the Written Word, 1120-1283', pp. 75-88 of Peter Thorau, Sabine Penth and Rüdiger Fuchs (eds.), *Regionen Europas – Europa der Regionen: Festschrift für Kurt-Ulrich Jäschke zum 65. Geburtstag* (Böhlau Verlag Köln Weimar Wien, 2003); p. 85.
[8] Huw Pryce (ed.), *The Acts of Welsh Rulers 1120-1283*, p. 86.
[9] Alexander Grant, *Independence and Nationhood: Scotland 1306-1469* (Edinburgh, 1984), p. 148.
[10] *The Royal Commission on the Ancient Monuments in Wales and Monmouthshire, Vol. 6: Merioneth*, p. 40.
[11] J. B. Smith, *Llywelyn ap Gruffudd: Prince of Wales*, pp. 283-5.
[12] David Stephenson, *The Governance of Gwynedd*, p. 113 and note 86.
[13] A. D. Carr and Glenda Carr, *Cestyll Gwynedd* (Cadw, 1985), p. 11.
[14] Cynthia J. Neville, *Native Lordship in Medieval Scotland: The Earldoms of Strathearn and Lennox, c. 1140-1365*, p. 193.
[15] David Stephenson, *The Governance of Gwynedd*, pp. 11-14; also J. B. Smith, *Llywelyn ap Gruffudd: Prince of Wales*, pp. 201-205, and references therein.
[16] Francis Jones, 'Welsh bonds for keeping the peace, 1283 and 1295', pp. 142-4 of *Bulletin of the Board of Celtic Studies* Vol. XIII (1950); Cledwyn Fychan, 'Bleddyn Fychan a Gwrthryfel Madog ap Llywelyn, 1294-5', p. 16.
[17] *Calendar of Court Rolls 1292-1301*, p. 132.
[18] For William Wallace' diplomacy, see Peter Reese, *Wallace: A Biography* (Canongate, 1996), p. 67; for Owain Glyndŵr's diplomacy, see R. R. Davies, *The Revolt of Owain Glydŵr*, pp. 169-70, 190-1; the presence of a Spanish envoy at Machynlleth in 1404 is noticed in J. E. Lloyd, *Owen Glendower* (Oxford, 1931), p. 82. For Owain Gwynedd, see Huw Pryce, 'Owain Gwynedd and Louis VII: the Franco-Welsh diplomacy of the first Prince of Wales', pp. 1-28 of *Welsh History Review* Vol. 19 No. 1 (June 1998); for Llywelyn I, see Roger Turvey, *Llywelyn the Great* (Gomer, 2007), p. 58; for Dafydd II, see J. G. Edwards (ed.) *Calendar of Ancient Correspondence concerning Wales*, p. 22.
[19] R. F. Walker, 'The Welsh War of 1294-5', p. xxxv.
[20] Sean Duffy, 'The Bruce Brothers and the Irish Sea World, 1306-29', pp. 55-86 of *Cambridge Medieval Celtic Studies* No. 21 (1991), p. 80 notices that reports that Rhys ap Maredudd planned to flee to Ireland were circulating in England in early 1289. Edward Lewis, *The History of Little England beyond Wales* (1888; Dyfed County Council, 1995), p. 171 alleges that Rhys returned from Ireland in 1292, raised another revolt, and fought a battle in which 4,000 of his men were killed before being captured. G. T. O. Bridgeman, *History of The Princes of South Wales*, p. 197 gives a slightly different version of the same event, dating Rhys' return

to 1290. The report of a battle is based on a single (unreliable) source, and even the notion that Rhys fled to Ireland is far from certain.

[21] Michael Altschul, *A Baronial Family in Medieval England: The Clares, 1217-1314* (John Hopkins Press, 1965), pp. 153-4. The revolt was recorded in at least one contemporary Irish chronicle, and must have been a serious threat to English security, as it caused the earl of Gloucester to visit his lands in Ireland, and to remain there until April 1294, and perhaps later (p. 154).

[22] See Avril Thomas, 'Interconnections between the lands of Edward I: A Welsh-English Mercenary Force in Ireland, 1285-1304', pp. 135-47 of the *Bulletin of the Board of Celtic Studies* Vol. 40 (1993).

[23] G. W. S. Barrow, *Kingship and Unity: Scotland 1000-1306* (Edward Arnold, 1981), pp. 161-2.

[24] R. R. Davies, *The Age of Conquest: Wales 1063-1415*, p. 387.

[25] Huw Pryce, 'Owain Gwynedd and Louis VII: the Franco-Welsh diplomacy of the first Prince of Wales', pp. 1-28.

[26] Ken Lloyd Gruffudd, in 'Maritime Wales' import trade during the later Middle Ages Part I' (*Cymru a'r Môr/Maritime Wales* No. 27 (2006), pp. 7-28) suggests that evidence in the *Calendar of Patent Rolls 1292-1301* can be interpreted as suggesting that the rebels were purchasing supplies from overseas (p. 10). The suggestion primarily rests on the phrasing of the entries in the *Calendar of Patent Rolls* (pp. 129-34), in which the words 'the king's enemies' is utilised in several entries. This may well, as Gruffudd implies, refer to the Welsh; it might also equally be a reference to the Scots or French. However, a further entry (p. 133) which is so worded as to explicitly prohibit one Peter de Lamegge, a merchant from Gascony, from supplying the Welsh, 'nor communicate in any wise with them', arguably strengthens the theory.

[27] Robert's nickname is noticed in J. D. Mackie, *A History of Scotland* (Penguin, 1964), p. 72.

7 – MORGAN AP MAREDUDD AND THE REVOLT IN THE SOUTH-EAST

One important aspect of the revolt has thus far been overlooked: the activities of the rebels of the south-east under Morgan ap Maredudd. Next to Madog's remarkable exploits in Gwynedd, the feats of Morgan and his men were the most spectacular of the entire revolt, as well as the most alarming to the English. It was arguably in the south-east that the English forces met with the staunchest resistance, and it was at Brecon that the final mass surrender of the revolt occurred, in the presence of Edward himself, in mid-June 1295. However, it is virtually impossible to fit an account of the revolt in the south-east into any sort of rigid time-scale, because dating evidence has simply not survived. As will be seen, other considerations too make a separate assessment of Morgan's part in the revolt the more prudent option.

As with Maelgwn and Cynan, Morgan's military successes are poorly attested in the historical record – indeed, most chroniclers devote little more than a sentence or two to him and his men. Yet the revolt in Morgannwg and Gwent was clearly a very serious affair, so much so that Edward had 4,000 men sent to Cardiff as early as November.[1] Indeed, if it had not been for the timely appearance of the king himself in the region in June, the revolt there might have lasted for a good while longer, for Morgan's adversary, the earl of Gloucester, seems to have met with precious little success in his attempts to quell the disturbances. In the light of the maddening absence of detail in the chroniclers' accounts, however, we must resort to somewhat more obscure historical records to piece together Morgan's story.

Identifying Morgan's objectives

English and Welsh sources alike agree that the revolt in the south-east began in the first days of October, as it did in other parts of Wales. What is less certain is how Morgan proceeded during those first crucial days. The Annals of Worcester and the Annals of Dunstable are the only two chronicles to give precise locations for the castles assaulted by Morgan: Abergavenny, which was under siege by the rebels in February 1295, and Morlais castle near Merthyr Tudful.[2] Given that native power had survived until the early 1270s in the uplands of Morgannwg, it seems reasonable to assume that Morgan's capture of Morlais castle was the first action of his campaign. Morlais would have presented an attractive target. Being virtually the only castle situated in the Rhondda valleys, it could be easily isolated and attacked. Morlais also appears as a good candidate for the first assault because the English were not as numerous in the uplands as in the lowlands. In the eleventh century, it had been the policy of the incoming Normans to eject the Welsh of the fertile lowlands, driving them into the valleys in numbers. It seems to make more sense that it is to this particular section of the local population that the chroniclers are referring when they speak of the willingness of the people to follow Morgan instead of their combative English earl, particularly when one considers that the uplands would provide the lion's share of Llywelyn Bren's force during his revolt of 1316.

After the fall of Morlais, however, Morgan's movements are a matter of conjecture. Frustrating discrepancies in accounts of the revolt do not help matters. Several sources assert that the earl of Gloucester was ejected from his lands in Wales and fled to his English estates for a period along with his family, and that the population of Morgannwg and Gwent acknowledged Morgan and not Gloucester as their rightful lord. Yet the fact that a great many castles and settlements apparently remained untouched by the revolt – including the substantial fortifications at Coety and Monmouth, and towns such as Cardiff – leads us to question these assertions; for if the lowlands stayed in English hands throughout the revolt, it would seem to make more sense for Gloucester to have retreated to one of his strongholds there.

The question of Morgan's strength in southern Morgannwg is further complicated by the aforementioned fact that Cardiff provided a base to several thousand English soldiers from November onwards. From this we might reason that Morgan's sphere of influence cannot have extended very far to the south; but many historians have inferred from accounts of Gloucester's attacks in April 1295 that he had by then lost control of Cardiff for a period.[3] As there are no firm references to an attack on Cardiff by Morgan, this supposition cannot be substantiated. Even so, it may be pertinent to point out in connection with this point that Morgan raided well to the east of Cardiff, indeed, right up to the English border. This fact leads one to doubt both the security of the coastal strip east of Cardiff, and, more importantly, the viability of English supply lines in Gwent. Though Cardiff was supplied by ship throughout the revolt, provisions would undoubtedly have been transported to the town by land as well, and the most practicable route for such an operation would have been through Gwent. The possibility of disrupting English supply lines must have occurred to Morgan, but if this is so, one struggles to reconcile his ability to wreak havoc in Gwent, which was well beyond the traditional heartlands of Welsh power in the Morgannwg uplands, with the fact that English supply lines to Cardiff seem to have remained unimpeded.

Finding resolutions to these issues is exceedingly difficult, and it may be that we will never obtain a substantially clearer picture of how events unfolded in the south-east in late 1294 and early 1295. All that can be done is to identify the various castles and settlements known to have been assaulted or attacked during the revolt. As has been noted, Morlais was one. The castle of Kenfig was another. Situated a few miles south-east of Neath, Kenfig's history had been an unhappy one from an English perspective. Both town and castle had been attacked and burned by the Welsh on no less than five occasions, in 1167, 1183, 1228, 1232 – when an attack by the forces of the local Welsh ruler Morgan Gam may well have necessitated the rebuilding of the entire south wall of the castle's keep – and 1243. The fact that Kenfig castle had been burnt down is recorded in an administrative record of 1295-6, from which it can be deduced that Morgan's men captured it, but there are no further details of the attack or its date. Probably at the same time, Llangynwyd (also known as Tir Iarll) castle, a few miles east of Kenfig and two miles south of Maesteg, was also attacked and burnt, but unlike Kenfig, the damage was such that the stronghold was apparently deemed not worth rebuilding, for the site was subsequently abandoned.[4]

Such was Morgan's campaign against the castles in the west of Morgannwg. In the east, the rebels' objectives are more difficult to identify. West of Cardiff, Llantrisant castle was sacked, as is suggested by a 1297 petition relating to the release of a number of local Welshmen who had been imprisoned pending the rebuilding of the castle. In the Cardiff area, the only attacks made by Morgan which can be substantiated were at Caerffili and Whitchurch. The former attack was the grander affair, for at this time Caerffili held over one hundred burgages. The rebels, however, succeeded in burning eighty of them, so that in 1306 only forty-four are recorded as having existed. Two of the town's mills were also rendered useless. Oddly, surviving records contradict one another on the question of whether or not Caerffili castle itself was attacked, but a number of modern historians have expressed the opinion that the castle was assaulted unsuccessfully by Morgan.*[5]

Caerffili lay within the old Welsh lordship of Senghennydd , in which a minor Welsh royal family had ruled in a state of semi-independence until as late as 1267. The lordship suffered badly during the revolt, though whether this was due to the rebels or because of the ravages of the earl of Hereford's troops after the lifting of the siege of Abergavenny is unclear. Whitchurch, three miles south of Caerffili, was however indisputably a target of the rebels. Now a suburb of Cardiff, Whitchurch was nothing more than a hamlet in 1294, but it did have a mill, known as Melin Griffith, which was burnt by Morgan's men. Whitchurch also boasted a castle, which may have been sacked in the same assault. A later record of 1314 certainly makes reference to the castle's dereliction due to war, but whether it was caused by Morgan in 1294-5, or by the instigators of a minor revolt in

* In *Old Whitchurch: The Story of a Glamorgan Parish* (1945), Chappell also suggests that the nearby stronghold at Castell Coch was assailed by Morgan (p. 18), but gives no authority.

Morgannwg earlier in 1314, is open to question (but see below). These raids, and perhaps other raids in the area that have gone unrecorded, had a negative effect on trade in nearby Cardiff, which faltered during the revolt.[6]

Further east, we find evidence for Morgan's presence at Llangybi castle, a small and little-known fortification two miles south of Usk. The castle, which was known as Tregrug throughout the Middle Ages, was in the hands of the Clare family by 1262. It was garrisoned during Llywelyn II's campaigns in the south-east in the same year, and in 1287 during Rhys ap Maredudd's revolt in the south-west. We may infer that Morgan occupied and burnt the castle because of a number of accounts pertaining to the castle made between 1301 and 1306, which show that a number of repairs were carried out during this period. These included the plugging of a breach in the castle wall (work which took thirteen days to complete), the repair of fire damage, and the replacement of a roof in one of the castle's towers. Though the amount of money spent on these repairs was small – less than fifteen pounds – one wonders precisely what could have caused such extensive damage. It has recently been asserted that these repairs were effected as a result of an attack by Morgan (the gap of several years between the assault and the repair work may be explained by the fact that the castle was in the hands of escheators after the death of the earl of Gloucester in late 1295).[7]

We know that Morgan attacked at least one other castle, for the Annals of Worcester recounts the relief of a siege of Abergavenny, the only siege known to have been conducted by Morgan:

> On the 13th of February the Earl of Hereford, with other nobles and the levy of the district, raised the siege of the castle of Abergavenny in which the Welsh were engaged, and burnt their land, carried off a great deal of plunder, and slew innumerable people.[8]

Abergavenny's walls were made of wood in the 1250s, but a rebuilding in stone may have taken place in the 1290s, which, if true, is presumably why the castle needed to be besieged rather than directly assaulted.[9] In considering reports of the earl of Gloucester's flight from Morgannwg during the revolt, it may be of note that in this account, it is the earl of Hereford rather than Gloucester who takes the initiative.

Aside from these assaults on prominent castles, it is known that Morgan raided several towns and settlements also. Newport suffered badly; at least sixty-six of the town's 257 burgages were destroyed in the attack. Furthermore, thirty-five burgages in the hamlet of Llantrissent, four miles south of Usk, were burned. Usk itself lost 180 burgages, and saw its trade profits fall from £44 in 1292-3 to £24 12s in 1296-7, though its castle seems to have escaped unscathed. Finally, the town of Trelech was assaulted by the rebels. Though today little more than a hamlet, in Morgan's time the settlement was an important base in the administrative machinery of the region, being home to the local receivership – taxes from three neighbouring manors were brought there before being forwarded to Cardiff. Furthermore, it was a town bustling with inhabitants and traders, boasting no less than 378 burgages in 1288. By 1296, however, this figure had dropped to 276 as a result of Morgan's attack. A raid on Trelech would have been an attractive proposition – aside from its local importance as an administrative centre, the town was a soft target, being defended by nothing more substantial than a ditch and a wooden palisade, and having only the small and easily assailable 'Twmp Terret' fortification for a castle, which may have been attacked and destroyed by Morgan. Though the town's population more or less stabilised in the twenty years or so following the attack, its expansion was checked, and in the fullness of time, all that would remain of its pretensions to grandeur would be the rectilinear layout of its streets.[10]

Morgan's motives

Like Madog, Morgan was the head of a dispossessed royal Welsh house, that of Gwynllŵg. His distant ancestor, Caradog ap Gruffudd (d. 1081), had ruled over Morgannwg in its entirety, but after the arrival of the Anglo-Normans in south-east Wales in the late eleventh century the house had suffered a fall from grace. As early as the opening decades of the twelfth century, the house had lost control over all but the commote of Machen in the uplands north of Cardiff. The occasional expansion of control over neighbouring districts in the following decades, and the assumption of the rather grandiose title of 'king' by Morgan ab Owain (d. 1158), were high points in a long but inevitable decline, as the grip of the Anglo-Normans strengthened on the lowlands.[11]

It was against such a background of past glories that Morgan was doubtless raised; and it is in Morgan's quarrel with one of the victors in the struggle to dispossess the house of Gwynllŵg – the earl of Gloucester – that we find a most intriguing aspect of the revolt. In 1294 Gloucester's family, the Clares, was among the most powerful of English families in Wales. The earl himself owned the lordship of Morgannwg in its entirety from Neath to Caerffili, as well as Gwynllŵg to the east and a large swathe of land in Gwent that formerly belonged to Morgan's ancestors. It has thus been suggested that Morgan waged the revolt in Morgannwg as much for personal as for patriotic reasons.

This claim primarily rests on the report of Morgan's surrender to Edward in June 1295 contained in the Annales Monastici. The fact that Morgan surrendered not to Gloucester but to the king himself, and 'against the earl's will', was evidently considered important enough by the chronicler to be of note. Reports that Morgan declared that his men had been waging a campaign against Gloucester are also connected with the occasion of Morgan's surrender to Edward, and seem to confirm the notion that the attacks instigated by Morgan were carried out in order to obtain a local, rather than a regional, objective.[12] While it is equally possible that Morgan was lying, and simply using a convenient local quarrel as a cover to hide his more patriotic motives, the theory certainly should not be dismissed out of hand. An assessment of the targets of his campaign helps us to evaluate its soundness. One point in particular is worth exploring – namely, that with the sole exception of Abergavenny, every castle assaulted by Morgan was owned by the Clare family, or had been constructed by Gloucester or one of his ancestors (see map on page 224). Morgan's men avoided the heavily-defended lowlands of Morgannwg more or less completely, contenting themselves with a foray westwards as far as Kenfig and Llangynwyd, which were both perhaps assaulted during the same raid. Both were Clare castles. The latter was almost certainly Gloucester's first fortification, begun in 1262 on the site of the earlier Norman construction, while Kenfig was built by his ancestor William. Caerffili was Gloucester's masterpiece, built in the early 1270s. Llangybi was in the earl's hands until 1294, when he gave it to his brother, Bogo. Morlais, meanwhile, was the castle whose construction by Gloucester sparked off the confrontation of the early 1290s between him and the earl of Hereford, who claimed the area as his own.[13] (It is conceivable that Hereford's discomfiture of Gloucester after the latter's submission to the king first planted an idea of Gloucester's weakness in the minds of Morgan and his rebels.) Whitchurch was also a Clare castle, which seems to argue in favour of placing its assault and destruction in 1294 rather than 1314. Furthermore, the settlements of Trelech, Usk, Newport and Llantrissent all lay within the earl's territories, and assaults on former monastic granges at Resolven and elsewhere are more easily explained by the fact that it and others had come into Gloucester's possession in the early 1290s through an agreement with the abbot of Cîteaux.[14] The theory that Morgan was rebelling against Gloucester only also helps to explain why Newport castle was apparently not attacked while the borough itself was ravaged – the castle was, after all, not a Clare construction.

However, a very large number of other military targets built by the Clare family do not seem to have been attacked by Morgan. Why, for example, was Llangybi apparently assaulted, while Gloucester's castle at Usk only three miles to the north, whose North Tower was rebuilt in the late 1280s by Gloucester to store his valuables, would have presented a rather more attractive target? If, as has been noticed, the Welshmen of Afan were among the rebels in Morgan's force, why did they leave alone the castle at Neath, which was built by Gloucester's ancestor Richard, and which lay immediately adjacent to their homesteads?[15] Such inconsistencies can only re-admit the possibility of there being some other motivation for Morgan's part in the revolt.

Evaluation of Morgan's motives is made even more difficult by his apparent involvement in a curious addendum to the revolt – the treasonable actions of one of Edward's knights, Thomas Turberville.[16] Having served in France with an English force under John of Brittany since late 1294, Turberville was captured by the French at the fall of Rions in April 1295. By August he was back in England, and had enjoyed at least one audience with Edward before being captured in September on charges of treason and subsequently executed. Turberville had been found to have written letters in his capacity as a go-between in the pay of the French, in which he attempted to establish contact with parties in Scotland, Ireland and Wales who would be willing to make war against the English. Of particular interest is the fact that the one person he names as his contact in Wales is 'Morgan' – who can, of course, be none other than the man who led the revolt in the south-east.

According to Turberville, Morgan had promised to raise a revolt in Wales on the understanding that the action should coincide with a simultaneous uprising by the Scots. The date on which the intrigue between the two men began cannot, unfortunately, be settled; Turberville's letter was written around 7th August, but the fact that the letter has Morgan proposing to revolt rather than to continue a revolt already in motion suggests that the proposal may well have been put forward some time after 15th June, on which date Morgan surrendered.

Two other letters are known to have been sent to a Welsh leader or leaders advocating revolt, one from Turberville and one from the French king, Philip IV. Their recipients are not recorded; however, in view of Turberville's previous claim regarding Morgan, he would seem to be the likeliest candidate.

The veracity of Turberville's claim to have made an agreement with Morgan is open to question. As has been pointed out, even if he had refused to agree to Turberville's plan Morgan would have been duty-bound to report any treasonable communications to one of the king's representatives directly he received them, for if he did not he would be accused of treason himself. Though he seems not to have done so, it is equally true that he was not tried for treason, and so it may well be the case that Edward found Turberville's claims regarding Morgan to be sufficiently unconvincing (or, indeed, Morgan's protestations sufficiently persuasive!) to let the Welshman go free.

Whatever the truth about Morgan's attitude towards Turberville's plans, the episode is of great interest as it provides evidence that the 1294-5 revolt was looked upon by parties outside Wales as an opportunity to destabilise Edward's realm. Of equal interest is the fact that Madog seems not to have been contacted by either Turberville or Philip IV. One obvious explanation is that by the time the letters were written, it had become obvious that Welsh resistance in the north was a broken reed; by mid-June Madog had in all likelihood gone to ground. As for the other rebel leaders, there is nothing but silence regarding Cynan's actions by mid-1295; Maelgwn, meanwhile, may well have been dead before the end of June. This, one presumes, left Morgan as the only available native Welsh leader in a position to raise revolt. Without a proper resolution to these questions, however, we are forced to view Morgan's actions through a haze of supposition and speculation, and until further evidence comes to light, the fine detail of what happened in the south-east during the revolt will remain a mystery.

[1] R. A. Griffiths, 'Morgan ap Maredudd', p. 95 of *The Oxford Dictionary of National Biography* Vol. 39 (Oxford, 2004).
[2] An English translation of the account in the *Annales de Wigornia* (Annals of Worcester) is given in Mary Salmon, *A Source-Book of Welsh History* (Oxford, 1927), pp. 190-1.
[3] J. Barry Davies, *The Freemen and Ancient Borough of Llantrisant* (Llantrisant and District Local History Society, 1989), p. 10; Michael Altschul, *A Baronial Family in Medieval England: The Clares, 1217-1314*, p. 155.
[4] The attack on Kenfig is noticed in C. J. Spurgeon, 'The Medieval Town Defences of Glamorgan', pp. 161-212 of *Studia Celtica* Vol. XXXV (2001); p. 189; the attack on Llangynwyd is noticed in Julian Pettifer, *Welsh Castles*, p. 98.
[5] J. Barry Davies, *The Freemen and Ancient Borough of Llantrisant*, p. 10; C. J. O. Evans, *Monmouthshire: Its History and Topography* (William Lewis, 1953), p. 88; H. P. Richards, *A History of Caerphilly* (Cowbridge, 1975), p. 15. One example of speculation of an attack on Caerffili castle can be found in Edgar L. Chappell, *Old Whitchurch: The Story of a Glamorgan Parish* (Merton Priory, 1945 (1994)).
[6] Edgar L. Chappell, *Old Whitchurch: The Story of a Glamorgan Parish*, p. 17. For the notion that Whitchurch may have been attacked, see Julian Pettifer, *Welsh Castles*, p. 111.
[7] For a full discussion of the issues involved, see D. J. Cathcart King and J. Clifford Perks, 'Llangibby Castle', pp. 96-132 of *Archaeologia Cambrensis* Vol. 105 (1956); also S. G. Priestley and R. C. Turner, 'Three Castles of the Clare Family in Monmouthshire during the thirteenth and fourteenth centuries', pp. 9-52 of *Archaeologia Cambrensis* Vol. 152 (2003), particularly p. 24.
[8] Translated in Mary Salmon, *A Source-Book of Welsh History*, pp. 190-1.
[9] Neil Phillips, 'Abergavenny Castle 1087-1537', pp. 17-31 of *Gwent Local History* Vol. 88 (Spring 2000); p. 18.
[10] For records of the destruction in the Gwent area, see C. J. O. Evans, *Monmouthshire: Its History and Topography*, especially p. 88, and elsewhere; Ian N. Soulsby, 'Trelech: A Decayed Borough of Medieval Gwent', pp. 41-4 of *The Monmouthshire Antiquary: Proceedings of the Monmouthshire Antiquarian Association* Vol. 4, Parts 3 and 4 (1981-2).
[11] For a brief history of the house, see Huw Pryce (ed.), *The Acts of Welsh Rulers 1120-1283*, pp. 34-6; for Morgan's assumption of the title of king, see David Crouch, 'The slow death of kingship in Glamorgan', pp. 20-41 of *Morgannwg* Vol. 29 (1985).
[12] *Annales de Wigornia* (Annals of Worcester), pp. 520-1.
[13] For the construction of Kenfig, Llangynwyd, Caerffili and Llangybi, see C. J. Spurgeon, 'The Medieval Town Defences of Glamorgan', p. 189; Julian Pettifer, *Welsh Castles*, p. 82, p. 131; S. G. Priestley and R. C. Turner, 'Three Castles of the Clare Family in Monmouthshire during the thirteenth and fourteenth centuries', p. 24 and elsewhere; Michael Altschul, *A*

Baronial Family in Medieval England: The Clares, 1217-1314, pp. 148-50.
[14] F. G. Cowley, 'Gilbert de Clare, earl of Gloucester (the Red Earl) and the Cistercians of south-eastern Wales', pp. 115-24 of *Archaeologia Cambrensis* Vol. 154 (2005); p. 119. Cowley lists the granges attacked by Morgan; they included Crynant, Blaendulais, Aberpergwm, Rheola, Pwll y Wernau and New Grange.
[15] Edgar L. Chappell, *Old Whitchurch: The Story of a Glamorgan Parish*, p. 17.
[16] Much of what follows can be found in J. G. Edwards, 'The Treason of Thomas Turberville', pp.296-309 of R.W. Hunt et al (eds.), Studies in *Medieval History presented to Frederick Maurice Provicke* (Oxford 1948).

8 – THE SIEGE OF CONWY

While Morgan was facing down the earl of Gloucester in the south-east, Edward continued his penetration of northern Wales. Doubtless he was anxious to complete the job of reducing the rebels as quickly as possible. Every moment he spent on Welsh soil could be put to better use in Gascony, or in Scotland, where a group of disaffected barons would, in a very few months, take the reins of government out of the hands of their king, John Balliol, and form an alliance with France against England. Furthermore, the subjugation of the Welsh was proving to be an extremely expensive undertaking – keeping over 30,000 men in the field for weeks at a time would drain even the deepest of pockets. After successfully pacifying the rebels in the Denbigh area, he continued his march down the Vale of Clwyd, joining forces with a detachment of Reginald de Grey's Rhuddlan army. He was at Derwen Llannerch on 17th December, and reached the coast at Abergele the day before Christmas Eve. He celebrated Christmas Day at Conwy castle, undoubtedly buoyed by the news that John de Havering had been able to land seven extra men at the besieged Harlech castle, boosting the garrison's size to thirty-six fighting men.[1]

Edward's next move has baffled historians for centuries, for on 6th January 1295 he marched west into Gwynedd with a portion of his army. Records showing the precise number of troops he took with him have not survived, but the force cannot have been substantial enough to reduce the area which it penetrated – the *cantref* of Arfon – on its own. By 8th January he was at Bangor, and pressed on along the northern coast of the Llŷn peninsula as far as Nefyn, at which he arrived on 12th

January. Not even on his subsequent march in the spring would Edward push his northern army so far to the west (see map on page 225).

Quite what the king hoped to achieve by this manoeuvre is unknown. John Griffiths postulates that the march was meant 'as a reconnaissance in force'.[2] In any case, it was not the first time that an English army had made a rash advance in northern Wales. During Edward's Welsh campaign of 1282-3, a force composed of English and Gascon troops led by Luke de Tany had been stationed on Ynys Môn. Apparently acting on his own initiative, de Tany ordered a crossing of the Menai Straits on 6th November 1282 on a pontoon bridge erected somewhere in the Bangor area. In the afternoon the Welsh emerged from cover in the mountains overlooking the bridgehead and advanced, ingeniously timing their attack to coincide with high tide. How the battle developed is not recorded, but the Welsh onslaught was of sufficient ferocity to induce the English army to retreat towards the bridge. As they fell back, the bridge broke under the strain of increased water flow and the combined weight of knights and infantry, and a very large number of men were drowned, including Luke de Tany himself. The action later came to be known as the battle of Moel-y-Don, and was a very serious reverse for the English – indeed, the almost hysterical response to the disaster in England has been compared with that which greeted news of the later rout of an English army by a Scottish force under the command of William Wallace at the battle of Stirling Bridge in 1297.[3]

Memory of the rout at Moel-y-Don ought to have warned Edward against a hasty march into Gwynedd, but he pressed on, and paid the price. At some point during the march, he was attacked by the Welsh, who captured the royal supply train. While this skirmish does not seem to have inflicted many casualties among Edward's force, it denied them supplies, and may well have been a factor in forcing Edward's retreat to Conwy, where he arrived on 20th January.

Successive historians have disagreed as to the date of the Welsh attack. R. F. Walker concurred with J. E. Morris' view that the loss of the supply train most likely occurred between Conwy and Bangor, an area which, in the opinion of Morris, 'gave the Welsh an admirable cover from which to attack [Edward's] flank and rear'. Morris, however, was unaware of the fact that Edward pushed further west than Bangor, and therefore also suggests that the attack occurred on 9th or 10th January, immediately after Edward's arrival in Bangor.[4] This seems improbable to say the least: it would be a foolish commander who embarked on a ten-day march of over eighty miles in mid-winter having lost his army's supplies. John Griffiths' theory that the Welsh attack took place during Edward's march back towards Conwy seems a more likely scenario[5] – it is arguably reinforced by the fact that Edward's homeward journey took a day longer than the march westwards. If Morris' supposition that the attack was launched in the Penmaenmawr area is also correct, it ought to possible to very tentatively place the attack as having occurred a day or two before Edward reached the safety of Conwy.

However, there are some grounds for assuming that the Welsh attack on Edward's supply train did not take place near Penmaenmawr, but much further to the west. In reaching Nefyn, Edward had to pass by the town of Caernarfon, which had been attacked and captured by the rebels at the beginning of the revolt. Indeed, on 9th January he was at the village of Llanwnda, only two miles or so to the south of Caernarfon. This raises the very important question: was the town still occupied by rebel forces at the time, and if so, why did they not take the opportunity to harass Edward as he passed through the area, or even cut off his route back to Conwy once he had reached Nefyn? It must be stressed that Edward's decision to push west flew in the face of military thinking at the time. Every modern historian to examine the episode has emphasised the utter folly of the march to Nefyn – R. F. Walker described it as 'certainly a risky undertaking in the face of an active enemy',[6] while Michael Prestwich calls the decision to embark on the march 'astonishing'.[7] It would have been equally foolish of Madog not to take advantage of Edward's weakness while he was split from the major part of his army. To implement some sort of manoeuvre whereby a portion of the army commanded by the king himself was surrounded or at least attacked in its rear would seem to be a logical step after the English force moved west, and given Edward's inclination to keep to the coastline, Caernarfon was an ideally situated spot from which to attack. That no such attack seems to have been launched stretches credulity. There are four possibilities. Either Edward's force was too large for Madog to sanction an attack; or an attack or attacks were made which are not attested to in the surviving records; or there were no rebels in the area of either Caernarfon or the Llŷn.

The fourth possibility – one, it seems, which has hitherto lain unconsidered – is that the rebel attack on Edward's supply train was launched not between Bangor and Conwy, but in the Caernarfon area on his return from Nefyn. This would place the attack several days earlier in the month, perhaps on 16th or 17th

January. There is much to discount this theory, though it ought to be noted that none of the four seem very plausible. If true, however, it would at least refute the absurd notion that Edward was able to march past a supposed base of the rebels without being harassed by Madog's men. Sadly, the lack of evidence precludes any firm conclusions; and the truth is that we may never be able to account for these strange inconsistencies surrounding Edward's perilous journey deep into the heart of rebel-held territory.

The rebel siege

All this time, the rest of Edward's army had not ventured further west than Conwy. A precise identification of its movements is not possible, but it seems likely that the force was spread out and well to the east of Conwy by the time Edward and his men made it back to the castle on 20th January, with the Welsh not far behind.[8] Presently Madog's men reached the town, and set fire to part of it before laying siege to the castle. Edward's response was pragmatic. The loss of his supplies a couple of days earlier was a blow, but he knew that it was by no means a decisive one. As has been noticed, letters written by Edward at Conwy in late January exhibit few signs of anxiety or urgency, despite the fact that his raiding force had been unable to rejoin the rest of his army before the Welsh descended on the town. Combined with the castle's garrison, Edward's force would still be more than sufficient to repel any attack.[9]

There were only two obstacles to overcome. One was the weather. The winter had been an exceptionally wet one, and by the time the rest of Edward's army had heard of Edward's return and returned to the vicinity of the castle, the river Conwy was in flood and prevented them from crossing to lift the siege on the stronghold.

Edward's other worry was the state of his supplies. The number of men sheltering in the castle almost certainly numbered in the high hundreds, perhaps even running into four figures, and they began to run out of food. But Madog's men had no siege engines with which to batter the walls of the great castle, so the obvious course of action was for the king to wait for help to arrive. All the same, Edward would have been less than human had he not experienced the odd twinge of anxiety whilst waiting for provisions. As long as the river Conwy remained impassable, no help could come over land; and a provisioning by sea in the depths of winter could be a risky business – navigation was not always possible in bad weather, and indeed, one of the English ships supplying Conwy sank during the winter months. Also, it seems likely that many of his infantrymen had died due to malnutrition and the privations suffered on the punishing march to Nefyn, as is intimated in one of the English chronicles. Tents had been provided for the troops at Conwy as early as 6th January, but their state of repair, and whether or not enough of them were taken on the march to accommodate all of Edward's men, is unknown.[10]

One account of the siege is notable for its brief comment on Edward's stoic response to the shortage of food and drink. Supplies of wine had apparently run out, but at length a small barrel was located and set aside for the king's use. Edward refused to drink it, opting for the only other available fare of water mixed with honey, and insisting that the wine be shared out amongst his men instead. In the days before water became a natural part of one's diet due to the ever-present possibility of contamination by bacteria, and armies were therefore reliant on a constant supply of beer or wine, this was no small sacrifice on the king's part. It is a good story, and its appearance and re-appearance down the ages is a testament to its appeal to successive generations of English historians.[11]

In any case, the waters of the Conwy soon dropped, and the main part of Edward's army crossed the river in the last week of January, driving off the besiegers and putting the days of Edward's hardship to an end. In writing his account of the siege, J. E. Morris assumed that the relief of the castle was accompanied by a battle in which the Welsh were routed.* It is now known, however, that this was a misinterpretation of the surviving evidence – acting on a mistaken assumption, Morris located an account of the later battle of Maes Moydog in the Conwy area.[12] In all probability, the Welsh besieging force saw the body of Edward's army bearing down on their position from the east, and did what they were to do on most occasions during the revolt in the face of a larger and well-equipped enemy – they retired.

In all, the siege of Conwy probably lasted for less than a week, but even so, it created considerable difficulties for Edward. Aside from the loss of face engendered by his having to submit to a siege in one of the castles in his great chain of fortresses along the northern Wales coast, he lost valuable time which could have been put to better use planning the next stage of the campaign. Undoubtedly the experience also had a great bearing on his thinking, for after the siege was raised he never

* Writing in 1932, John Griffiths concurred with this viewpoint, suggesting that 'the King was relieved... near Conway and a battle was probably fought', but he later retracted this contention somewhat. See 'The Revolt of 1295 and its effects upon the Edwardian Settlement in the Principality of Wales', unpublished BA thesis, University of Liverpool, 1932, p. 55.

again left Conwy except in force, establishing his headquarters at the castle and remaining there until April. The high-risk strategy heralded by his 'reconnaissance' to Nefyn was abandoned in favour of an altogether safer approach of consolidation. Edward's decision, taken in late 1294, to send the biggest of the three English armies into Gwynedd may be seen as a premeditated one, a deliberate attempt to strike at the heart of Welsh resistance and end the conflict with the minimum of fuss. But as it became clear that Madog was one of his more stubborn opponents, it seems that the king reconciled himself to the task of re-conquering the country a piece at a time.

[1] For Edward's itinerary in Wales during the 1294-5 revolt, see E. B. Fryde (ed.), *Book of Prests of the King's Wardrobe for 1294-5* (Oxford, 1962), pp. 222-4; for John de Havering's success at Harlech, see A. D. Carr, 'Madog ap Llywelyn: The Revolt of 1294-5 in Caernarfonshire', p. 40 and references therein.
[2] John Griffiths, 'The Revolt of Madog ap Llywelyn, 1294-5', p. 17.
[3] For a thorough examination of the battle, see J. Beverley Smith, *Llywelyn ap Gruffudd: Prince of Wales*, pp. 536-42.
[4] R. F. Walker, 'The Welsh War of 1294-5', p. xxxiii.
[5] John Griffiths, 'The Revolt of Madog ap Llywelyn, 1294-5', p. 17.
[6] R. F. Walker, 'The Welsh War of 1294-5', p. xxxiii.
[7] Michael Prestwich, *Edward I*, p. 221.
[8] J. E. Morris, *The Welsh Wars of Edward I*, p. 255.
[9] R. F. Walker, 'The Welsh War of 1294-5', p. xxxiii.
[10] A. D. Carr, 'Madog ap Llywelyn: The Revolt of 1294-5 in Caernarfonshire', p. 38 and references therein.
[11] David Powel (rev. Richard Llwyd), *The History of Wales*, pp. 271-2. The original source for the anecdote is to be found in the writings of Walter of Guisborough.
[12] J. G. Edwards discusses the evidence that led Morris to this conclusion in 'The Battle of Maes Madog and the Welsh Campaign of 1294-5', particularly pp. 5-8.

9 – THE BATTLE OF MAES MOYDOG

Madog's position in the early months of 1295 was much like that of Llywelyn II in the autumn of 1282. A sustained effort had been made to shake off the shackles of English rule, and some notable military successes achieved; but with the appearance of a massive English army in the field under the overall command of no less a personage than the king of England himself, Madog's bluff had been called. Nor is 'bluff' too harsh a word to use, for there is no way that Madog could possibly have matched Edward in numerical terms. He was almost certainly outnumbered in both the north and the south by the various royal armies and forces raised by the local English lords, which were around 35,000 strong in total at one point. As Wales' population in the early fourteenth century has been estimated at around 200,000,[1] in order to achieve parity around one-third of the entire native male population would have had to have joined the rebels. In the previous half-century, the only Welsh army of comparable size was the force of 30,000 men and 300 cavalry assembled by Llywelyn II in late 1262 for a campaign in Maelienydd, at a time when the prince's power was nearing its zenith.[2] It seems highly unlikely that a rebel leader such as Madog, contesting an established English system of government and with limited resources at his disposal, was able to bring such a large force into being, still less to adequately arm them. (In this regard, it is worth noting that the largest army assembled under Owain Glyndŵr in his first three years as prince of Wales numbered around 8,240 during the Tywi valley campaign of July 1403.)[3] Aside from the unconfirmed figure of 10,000 men given in the Hagnaby chronicle, there is no evidence to suggest that the forces assembled under the personal command of Madog were ever counted in more than four figures. Given the perilous nature of the mismatch, Madog, it seems, searched for ways to alleviate the pressure Edward was bringing to bear on Gwynedd. In late February he appears to have decided to take a leaf out of Llywelyn II's book by breaking out of Gwynedd and moving south.

We know little of Madog's military credentials, but it does not stretch credulity too much to suggest that he looked to Llywelyn's highly successful campaigns for inspiration. Not only did his forces use the 'hit-and-run' tactic to great effect in capturing Edward's supplies in January, but it may also be the case that Madog looked carefully at considerations of terrain, trying to second guess Edward's route through northern Wales. It has been argued that Madog anticipated Edward's use in 1294 of the same route his army took into Gwynedd in 1282, through Denbigh and Llanrwst, which would take him into a small, steep valley in the area of Pont Garregnewid. With an army confined in such a small space, there would be little room for manoeuvre, and the rebels could take Edward by surprise, and might stand a chance of repelling the invaders. Madog's grant of a parcel of land containing Pont Garregnewid to Bleddyn Fychan in the Penmachno document therefore may have had a double purpose – as an enticement to Bleddyn, and as an assurance that the area in question would be in friendly hands if the opportunity for an ambush arose.[4] As it happened, Edward and his men never strayed from the coast after reaching Abergele in mid-December, but it nevertheless seems that Madog expended a great deal of thought on strategies of this sort.

Madog's other major borrowing from Llywelyn may have been the use of a diversionary tactic. Knowing that any direct confrontation between the king's army and his own would put him at a massive disadvantage, he sought to draw Edward's attention away from Gwynedd, just as Llywelyn did in 1282. In late February, Madog marched southwards from Gwynedd with a body of men. Like Llywelyn, his objective was the Marches, where he probably hoped to shore up morale among the local Welsh – it is conceivable that he hoped to confer with the leader of the revolt there, Cynan ap Maredudd – and hopefully cause enough of a commotion to force Edward to divert troops from the long-planned attack in the north-west. Like Llywelyn, it seems unlikely that he actively sought to fight a pitched battle; and just like Llywelyn, the decision to march south would prove to be the turning-point of the campaign.

'The Earl surrounded them on all sides': preparations for battle

Piecing together an account of the battle – the preparations for it, the action itself, and what happened afterwards – is extraordinarily difficult. Until recently, only one account, that of Trivet, was deemed to be of any great worth, though it has now been supplemented by that contained in the Hagnaby chronicle. Taken together, the accounts provide a wealth of detail about the battle itself, but their brief comments about the preparations for battle make more difficult the task of assessing the movements of Madog's opponent, the earl of Warwick.

Warwick had been stationed for some time at Montgomery on the Welsh border with a force of about 2,700 infantry, 120 or so lances, and thirteen crossbowmen and archers. At the height of the crisis in mid-winter, the size of this force had swelled to well over 10,000 soldiers, but many had been paid off or transferred to other parts of Wales in the interim. Since then Warwick's men had been busy in the middle Marches, guarding the approaches to the castle at Montgomery and patrolling in the adjacent Welsh territory to good effect.[5]

Among the most useful men in Warwick's pay were a number of Welsh spies who had been charged with tracking down Madog. To begin with they had drawn a blank, but at the end of February they reported that they had located Madog, together with part of his army.[6] Here the record is confusing; in later times, David Powel asserted that Madog was raiding the lands around Knockin in Shropshire when Warwick received notice of his whereabouts, but there is reason to doubt this supposition (see Epilogue). Wherever the spies reported Madog to be, we know that Warwick, leaving a force of around two hundred men to garrison Montgomery castle, marched north to Oswestry, where he is are recorded as having stayed on 1st March. Finding nothing, and probably at the prompting of a further report, Warwick left Oswestry a few days later, arriving back at Montgomery on 4th March, the day before the battle.[7]

At this point it is necessary to relate the accounts of the preparations for battle as contained in the two principal chronicle sources. Trivet's account begins thus:

> The Earl of Warwick, hearing that the Welsh were massed in great numbers in a certain plain between two forests, took with him a picked body of men-at-arms, together with crossbowmen and archers, and, surprising them at night, surrounded them on all sides.[8]

The Hagnaby chronicle, meanwhile, has this to say:

> ... the prince came into Powys with the elite of his Welshmen, and our spies came by night to Oswestry, and told us that the prince had gone as far as Cedewain. They [the English] went as quickly as they could to Montgomery, on the Friday and Saturday, 5th March. The prince's host awaited our men on open ground and they fought together, our men killing a good six hundred. Then our men from Thesseweit joined battle with those who were transporting the prince's victuals, and killed a good hundred, and took from them over six score beasts laden with foodstuffs.[9]

Previous assessments of the battle have placed emphasis on the fact that Madog's men were surrounded by Warwick. More recent interpretations, however, have sought to modify this notion in the light of the new information provided by the Hagnaby chronicle relating to the previously unknown action fought between a detachment of Warwick's force – based in 'Thesseweit' (see below) – and those guarding Madog's supply train. R. F. Walker has used the report to lend further credence to Trivet's contention that the Welsh were surrounded. Yet Trivet's account relates very specifically to happenings on the battlefield itself; it is unlikely that, had he have known of the second engagement, he would not have inserted a short account of it into his narrative to qualify his statements. It seems certain that Warwick's main force were responsible for encircling Madog's army, and that they did so by dint of a night march from Montgomery.[10]

The route they took to the site of battle is unclear. The area in which the battlefield sits is a few miles to the south-west of Welshpool, and is dominated by a network of shallow valleys running east-west, many of which contain rivers. The largest of these is the river Banwy, which meanders through a valley in which stands the villages of Llanfair Caereinion and Llanerfyl, and to the east are a number of smaller wooded valleys. On 4th March, Madog and his men were, it seems, in one of these, at the head of which was the source of a small stream – now called Nant Moydog – that fed the larger river.

We do not know precisely what Madog was doing so close to Warwick's base at Montgomery, but it may be supposed that Madog's expedition into the Marches was already over and done with, and that he and his men had stopped briefly on their march back towards Gwynedd. It has been postulated that Madog's men may have traversed the ancient Roman road that passed by the settlement of Llanerfyl around seven miles to the west of the battlefield on their way back from Cedewain.[11] If that is so, however, one is driven to speculate as to why Madog and his men decided to venture so far to the east of it. After an expedition into the Marches, it would seem to make sense for his force to have made directly for rebel-held territory instead of feinting towards the border with England; but the site of the battle lies some considerable distance downstream from Llanerfyl, and well out of Madog's way. Even if one discounts the notion that Madog made use of the Llanerfyl road, a convincing explanation for his easterly position is hard to come by. Perhaps Madog diverted his troops in the direction of Montgomery with the intention of staging a raid on the settlement before turning for home. Alternately, it may be the case that Madog had greater warning of Warwick's approach than has previously been assumed, and marched a short way to meet him, as Richard Morgan implies; but this notion seems to agitate against the account of the Welsh being surrounded found in Trivet's report.[12]

Unfortunately, as the surviving accounts of the battle are all English they not unnaturally tend to concentrate on the tactics adopted by Warwick after his spies had informed him of Madog's whereabouts, as opposed to Madog's movements in the period leading up to the battle. These accounts shed some light on the nature of Warwick's actions before battle was joined. His discovery of Madog's precise position was the work of spies, apparently Welshmen. Armed with this information, he presumably concluded that a strategy of encirclement was feasible. In all probability, Warwick's main force marched north-west from Montgomery on the night of 4th March to gain the entrance to the valley at the earliest opportunity.

5th March: the battle

The site of the battle of Maes Moydog was broadly identified in the 1920s as being in the region just to the north of the village of Castle Caereinion, in which there are no less than four farmsteads bearing the name 'Moydog' in various configurations lying within a mile of one another. In the same area there is also a 'Moydog Wood' and the aforementioned 'Nant Moydog', a tributary of the river Banwy. The name 'Moydog' predates the battle, as a 1291 record shows that the abbey of Strata Marcella owned lands at 'M'dok' in Montgomeryshire. The fact that the placename predates 1295 need not necessarily conflict with the notion that it has some connection with the battle, however; and it has been convincingly argued that its appearance at so many sites within such a small area can be traced back to the 1295 action.[13]

Though only archaeological excavation can ultimately reveal the exact location of the battle, it was almost certainly fought somewhere in Y Figyn, a small valley around 600 yards wide at its wider end, with gently sloping sides and thinly covered with grasses. For Warwick, it was sufficiently large to allow him to organise his forces, yet thickly forested to the north and north-west. It also favoured the attacking force in terms of its topography; being relatively flat, Warwick did not have to worry about giving his opponents the advantage of the higher ground. It seems conceivable that Warwick and his men marched into the valley upstream from either the south or the west.

Trivet's report of Warwick's innovative battle strategy has become something of a *cause célèbre* among students of military history, yet our appreciation of it is severely handicapped by our lack of knowledge of Madog's responses. Having already seized the initiative by dint of an audacious night march, on the morning of 5th March Warwick's army was either in position on the battlefield or very close to it. The speed with which Madog came to know of Warwick's presence may well have dictated his decision to fight. Madog either moved forward to meet Warwick's army or – what seems more likely – was surrounded too quickly to do anything but occupy the field. Madog's decision to prepare for battle has been the source of much controversy, as it was not common practice for the Welsh to engage in pitched battles at this time in history. Only one other large-scale engagement occurred during the revolt, the battle at

Denbigh on 11th November, and the details of that action are unknown; but historians have tended to favour the view that it was less of a pitched battle and more of an ambush. For Madog, facing an enemy almost certainly superior in numbers and equipment, the prudent option would have been to withdraw. He did not do so, as the evidence in the English chronicles, which state that Madog very purposefully and deliberately stood his ground, attest. The obvious conclusion to draw is that reports of Warwick's advance came to Madog too late for him to do anything about it. If true, it was as abject an indictment of the work of his scouts, of which there must have been several, as could be; or perhaps even an indication that some of the men serving under Madog were not as steadfast in their loyalties as they seemed.

As the two forces squared up to one another, the size of Madog's task must have become painfully clear. Although the Hagnaby chronicle testifies to the fact that Madog's force contained his best men, such comments were not uncommon in reports of battles. Even if true, the context of these comments – allied, as they are, to the unexpected willingness exhibited by the Welsh to stand and fight – may allow one to interpret them as testaments to their bravery rather than to the quality of the implements with which they prepared to do battle.[14] The weapons used by Welsh soldiers were largely dictated by their poverty. Thus, swords were doubtless rare outside the ranks of the nobles, crossbows were unheard-of until at least the time of Llywelyn I, and armour and helmets were seldom worn. Spears and arrows, which only required a small amount of metal for the tip, were accordingly in favour,[15] and indeed, there were large numbers of Welsh spear-men present at Maes Moydog.

There were, however, no cavalry, and no archers either – none are mentioned in contemporary accounts.

Warwick, by comparison, had multiple options. His force at Maes Moydog included cavalry – ten horses are recorded as having been killed during the battle – and archers, as well as crossbowmen. The exact size of his force is uncertain, but it would appear that only part of his army of 2,700 fought at Maes Moydog.[16] Allowing for the men stationed at Montgomery castle, one may assume that Warwick had at his command some 2,500 infantry and sixty cavalry. The archers and crossbowmen who were to play such an important part in the battle may only have numbered around a dozen, though this does not deny Trivet's claim that their presence was pivotal. The size of Madog's army is unknown, but it may be presumed that Warwick would not have ventured into the field without making sure that he had numbers on his side, and so one may reasonably conjecture that the Welsh force was smaller. It must have been at least seven hundred strong, as that is the number of Welshmen recorded as having been killed.

At the onset of battle, Madog's men assumed a defensive posture, and formed into a square. This fact alone suggests a considerable amount of tactical acumen on Madog's part, and may indicate that his men were subjected to a certain amount of drilling. It took a considerable effort to train unskilled and inexperienced soldiers to assume such formations, as is demonstrated by the time William Wallace spent training his charges to adopt the schiltron formation – a grouping of spearmen formed into a circle – during his campaigns against the English in Scotland in the late 1290s.[17] Moreover, the tactic was a sound one to adopt against a force with superior numbers of cavalry.

It seems strange, therefore, that the first move in the battle appears to have been a cavalry charge into the Welsh ranks, ordered, it would seem, by Warwick. Though J. G. Edwards questions this version of events in his essay on the battle, it would seem to make sense in the light of the losses of English cavalry (about which Edwards may well have known nothing; the evidence for these losses only came to prominence in recent times). Madog's men planted the butts of their spears on the ground, thus presenting a row of spikes to the onrushing horsemen, and it may well have been at this point that the greatest English losses of the battle were sustained.[18]

As his cavalry came to grief at the tips of the Welsh spears, Warwick changed tactics. His next move would attract the attention of many writers in the years to come. Dispensing with convention, he placed his archers and crossbowmen not in a separate formation, but amongst his cavalry and infantrymen. Secreted in Warwick's main force in this way, the bowmen were essentially safe from the Welsh spears; and as Madog does not seem to have had bowmen of his own with which to retaliate, the law of attrition would gradually weaken the Welsh line.

We can perhaps forgive Madog for not drawing this conclusion himself – after all, this tactic was a completely new one, and immediately after the repulsion of the English cavalry charge, all must have seemed well. To maintain the element of surprise in introducing his new tactic, Warwick may have refrained from employing his small force of bowmen in the early stages of the battle, but even if he had not, to Madog's eye the disappearance of such a small band of men from the fray can hardly have been a cause for concern. What he could not foresee was that they would rejoin the battle (presumably surreptitiously) in the ranks of the cavalry after their failed charge. After all, according to conventional wisdom bowmen were simply not deployed singly, but as a body; and at first, the felling of a few Welshmen by arrow and bolt must have appeared to be isolated and insignificant incidents in the wider context of the battle.

Gradually, however, as more and more shots got home on Welsh bodies, Madog must have realised the damage that Warwick's seemingly trifling band of bowmen were inflicting on his force. His options were rapidly dwindling. A head-on attack was not feasible – Welsh spearmen were incapable of charging[19] – and to hold one's ground for any longer would be pointless. The Welsh began to retreat. Whether or not they had to fight their way out of an encirclement is a matter for speculation, but in any case, it was doubtless in this flight from the field, and the pursuit by Warwick's army that followed, that Madog lost most of his men.

Afterwards, there was the second, smaller engagement whose relation to the main battle remains a source of confusion – the attack of the English, coming from 'Thesseweit', on Madog's supply train. The struggle to identify this comprehensively mangled Welsh placename has produced half a dozen alternatives, none of which are very satisfactory. R. F. Walker theorised that 'Thesseweit' was synonymous with either Llystynwynnan, a hill fort just north of the village of Foel, or Llysyn, less than two miles to the east, at which there stands the site of a motte and bailey castle.[20] Both fortifications are within two miles of the Roman road at Llanerfyl, and Walker theorises that Warwick sent a detachment at night to the Banwy valley –

due west of Madog's location – to block any Welsh retreat. This would seem to place the attack on the supply train somewhere between Y Figyn and the Llanerfyl area. The theory has a certain amount of circumstantial evidence to commend it. No contemporary records document the history of Llysyn, though there is some archaeological evidence to suggest it may originally have been a construction of Rhirid Flaidd, a kinsman of the twelfth-century prince of Powys, Madog ap Maredudd (d. 1160).[21] It is conceivable that it, or Llystynwynnan, or indeed, another motte and bailey castle in the grounds of the Cann Office Hotel, was in a defensible state in 1295, and that one of them was used by Warwick's men as a temporary camp.*

However, it may be more likely that, as Richard Morgan later asserted, 'Thesseweit' was the Hagnaby scribe's attempt to render the Welsh name Y Tair Swydd, used to refer to the three commotes to the west and north-west of Llanfair Caereinion. In the southernmost of the three lies Welshpool, and as the settlement lay less than four miles from the site of the battle, it may make more sense to envisage this detachment of Warwick's men approaching from there rather than from the Llanerfyl area. The force may conceivably have been led by Gwilym de la Pole, who is known to have served in the area under Edward in early 1295.[22]

Yet this theory, too, is not without its problems. Morgan theorised that Madog swung his force southwards to meet the English force, and that, as it was usual to place supplies to the

* There are few surviving local traditions connected with either site, but Mrs. Laura Richards of Foel has recounted stories told to her in the 1960s of the Welsh and English lighting fires on the summit of the mottes at Llysyn and the Cann Office Hotel in times of war to warn of an approaching enemy. Such a story, while rather far-fetched, ought not to be wholly discounted; it is worth noting, for instance, that the story is not specific to a Welsh fighting force, and so admits the idea of an English use of either motte in 1295. Private communication with the author, 30th April 2007.

rear of a body of men in case that body itself came under attack, he placed his supply train immediately behind him, that is, to the north. However, a forest lies directly to the north of the battlefield. This would therefore seem to not only contradict Trivet's claim that the battle was fought between two forests, but would also require us to locate the battlefield rather further south than has usually been envisaged. Still, the notion of Warwick's detachment marching a short distance west from Welshpool seems more admissible than that of marching from the Llanerfyl area, or even from Cheswardine, as has also been suggested.

The efficacy of the second attack was crucial to the success of the battle as a whole. Though perhaps not as well-provisioned as that of Edward's army which was captured by Madog in January, the rebel supply train was just as important to Madog – without it, his men would go hungry. Warwick's detachment fell upon it, killing over one hundred of the men guarding it and capturing the supplies – more than one hundred and twenty beasts laden with food.[23]

As with most battles of the medieval period, losses are difficult to ascertain with any accuracy. The Hagnaby chronicle gives the absurdly small figure of seven men killed on the English side – one squire and six infantrymen – while noting that six hundred Welshmen died in the main attack and over one hundred in the assault on the supply train. These Welsh losses are at least corroborated by the Worcester annalist, who gives a figure of seven hundred; but the pay rolls for Warwick's army tell a different story regarding English losses. Twenty-six constables and 2,689 men were recorded as being in the infantry on the day of the battle, but by the following day, the numbers are twenty-seven and 2,597, thus producing a decrease of ninety-one. Therefore, according to the best available figures, the Welsh lost around six hundred men in the main attack to around one hundred men on the English side. J. G. Edwards has speculated that Welsh losses may well have been exaggerated by English chroniclers keen to underline the importance of the engagement.[24] But even if this is so, it is still clear that Maes Moydog was nothing less than a signal victory for the English, and the killer blow for Madog's revolt.

The battle's aftermath

The closing stages of the battle are sketchily attested. One of the few points of detail comes from the pen of the Worcester annalist, who notes that many of the fleeing Welsh drowned trying to cross a river, perhaps the Banwy itself, which would have been swollen with the rains of the exceptionally wet winter months. Madog himself, it was said, barely escaped from the field with his life. Nevertheless, the tenacity of the Welsh on this occasion earned the respect of a great many English observers. 'They [Madog's army] were the best and bravest Welshmen that anyone has ever seen,' noted the Hagnaby chronicler in tones of admiration.[25]

What became of the remnants of Madog's force? No account makes mention of them, but it may reasonably be speculated that some survived. The most persuasive piece of evidence in support of this point is the survival of Madog himself, who presumably made to the west with what remained of his army, perhaps after joining up with the survivors of the engagement between Warwick's detachment and the troops guarding Madog's supply train. No documentary evidence survives to corroborate the notion of a retreat westwards, but it seems logical; and there is in addition an interesting local tradition that may argue in its favour. Less than four miles to the north-west of Llangadfan is a small area of open pasture marked on today's maps as Tryfel. The pasture is bounded on one side by a small stream named Nant y Dwyslyn ('stream of the sorrowful lake/waters'). Mrs. Laura Richards of Foel has related the local tradition that the stream got its name after a group of soldiers, retreating after a battle, stopped in the area to tend to their injuries. According to the story, they washed their wounds in the stream, which ran red with blood. This last is, of course, an exceedingly common motif in oral history, and it also ought to be pointed out that there is nothing in the story to explicitly link it with the battle of Maes Moydog. Yet it is worth noting that history records no other battle of moment as having occurred in the area, and the source of the story is potentially of great antiquity.[26] As such, it is not wholly fanciful to envisage that it was indeed at Tryfel, a secluded spot away from the fray, that the remains of Madog's army, and perhaps Madog himself, stayed awhile to dress their wounds and reflect on what might have been.

[1] Quoted in Keith Williams-Jones, *The Merioneth Lay Subsidy Roll 1292-3*, p. lix, note 2. Williams-Jones himself suggests that, by extrapolating from other, later estimates, a late thirteenth-century population of 300,000 can be arrived at: 'But this latter figure, it must again be emphasised, is a very crude estimate indeed, no more reliable than a supposition

founded upon a supposition.'
[2] J. Beverley Smith, *Llywelyn ap Gruffudd: Prince of Wales*, p. 149.
[3] R. R. Davies, *The Revolt of Owain Glyndŵr*, pp. 230-1. Davies also notes a less reliable report of the battle of Grosmont in March 1405, at which the rebel army was said to number 8,000 men.
[4] Cledwyn Fychan, 'Bleddyn Fychan a Gwrthryfel Madog ap Llywelyn, 1294-5', p. 19.
[5] For the size of Warwick's forces, see J. G. Edwards, 'The Battle of Maes Madog and the Welsh Campaign of 1294-5', p. 11. Much of what follows is based on the account of the battle as suggested by R. F. Walker, 'The Hagnaby Chronicle and the Battle of Maes Moydog', pp. 125-38 of *Welsh History Review* Vol. 8 (1976).
[6] R. F. Walker, 'The Hagnaby Chronicle and the Battle of Maes Moydog', p. 128.
[7] The Hagnaby chronicle suggests that the army marched on Oswestry to plunder the town; see R. F. Walker, 'The Hagnaby Chronicle and the Battle of Maes Moydog', p. 128.
[8] Quoted in translation in J. E. Morris, *The Welsh Wars of Edward I*, p. 256.
[9] Quoted in translation in Michael Prestwich, *Edward I*, p.223.
[10] R. F. Walker, 'The Hagnaby Chronicle and the Battle of Maes Moydog', pp. 129-30.
[11] R. F. Walker, 'The Hagnaby Chronicle and the Battle of Maes Moydog', p. 136.
[12] Richard Morgan, 'Thesseweit', pp. 87-9 of *Montgomeryshire Collections* Vol. 68 (1980), espcially p. 89.
[13] J. G. Edwards, 'The Site of the Battle of 'Meismeidoc', 1295', pp. 262-5 of *English History Review* Vol. 46 (1931).
[14] Michael Prestwich, for example, provides a translation of the section of the Hagnaby chronicle's report of the battle that deals with the bravery of the Welsh; see *Edward I*, p. 223.
[15] See Sean Davies, *Welsh Military Institutions 633-1283* (Cardiff, 2004) for a discussion of the weaponry typically used by the Welsh during the thirteenth century.
[16] R. F. Walker, 'The Welsh War of 1294-5', p. xxxvii.
[17] Peter Reese, *Wallace: A Biography*, pp. 74-5 describes in greater detail the advantages and disadvantages of the schiltron formation.
[18] *Nicholae Triveti Annales* (ed. Thomas Hog; 1845), pp. 335-6; J. G. Edwards, 'The Battle of Maes Madog and the Welsh Campaign of 1294-5', p. 12. For a modern analysis of Trivet's commentary on the employment of Madog's spearmen, see J. E. Morris, *The Welsh Wars of Edward I*, p. 256.
[19] J. E. Morris, *The Welsh Wars of Edward I*, p. 257.
[20] R. F. Walker, 'The Hagnaby Chronicle and the Battle of Maes Moydog', pp. 130-6.
[21] *Royal Commission on the Ancient and Historical Monuments of Wales Vol. 1: Montgomery* (1911) notes that a seal bearing Rhirid Flaidd's herald was found at Llysun (p. 83). The context in which it was found has not been recorded, however, and so a definite connection with the motte itself is yet to be established.
[22] Richard Morgan, 'Thesseweit', pp. 87-9.
[23] R. F. Walker, 'The Hagnaby Chronicle and the Battle of Maes Moydog', p. 130.
[24] J. G. Edwards, 'The Battle of Maes Madog and the Welsh Campaign of 1294-5', p. 12.
[25] For the suggestion that the Welsh drowned crossing the Banwy, see J. G. Edwards, 'The Site of the Battle of 'Meismeidoc', 1295', pp. 264-5; the translation of the Hagnaby chronicle is from Michael Prestwich, *Edward I*, p. 223.
[26] Private communication with the author, 30th April 2007. Mrs. Richards learned of this story in the 1960s from Mr. Sidney Jones, a farmer living in the area of Tryfel, who took a keen interest in Welsh history, and whose family had lived in the area for generations.

10 – THE REBEL SUBMISSIONS

The beginning of Edward's march through Wales

Edward received word of the Welsh rout at Maes Moydog on 6th March from Adam Bernard. Since the lifting of the siege in January, the king had been biding his time, concentrating his energies on building up men and matériel at Conwy, and it was during this lull that he decided to wage war on Madog for the first time on the diplomatic front. Edward communicated with John Pecham to ask him if he could bring any pressure to bear on the rebel prince.[1]

Pecham is a figure of some controversy in Welsh history. As the Archbishop of Canterbury, in late 1282 he had attempted to act as peacemaker between Edward and Llywelyn, meeting with the Welsh leader near Bangor in early November. His mission ended in failure, but prompted Llywelyn to produce one of the most remarkable documents ever composed by a Welshman, variously referred to as 'the reply of the Welsh', the 'Garthcelyn Declaration', after the place at which it was written, or the 'Declaration of the Nobles'. The document communicated the determination of the Welsh to rule over themselves and their country: 'The prince is not obliged to abandon his inheritance.... The people of Snowdonia say that... they do not wish to do homage to a stranger [Edward] of whose language, manners and laws they are entirely ignorant...'[2] Up until this point Pecham seems to have carried out these negotiations in good faith, but on receipt of this letter he condemned the Welsh as uncivilised, chastised them for continuing to practice their native laws, and advised Edward to bring them to heel as quickly as possible.

It is not, however, this outburst for which Pecham is chiefly remembered in Welsh history. Later writers alleged that Llywelyn was betrayed by members of the church shortly before his death. Evidence is scanty, but a number of historians have noted that Pecham left a friar, Brother Adam of Nannau, in Gwynedd after concluding negotiations with Llywelyn, and that Adam was recalled by Pecham immediately after Llywelyn's death. Though there is no proof of a connection between the clergy and Llywelyn's move to the middle March, this fact has caused many to call Pecham's intentions into question.[3]

Now Pecham was once again involved in Welsh affairs, for on 6th February he wrote to the Bishop of St. Asaph, ordering him to excommunicate Madog if he did not bring the conflict to an end within eight days. This sort of threat was a common in situations of this sort – indeed, Pecham himself saw fit to excommunicate both Llywelyn and Dafydd during the conflict of 1282-3 – and in essence it meant that the subject of the order was expelled from the church. There is no evidence that Madog responded to this threat, and so what seems to have been the only attempt to bring the revolt to an end by peaceful means ended in failure. (This episode also brings to light the interesting fact that, unlike either Llywelyn Bren or Owain Glyndŵr after him, Madog seems to have garnered little ecclesiastical support for his cause. The Bishop of St. Asaph – a man by the name of Llywelyn – seems to have been on the English side throughout. Neither is there a clergyman listed among the signatories of the Penmachno document, though the document may well have been drawn up by one (and the phrase 'and many others' *(et multis aliis)* appended to the document's witness list, though a standard wording in such lists, leaves open the possibility that ecclesiastics may have been in attendance).)

The failure of this ploy was, however, effectively rendered irrelevant by the victory at Maes Moydog. On the same day that he received word of the rout, Reginald de Grey marched south from Rhuddlan with around one hundred cavalry and 2,500 infantry. Now that the area north of Caereinion was once again firmly under English control, he could afford to lead his men on an expedition into the Berwyn mountains to pacify any rebels remaining there, safe in the knowledge that he was secure from attack from the south-east. At the same time, Adam de Riston left for Lancashire to raise more troops, and in due course 2,000 men from Lancashire and Cheshire arrived for duty in the Conwy valley in late March, where they seem to have spent at least some of their time plundering the local inhabitants.[4]

In the meantime, Edward was busy preparing for his long-awaited advance from Conwy into Gwynedd and across the Menai straits to Ynys Môn. The Welsh of the island were evidently expected to put up a great deal of resistance, for the preparations of the English left nothing to chance. The royal architect James of St. George had been at work since February on the Wirral peninsula building pontoon bridges for the crossing of the Menai; these were evidently ready by 4th March, when orders were issued to have them transported to Conwy. His counterpart Thomas de Houghton busied himself by supervising a number of carpenters engaged in the construction of siege equipment. Barges were being built at Chester and fitted out at Conwy, where several of the 140 ships that were due to be used for the crossing were being repaired. Henry de Lathom, who had set off for the island in December with a small invasion force, was entrusted with the task of patrolling the Menai with a squadron of ships to protect the royal army during the crossing.[5]

Yet it would be another month before Edward felt confident enough to move from Conwy; and in the interim period sections of his army grew increasingly restless. A number of his infantrymen pleaded with Edward to be given permission to leave the confines of the town for a punitive raid on the Welsh, and the king consented, sending forth a combined infantry and cavalry force on 10th March. That night, the force surprised a large group of rebels in their beds – the location of the rebel camp is not recorded – and killed 500 of them in their sleep. According to the chronicler, the English recaptured the plate and utensils that had been stolen in the attack on the king's baggage train two months earlier. No other details are available, and so questions relating to the preamble to the incident – such as, for example, whether or not the English had somehow gained a foreknowledge of the position of the Welsh camp – must remain unanswered.[6]

This episode is recorded only in the Hagnaby chronicle, but if true – and, given the substantially accurate account of the revolt contained elsewhere in the chronicle, there is no reason to doubt its authenticity – it represents a blow to Madog's forces of a similar magnitude as the rout at Maes Moydog. It is therefore worth speculating as to why no other account of it survives. The inclusion of what seems at first to be an insignificant detail – the recapture of utensils unlawfully taken by the Welsh in their January attack on Edward's force near Conwy – gains importance when examined as part of a wider discourse on the nature of justice: 'one reaps what one sows' is the unspoken moral. But from an English perspective, even the value of the story in upholding this tenet must have been eclipsed by the nature of the English retaliation. If the event was well known to English writers, its absence from their works may stem from the fact that they may have simply considered it more seemly to omit a description of a massacre perpetrated by men under the command of the king himself from their accounts of the revolt.

This is not to claim the moral high ground for the rebels – as has been recounted, Madog's men were responsible for some outrages of their own. Nevertheless, some acts of war cause particular offence to both heart and intellect on account of their callousness, and the scale on which they are perpetrated. For Walter of Guisborough or Nicholas Trivet, the images of Edward I stoically sitting at a table bearing salted meat and water mixed with honey, and the earl of Warwick cunningly directing his bowmen to stand among the battle-hardened ranks of the English cavalry, presented an altogether more attractive picture of the English at war than did the massacre of 10th March 1295, which in scale exceeded that of Glencoe.

The submission of Ynys Môn

While Edward prepared for the crossing to Ynys Môn, Morgan ap Maredudd continued to cause problems in the south-east. By mid-February, he had apparently been in control of the uplands of Morgannwg for several months, and his forces had launched several attacks on English settlements in Gwent to the east. Now he lay siege to Abergavenny castle. The particulars, such as the numbers of rebels involved and whether or not they had access to siege equipment, are not clear. However, the siege was clearly a serious threat to the castle's well-being, for the earl of

Hereford was obliged to intervene, driving Morgan's men away in an engagement on 13th February. Afterwards, the Annals of Worcester inform us, he launched assaults on rebel-held territory.[7]

The seriousness of Morgan's reverse at Abergavenny is difficult to determine, but it seems as though Morgan retained his ability to strike at English positions in the vicinity at least until early spring, for the rebels were considered to be enough of a danger to sanction the laying of a trap. Quite what form this ambush took is unknown, but the fact that its success rested on the shoulders of a spy in the pay of the English allows us to deduce that Morgan was bested on this occasion through treachery rather than from any shortcoming on his part as a tactician. Thereafter the English gained the upper hand in the south-east. A counter-attack in late spring drove the rebels away from the Cardiff area, and may well have caused them to retreat into the fastnesses of the Morgannwg uplands.[8]

In the west, Maelgwn too was facing difficulties. Although the siege of Aberystwyth castle had reduced its defenders to dire straits due to the shortness of food, in April 1295 the garrison was at last re-provisioned by ships from Bristol, and by late spring Maelgwn's activities were probably confined to Ceredigion and the northern districts of Carmarthenshire. In any case, by this time he cannot have presented much of a threat to English military installations in the area, for a number of letters written by William de Valance at Carmarthen in late April make no reference to the disturbances, and by the spring de Valance was perfectly able to travel long distances in Carmarthenshire – between Carmarthen and Dryslwyn castle, for instance – without being hindered by the rebels, as the existence of another letter written by him at Dryslwyn in May proves. What was on more than one occasion described as a 'war' in west Wales does not therefore seem to have unduly taxed the English forces in the area during the spring. In the area around Builth that was the preserve of Cynan, meanwhile, the revolt appears to have completely collapsed after the battle of Maes Moydog – no other rebel attacks are recorded in the area after 5th March, and three days later local landowner Edmund Mortimer received orders to allow the submission of the rebels in his lands, particularly those in Gwerthrynion and Ceri.[9]

It is clear, therefore, that the rebel cause was beginning to peter out across Wales by early April, and it was now that Edward decided to act. He left Conwy for Bangor on 8th April. Two days later he crossed the Menai Straits, and established a military headquarters at Llanfaes.[10]

Unbeknownst to Edward, the equipment readied for the Ynys Môn campaign was to go unused. Sixteenth-century writer Elis Gruffudd described the king leading the English to a great battlefield victory on a plain on the island, but the truth was almost certainly far less dramatic. In the event, the Welsh of Ynys Môn were in no condition to put up much resistance. One of the few indications of trouble on the island can be found in the *Itinerarium of William Worcester*, a fifteenth-century chronicle that contains a reference to the felling of woods 'which afforded cover for the natives' after Edward's crossing.[11] The evidence supplied by other sources, however, shows that these committed rebels were apparently in the minority. The unusually wet conditions of the previous year meant that food was scarce, and with the appearance of the royal army, the popular will to put up a fight crumbled. According to the

Annals of Worcester around 11,000 men – surely more than had actually participated in the revolt on the island – hastened to make their peace 'after Easter' with the English king. Ever the pragmatist, Edward saw the opportunity to kill two birds with one stone, and granted them a pardon on the condition that they enter into military service. Many agreed, and for the remainder of the campaign Edward's forces were bolstered by six hundred inhabitants of Ynys Môn. To keep the peace, thirty-six hostages were taken from the island, to be transported to distant castles in England at a later date.[12]

It was now that Edward made the decision to construct a new castle on the island to prevent the locals from rising again. The site he chose was already occupied by a hamlet called Cerrig-y-gwyddyl, but the inhabitants were forced to move to a site several miles further down the coast, where a 'new borough' was built for them.* On 17th April, work began on the project, and by the following day, the name 'Beau Mareis' appears for the first time in the historical record, in a document sent to the clerk of the works. The castle was to be no trifling affair, with a concentric wall system and a dock to allow it to be provisioned by sea.[13]

Meanwhile, the earl of Warwick advanced into mid-Wales from Montgomery with his men. The Montgomery army had been reinforced by a contingent of 3,650 infantry from Shrewsbury and Ludlow on 14th April, and from then until the end of the month Warwick had around 7,000 men with which to stamp English authority once again on the people of northern Powys. As on Ynys Môn, it seems that there were a few devoted rebels still at large in the area, for Warwick also employed a

* The settlement created for them still bears the name Newborough.

force of over two hundred carpenters and wood-cutters in late April to fell woods in order to deny shelter to the rebels. By 30th April, the business was concluded, and a large proportion of Warwick's army was paid off.[14]

On 13th May, Warwick marched west into Meirionydd with only 2,350 men. Not that the reduction in the size of his army mattered: Reginald de Grey had got there first, and had already accepted the surrender of every commote in the county with the exception of Ystumanner in which Castell Y Bere stood.[15] By this time Edward was likewise moving south towards Meirionydd, having left northern Wales in the care of his brother, the earl of Lancaster. As J. Beverley Smith notes, 'the routes taken by the three English armies in May 1295, converging upon Merioneth as their common objective, underlines the importance of the county as Madog ap Llywelyn's stronghold'.[16] Indeed, the likelihood that Madog was brought to heel in the county in July, either through surrendering to John de Havering or due to capture by Ynyr Fychan, provides additional evidence for the theory that the English expected stout opposition in the area.[17] One might also point to the prolonged sieges of Harlech and Cricieth – though both were in far less danger now than previously, having been successfully re-supplied by ships from Ireland in early April – and the loss of Edward's prized Castell Y Bere, which would undoubtedly have planted fears about the fierceness of the rebels in Meirionydd in English minds. That only the rebels of Ystumanner should have resisted for any length of time is therefore puzzling, but perhaps no more puzzling than the rapidity with which Ynys Môn's inhabitants – many of whom would have been tenants, friends or even relatives of the prominent rebels under Madog's command, and who would have known them by reputation if not by sight – had earlier come to the king's peace.

Edward's march through southern Wales

By the first week of May at the very latest, the revolt was over in the north, and Edward continued south along the coast of west Wales, receiving submissions from rebels as he went. His route through Meirionydd and Ceredigion can be traced with a fair degree of accuracy (see map on page 226). After leaving Conwy and moving through Caernarfonshire, he passed through Llanrug and Cricieth, at which time the castle was probably relieved. He had reached the fledgling settlement of Dolgellau by 11th May, where he probably joined forces with Reginald de Grey (see map). The following day, a ceremony was held in which the erstwhile rebels of the area formally submitted to the Crown – the fierce resistance expected in Meirionydd had failed to materialise – and more hostages were given over to the English to keep the peace. It must have been around this time that the siege of Harlech was lifted – as there are no records of an engagement, we can assume that the Welsh siege party abandoned the stronghold in the face of the advancing English – and the long-suffering garrison was at last relieved after a period of over six months, together with the fifty-eight inhabitants of the town who had taken shelter in the castle. Edward was in the Tywyn area six miles or so north of Aberystwyth by mid-month, where he was met by the earl of Warwick and his army, and the king felt sufficiently secure to leave for Ceredigion on 18th May.[18]

Ceredigion and Carmarthenshire, which had to all intents and purposes been pacified by the time of Edward's arrival, similarly provided no resistance, although the siege of Aberystwyth seemed to have been particularly well observed by the rebels – one account describes those inside the castle being forced to eat horseflesh at one point. Supply ships from Bristol finally reached the castle on 12th April, and the royal army reached the town on 20th May. An interesting and well-known episode recorded in the Annals of Worcester occurred around the end of the month, when the abbot of Strata Florida met with Edward and promised to bring the leading rebels of the area to surrender to the king in person. When he failed to produce the men, Edward ordered that the abbey be burned to the ground.[19]

By 2nd June the royal army reached Cardigan castle. The date of this castle's fall the previous year is uncertain, but in any case Maelgwn's men seem to have abandoned it by this time. Edward reached Carmarthen by 3rd June, and after a brief meeting with the local military commander the earl of Pembroke at Dryslwyn castle on 6th June, he continued through the Tywi valley. The following day the king wrote to the earl of Lancaster that the rebels in Cardiganshire, Carmarthenshire, and Builth had surrendered. He stayed at Merthyr Tudful from 13th to 15th June, during which time Morgan is known to have surrendered, and then proceeded north through the Marches, paying off and dismissing large numbers of his now superfluous infantrymen as he went.[20]

Wales was at peace again, and it was now Edward's responsibility to make sure it stayed that way. By 30th June he was back at Conwy, and from there proceeded to make a whistle-stop tour of northern Wales, surveying the new construction works at Beaumaris and the repairs at Caernarfon.

Overseeing the works was the mercurial James of St. George. Beaumaris has long been recognised as his crowning glory, one of the most impressive castle designs of the Middle Ages. The castle was given priority over the repairs at Caernarfon by Edward, the lion's share of the money earmarked for rebuilding being expended on the new fortification. Accordingly, James personally supervised the construction works at Beaumaris himself, assigning his understudy, one 'Walter of Hereford', to the works at Caernarfon. Both men were under considerable pressure to finish their jobs as quickly as possible. A deadline of 11th November had been set, by which time both castles were ordered to be in a defensible state. By the time of Edward's visit to Caernarfon on 9th July, rebuilding work had been in progress for over a month, with a total of £149 spent on the town wall alone; the wall was completed on 10th September, and it was only after this that efforts were concentrated on the castle. For the town itself, recovery was clearly going to be a slow process. The town's burgesses were excused from paying rent for a period of ten years in order to foster economic growth, but records from 1306-7 show that much agricultural land in the surrounding countryside remained uncultivated as a result of the revolt.[21]

However, it was not Caernarfon but Beaumaris that occupied Edward's interest. His eagerness to add another link to his 'Ring of Steel' is underlined by the fact that he spent three days there from 10th July onwards. Though the castle was fated never to be completed, the astronomical sum of £11,289 9d. was spent on it from April 1295 to September 1298, over half of this being spent between April and September 1295; and 2,600 masons, diggers and quarriers were employed in its construction.[22]

Elsewhere, modifications and improvements were made. At Denbigh, the earl of Lincoln completely rebuilt the castle, strengthening the town walls and ensuring that in the event of another revolt, besieging the town would be a more difficult proposition. Chirk castle was begun in 1295, and its resemblance to Beaumaris in layout suggests that it too was a product of the fertile mind of James of St. George. Castell Y Bere was deemed to be too difficult to supply in times of war and abandoned, as were Morlais and Llangynwyd castles in Morgannwg. Another Morgannwg castle, Llantrisant, was rebuilt in the late 1290s, only to be sacked during the revolt of Llywelyn Bren twenty years later. Llangybi probably remained derelict for several years after 1295. Even so, it was clear that the castles of Wales had, with only one or two exceptions, proved their military worth during the revolt. Ultimately it was Edward's meticulous approach to their resupply that ensured the recovery of Wales in the uncertain winter months of 1294.[23]

What is less well documented is the impact of the revolt on the people of Wales, but what little evidence we have suggests that the destruction caused in some parts was nothing less than horrific. Neither the English armies nor the Welsh rebels refrained from ravaging settlements across the country. The depredations wrought by English soldiers on their countrymen in the town of Flint have been noted already, but the Hagnaby chronicle also states that the earl of Warwick's men marched on Oswestry in order to plunder the town (and this at a time when it was not even in rebel hands!). Some sources reporting the progress of Edward I through northern Wales also mention in passing the fact that the main body of his army was pillaging the Vale of Clwyd while the king was being attacked west of the Conwy by Madog's men; and then there is the destruction of Strata Florida on the orders of Edward. The Welsh, for their part, were little better: quite aside from the barbarity of the attack on Caernarfon, the areas of Denbigh and Overton and the island of Ynys Môn in the north, Pembroke, Carmarthenshire and northern Ceredigion in the south-west, Senghennydd , Tal-y-Fan and much of lower Gwent in the south, and Ceri and Gwerthrynion in the Builth area were all devastated. Most areas would take months or even years to recover. After the poor harvest of 1298 boatloads of wheat had to be sent to Beaumaris, Caernarfon, Cricieth and Harlech; 'it seems that the resources of the district[s] in corn, recently devastated by warfare... were unequal to the task of supplying the... population'.[24] In mid-Wales in 1304 a commission conducted after the death of landowner Edmund Mortimer revealed that no less than nine burgages in the town of Rhaeadr returned no money because they had been destroyed during the 'war', while much of the farmland in the Caernarfon area remained unused because of the revolt until as late as 1306. Two mills burnt at Aberconwy remained unrepaired in 1307.[25]

The English treated the widespread nature of the revolt as an excuse to introduce even more laws to discriminate against the Welsh. There was the occasional acknowledgement on Edward's part that the feeling on the Welsh side that justice was not being done to them contributed to the popularity of the revolt, and concessions were made accordingly. In early 1297, and after hearing a plea brought to him by the men of Maelienydd against their lord Edmund Mortimer, the king ordered Mortimer to grant the men in Maelienydd the rights to have cases heard at his court in Cymaron, with the proviso that claims to his authority in Cefnllys, Knucklas and Pilleth be dropped.[26]

Such a favourable decision, however, was the exception rather than the rule, and the response of Edward's government overall was less than amenable to the Welsh. Hundreds of hostages were taken away for long periods of confinement in castle in remote parts of England, and communities across Wales were forced to pay fines for their involvement in the revolt. The Welsh of Tir Iarll and Neath in Glamorgan were still paying instalments until well into the fourteenth century, a factor that was surely instrumental when they revolted in 1314, and declared their support for Llywelyn Bren during his revolt in 1316.[27] This bitter conclusion to the revolt of 1294-5 gave the peace that followed a fragility that would be exposed less than twenty years later.

Madog's end

The one remaining mystery is the fate of the four rebel leaders, and rarely can such an apparently simple question have produced so many different answers. The sheer number of contradictory statements regarding the surrenders and captures of June and July made it almost impossible to sort out the erroneous reports from the truthful ones until very recently, and even now we must be wary of committing ourselves to certain versions of events over others. Nevertheless, a not too misleading account of the end of the revolt can be constructed.

In the middle march, English forces were despatched in all directions to hunt down Cynan. Though the revolt was over in the area of Builth by 7th June, he is known to have been at large as late as 21st June, but was eventually apprehended, probably in late July, possibly after feigning leprosy in a bid to escape capture. The location of his capture is a matter of debate, with some writers favouring Hereford, but the balance of evidence suggests that it was in Brecon that Cynan was brought to heel. Though some sources record him as having been imprisoned indefinitely, these confuse Cynan with another imprisoned Welshman of the same name, and it seems highly likely that he was in fact hanged at Hereford on 14th September[28] along with two other rebels.*

There is at least less uncertainty about the circumstances of Maelgwn's death in the south-west. He was killed in a skirmish near Carmarthen, possibly while fighting a group of Welshmen on the English side, and was thus the only one of the four rebel leaders to meet his death in combat. Assigning a date to this engagement is more difficult. Maelgwn must have been still alive on 7th June, for on that date Edward wrote a letter to the earl of Lancaster in which he expressed his wish that 'he will soon have good news of Madog and Maelgwn, either by causing them to come to the peace, or in some other way'. Presumably this final skirmish therefore occurred in mid-June or early July. Further investigations may yet ascertain the location of the skirmish, which was said to have occurred between a mill-pond and the prior of Carmarthen according to a late source.[29]

Morgan ap Maredudd was destined to be the luckiest of the rebel leaders. It was in early summer that he met with the earl of Warwick, who escorted him along with seven hundred men of his rebel force to Merthyr Tudful, where he surrendered to

* Though some sources suggest the hangings occurred on 14th December.

Edward in mid-June. According to one chronicler, Morgan now claimed to have been in revolt only against the earl of Gloucester, and not against Edward himself. Whether or not Morgan was sincere in this, or indeed whether Edward believed him, is a matter for debate. What is certain is that in his acceptance of Morgan's surrender, Edward saw an opportunity to embarrass an earl whose overweening sense of power caused the English king so much discomfort in the early 1290s, and with whom he was even now embroiled in a long-running dispute regarding the bishopric of Llandaf. The earl's lands were temporarily forfeited to the king, and not only did Morgan find himself a free man in short order, but he was also enlisted to serve as an esquire in the royal household, even fighting with the English army in Flanders in 1297.[30] In 1317 he helped to raise levies for service in Scotland from the Welsh population of Morgannwg. He was even granted some of the ancestral lands whose possession he so coveted – he held a life interest in Edlogan worth £15 per year until 1307.[31] Though Morgan's revolt was a failure, the goodwill of the king was a splendid consolation prize. A veteran of two revolts to reinstate Welsh rule, Morgan inclined towards an altogether quieter middle age, and he remained faithful to the English Crown for the rest of his life.

Madog for his part managed to elude capture until mid-summer, but his movements after his escape from the battlefield at Maes Moydog are unknown. Edward clearly considered Madog to be a threat to peace in Wales while he was still at liberty, for he offered a reward of 500 marks to anyone who could capture or kill the rebel leader. By June Madog's sons had already been captured on Ynys Môn, and were languishing in

Hereford castle at the beginning of what would turn out to be a long imprisonment. Such news can hardly have lifted his spirits. Possibly after a final unsuccessful raid in the northern march, he submitted in late July. Some sources suggest he surrendered to the newly-appointed justice of northern Wales, John de Havering, on 31st July 1295, but in later times Ynyr Fychan of Nannau – who remained loyal to the English cause throughout the revolt – was to claim that he was responsible for Madog's capture. Whichever version of events is true, Madog was not hanged and quartered, as is asserted in two Welsh sources, but was instead taken to the Tower of London, where he was to spend the rest of his life. He is still noted as being a prisoner in a record of 1312, but the exact date of his death is not recorded.[32]

The fate of former rebels

Although Madog's revolt was a failure, it nevertheless had very grave repercussions for the remainder of Edward's reign. It cost the king £55,000 in wages for his troops, the procurement of provisions and ships, and the construction and repair of castles throughout the north, thus setting him inexorably on the path to bankruptcy. Indeed, more than one historian has speculated that the drain on royal resources caused by the revolt directly contributed to the difficulties experienced by Edward and his successor in the twenty years after 1295 in prosecuting campaigns in Scotland, and so assisted Robert the Bruce in the long run in his quest to safeguard Scottish independence.[33] Expressed in such simple terms this theory appears rather crude, and even a superficial examination of events in Scotland after the revolt reveals some significant sticking-points. Edward's 1296 invasion of Scotland was a completely successful one; after a Scottish raid into Cumberland and Northumberland in March, an English victory at Dunbar sealed the fate of John Balliol, who was stripped of his title of 'King of Scotland' in July and sent to the Tower of London.[34] Given the remarkable ease with which the English gained this victory, the theory that Madog's revolt fatally undermined Edward's ability to fight seems shaky at best.

Even so, it may contain a kernel of truth, for in the end English aspirations outstripped the country's wealth. The ramifications of overspending do not become apparent overnight, and it can be some time before one feels the pinch. There is no doubt that Edward's pocket was very sorely taxed by his campaigns in France and elsewhere, and the high taxes imposed on his subjects even before Madog's revolt began, combined with his increasing reliance on Italian bankers to fund his military forays, was a clear sign of his predicament. The aftermath of the revolt brought numerous complaints from royal officials and traders alike that they were not being paid according to the work they had done. In 1296 the constable of Bristol, who had carried out the resupply of the Welsh coastal castles with such alacrity the previous year, was still owed £398. During Edward's invasion of Scotland in the early 1300s, work on his castles across northern Wales simply ground to a halt for sheer lack of money. The works at Beaumaris had already lain unfinished for several years, and the stunted appearance of the castle's towers today is due to the fact that they were originally to have been one storey higher. By the time Edward's throne passed to his son, Edward II, in 1307, the crown had amassed huge debts which left England's ability to effectively control its newest possession in the gravest doubt. Edward II's payments to his armies serving in Scotland or on the Continent were frequently late, a state of affairs which probably contributed to the propensity of some soldiers to desert – records attesting to the loss of troops on a Scottish campaign to desertion during Edward II's reign demonstrate how a chronic lack of money could directly aid one's enemy on the battlefield.[35]

The other beneficiary of the Welsh revolt was France. As has been seen, the revolt completely wrecked plans for a campaign in Gascony, ensuring that English authority in the area remained vestigial for many years to come. It also theoretically provided the French with another fissure to exploit in the internal politics of Britain, as it brought the Welsh desire for independence – a desire that could thwart English attempts to dominate Britain if fostered – to their attention. One source alleges that, shortly after the conclusion of the revolt, a plan was afoot to install Thomas Turberville as rightful leader of Wales in the event of a successful invasion of England.[36] Such rumours can only have increased the fears of the English, who kept a close watch indeed on affairs in Wales for some years after the revolt.

As for the Welsh themselves, the deaths of Welsh landowners during the revolt gave the English authorities a good excuse to confiscate their former lands; much of the commote of Dinllaen on the Llŷn peninsula was forfeited in this way.[37] In other areas, wealthy Welsh prisoners were allowed to buy their freedom; Roger de Knovil is on record as having received an allowance for £40 in 1296 in return for the freedom of two Welsh hostages.[38] Sometimes, rebels paid for their transgressions with their lives. The hanging of Roger de Puleston on the opening day of the revolt, for example, could not go unpunished. The two men who carried out the deed, Grono of Twrcelyn and Trahaearn ap Bleddyn, were themselves hanged.[39] However, the English response to individual rebels was remarkably even-handed. The lives of Maelgwn ap Rhys' brothers, Rhys and Gruffudd, were spared, though they were sent to languish in Norwich castle; they were still there in 1308.[40] Ieuaf ab Adda of Trefor, who killed an English soldier during the revolt, was pardoned and went on to prosper, so that at his death his grave was marked by an impressive effigy that can still be seen in Valle Crucis abbey (see plates). Likewise, it appears that the family of one of the men responsible for the destruction of Overton, Madog Goch, survived the revolt with their societal status intact, for a 'Madoc Vachan son of Madoc Goch' is recorded as holding land in the Overton area in 1316.[41]

Another example of how certain rebels escaped heavy punishments can be found in the fate of the eight signatories of the Penmachno document. Although the later life of one is not recorded, the other seven all survived. Tudur ap Gronw and his brother returned to their estates on Ynys Môn, the former dying in 1311. Gruffudd ap Tudur died around 1310, having held lands in Arfon and modern-day Flintshire. 'Deikyn Crach' is recorded as living in Caernarfonshire in 1304. Tudur ap Carwed, Gruffudd ap Rhys ab Ednyfed Fychan and Ieuaf ap Rhirid were among the fifty-seven Welshmen who appeared in front of the earl of Lincoln at Eglwys-fach near Denbigh on 29th June 1295 and swore on behalf of the communities they represented to keep the peace.[42]

They were joined by the irrepressible Bleddyn Fychan, who, despite his switch of allegiance to the Welsh cause, emerged from the revolt smelling of roses: along with Tudur ap Carwed, he secured a post within the administration of the lordship, and served the earl of Lincoln for many years. In 1299-1300, the pair's property was temporarily confiscated after they came under suspicion of having embezzled taxes from Rhos and Rhufoniog. The matter, however, seems to have been settled with a minimum of fuss, for the two men were vital to the smooth running of the lordship, and as such, the earl was disposed to overlook any wrongdoing.[43] Even in the face of defeat, life had to go on, and it would be odd indeed if there were no Welshmen in Wales who could not find ways of creating opportunities for advancement in its aftermath.

[1] For the report of the battle, see John Griffiths, 'The Revolt of Madog ap Llywelyn, 1294-5', p. 20, where it is also noted that Edward was later furnished with another report of the battle by two prisoners; for Pecham's activities, see ibid., p. 19.
[2] Huw Pryce (ed.), *The Acts of Welsh Rulers 1120-1283*, p. 627.
[3] R. R. Davies, *The Age of Conquest: Wales 1063-1415*, pp. 351-2 gives an overview of Pecham's role in the 1282-3 conflict. The *Brut Y Tywysogyon* (Pen. 20 version), p. 120 notes that Llywelyn was betrayed 'in the belfry at Bangor by his own men'. The events leading up to Llywelyn's death are considered at length in Llinos Beverley Smith, 'The Death of Llywelyn ap Gruffudd: The Narratives Reconsidered', *Welsh History Review* Vol. 14 (1982-3), pp. 200-214.
[4] R. F. Walker, 'The Welsh War of 1294-5', pp. xxxviii-xxxix; see also E. A. Lewis, *Medieval Boroughs of Snowdonia*, p. 227.
[5] For James of St. George's work, Thomas de Haughton, and Henry de Lathom, see R. F. Walker, 'The Welsh War of 1294-5', pp. xxxix-xli.
[6] Michael Prestwich, 'A new account of the Welsh campaign of 1294-5', p. 90.
[7] *Annales de Wigornia* (Annals of Worcester), pp. 519-20.

[8] Michael Prestwich, 'A new account of the Welsh campaign of 1294-5', p. 90.
[9] For the provisioning of Aberystwyth, see R. F. Walker, 'The Welsh War of 1294-5', p. xxxv; for de Valance' correspondence, see J. G. Edwards (ed.), *Calendar of Ancient Correspondence concerning Wales*, pp. 215-6; for Mortimer's orders, see Paul Remfry, *Castles of Radnorshire*, p. 60.
[10] John Griffiths, 'The Revolt of Madog ap Llywelyn, 1294-5', p. 20.
[11] Gruffudd's story can be found in both the Welsh original and in translation in John Griffiths,'The Revolt of 1295 and its effects upon the Edwardian Settlement in the Principality of Wales', pp. iii-iv; in it Gruffudd also recorded (wrongly) that Madog was executed and quartered. The evidence for the felling of trees is quoted by Hulbert-Powell in 'Allusions to the Isle of Anglesey in the Itinerarium of William Worcester', pp. 25-7 of *Anglesey Antiquarian Society Transactions* (1949); p. 26.
[12] *Annales de Wigornia* (Annals of Worcester), p. 520; Natalie Fryde, *List of Welsh Entries in the Memoranda Rolls 1282-1343*, p. xvi.
[13] Ian N. Soulsby, *The Towns of Medieval Wales* (Phillimore, 1983), p. 78.
[14] R. F. Walker, 'The Welsh War of 1294-5', p. xli.
[15] R. F. Walker, 'The Welsh War of 1294-5', p. xxxvii, p. xli.
[16] J. Beverley Smith (ed.), *A History of Merioneth Vol. 2: The Middle Ages* (Cardiff, 2001), p. 68.
[17] John Griffiths, 'The Revolt of Madog ap Llywelyn, 1294-5', p. 22.
[18] John Griffiths, 'The Revolt of Madog ap Llywelyn, 1294-5', p. 21; R. F. Walker, 'The Welsh War of 1294-5', p. xlii.
[19] *Annales de Wigornia* (Annals of Worcester), p. 520. For a modern assessment of the incident, see Michael Prestwich, Edward I, p. 224.
[20] R. F. Walker, 'The Welsh War of 1294-5', p. xliii.
[21] For figures relating to the rebuilding of Caernarfon's town walls, see J. G. Edwards, 'Edward I's Castle Building in Wales' (Proceedings of British Academy, 1944), p. 48, note 2; for the situation at Caernarfon in 1306-7, see Keith Williams-Jones, 'Caernarvon', p. 81.
[22] A. J. Taylor, 'Building at Caernarvon and Beaumaris in 1295-6', pp. 61-6 of *Bulletin of the Board of Celtic Studies* Vol. 15 Part I (1952).
[23] For the argument that leads us to presuppose Y Bere's abandonment, see E. D. Evans, 'Castell Y Bere', p. 43; for others see the appropriate entries in Julian Pettifer, *Welsh Castles.*
[24] B. H. St. J. O'Neil, 'Cricieth Castle, Caernarvonshire', pp. 1-51 of *Archaeologia Cambrensis* Vol. 98 (1944-5); p. 5.
[25] For Rhaeadr, see *Calendar of Inquisitions Post Mortem Edward I Vol. 4*, p. 161; for lands in the Caernarfon area and other reports of damage in Caernarfonshire, see E. A. Lewis, *Medieval Boroughs of Snowdonia*, p. 190.
[26] See E. J. L. Cole, 'The Castles of Maelienydd', pp. 3-19 of *The Radnorshire Society Transactions* Vol. 16 (Dec. 1946), particularly p. 6.
[27] Frederic Evans, *Tir Iarll* (Educational Publishing Company, 1912), p. 59.
[28] *Annales de Wigornia*, p. 522.
[29] 'Rhys ap Maredudd', pp. 202-7 of John E. Lloyd (ed.), *A History of Carmarthenshire* Vol. 1. The same article refers to Maelgwn as having been 'slain by the men of Gwent' (p. 207). For the letter of 7th June, see pp. 207-8 of J. G. Edwards (ed.), *Calendar of Ancient Correspondence concerning Wales* (Cardiff, 1935).
[30] J. Beverley Smith, 'Edward II and the Allegiance of Wales', p. 142.
[31] Michael Altschul, *A Baronial Family in Medieval England: The Clares, 1217-1314*, p. 278, note 126; p. 244, note 7.
[32] Madog's surrender to John de Havering is noticed in a variety of chronicles, for example the *Historia Anglicana* (ed. Luard, 1859; p. 282); the capture of Madog's sons is also recorded (p. 282). Natalie Fryde, *List of Welsh Entries in the Memoranda Rolls 1282-1343*, p. xvi notes that they were in custody by 11th June 1295, and seem to have spent at least the next nine

years at Hereford. They were housed in the Tower of London by 1311. For Ynyr Fychan's claim to have captured Madog and Edward I's decision to put a price on Madog's head, see John Griffiths, 'The Revolt of Madog ap Llywelyn, 1294-5', p. 22.

[33] R. F. Walker, 'The Welsh War of 1294-5', p. 1 notes that between 18th June 1294 and 19th November 1295, at least £55,453 was spent on waging war in Wales by Edward. This figure accounted for a quarter of his entire spending on military matters. Glanville R. J. Jones, 'The Defences of Gwynedd in the Thirteenth Century'. pp.29-43 of *Caernarvonshire Historical Society Transactions* Vol. 30 (1969), p.32 notes the deleterious effects the revolt of 1294-5 had on Edward's finances.

[34] G. W. S. Barrow, *Kingship and Unity: Scotland 1000-1306*, pp. 164-5.

[35] For desertions during Edward II's reign, see Natalie M. Fryde, 'Welsh Troops in the Scottish Campaign of 1322', pp. 82-9 of the *Bulletin of the Board of Celtic Studies* Vol. XXVI (1974-5), particularly p. 83.

[36] *Flores Historiarum* Vol. III AD. 1265-1326 (1890), p. 95.

[37] W. H. Waters, *The Edwardian Settlement of North Wales in its Administrative and Legal Aspects 1284-1343* (Cardiff, 1935), p. 140, p. 158, note 2.

[38] Natalie Fryde, *List of Welsh Entries in the Memoranda Rolls 1282-1343*, p. 13.

[39] A. D. Carr, 'Madog ap Llywelyn: The Revolt of 1294-5 in Caernarfonshire', p. 37.

[40] T. Jones-Pierce, 'Maelgwn ap Rhys', p. 610.

[41] H. Helen Davies, *Schedule of the Elwes Collection* (National Library of Wales, 1976), p. 1.

[42] Cledwyn Fychan, 'Bleddyn Fychan a Gwrthryfel Madog ap Llywelyn, 1294-5', p. 21.

[43] Cledwyn Fychan, 'Bleddyn Fychan a Gwrthryfel Madog ap Llywelyn, 1294-5', pp. 20-1.

EPILOGUE: MADOG'S LEGACY

It is easy to see why Madog ap Llywelyn's exploits mean nothing to the average Welsh person today. From one perspective, his is simply one more name in a long succession of failed leaders of revolt in native Wales after 1282: men such as Dafydd III, Rhys ap Maredudd, and Llywelyn Bren. Even on this list, his achievements were overshadowed by those of Owain Glyndŵr over a century later. Glyndŵr's revolt was shot through with pitched battles and dramatic incidents, and Glyndŵr himself played an important part in many of them: his forays across the whole of Wales and into the border counties during a revolt that lasted over ten years ensured that a folk memory of his actions would linger in dozens of locations across the country for centuries. This status was something that Madog, whose revolt was over in less than a year and who apparently never ventured further south than Cedewain, never attained. Furthermore, Glyndŵr's posthumous reputation was bolstered by a great deal more documentary evidence than that which survives pertaining to Madog. Lastly, during the remarkable resurgence of Welsh national feeling during the nineteenth century, a Welsh public eager to create a national hero sought a figure whose achievements were such that he transcended the realm of simple historical fact and assumed quasi-legendary proportions. Glyndŵr, whose mysterious disappearance after the suppression of his revolt defied all efforts to coerce him into surrender, fitted the bill perfectly, whereas the figure of Madog, who after his capture was fated to spend the rest of his life in the tower of London, bespoke nothing but subjugation and defeat. For later generations, the role of national figurehead was already taken. Madog's legacy could not possibly compare with that of the last legitimate claimant to the title 'prince of Wales'.

It was thus left to a handful of chroniclers and historians to recount the story of the 1294-5 revolt. Among the first to do so was Nicholas Trivet (Trevet; d. 1328), a Dominican friar from a wealthy Norfolk family. Trivet's studies of philosophy and theology at Oxford in the late thirteenth century held him in good stead when he came to write his *Annals*, a substantial work which covers the history of England from 1136 to 1301. His account of the revolt mentions Madog's sacking of Caernarfon, Maelgwn's forays into Pembroke and Carmarthenshire, and the earl of Lincoln's defeat at Denbigh; but the section that would have the most resonance for later historians was that which dealt with the battle of Maes Moydog. Trivet's description of Warwick's tactics and the Welsh response to them would in due course be seen as evidence of the vital development of tactics in the years preceding the battle of Crécy, fought in 1346 during the Hundred Years War, where a modified version of the integrated approach to the dispersal of archers and cavalry pioneered by Warwick would be used to great effect.[1]

Another important text was the chronicle of the monk Florence of Worcester. Though Florence had died in 1118, a copy of the manuscript now residing at Corpus Christi College in Cambridge shows that his work was later added to by an unknown writer of the early fourteenth century. This writer's sources cannot have been very reliable, for the revolt is described as having been led by one 'Meredudd ab Llywelyn' ('Mereduco ab Lewelini'); but other important events, such as Edward's arrival at 'Aberconewei' before Christmas, are faithfully related.[2]

Outside the British Isles the revolt attracted little attention, but one Continental writer who saw fit to commit an account of the revolt to paper was the Dutch chronicler Lodewijk van Velthem. His *Spiegel Historiael* (1316) included a narrative of Edward's campaigns in Wales. A poet by nature, van Velthem was less interested in providing a truthful account of the revolt than in telling a good yarn: instilling Edward with all the qualities of a thirteenth century Arthur, his text mingles elements of well-known historical events in Wales with aspects of the Arthurian legend. As such, its account of a battle between Edward's army and a Welsh force commanded by a man van Velthem identifies as 'Pierleward' – not a close match for 'Madog ap Llywelyn' by any stretch of the imagination – must be treated with extreme suspicion. The dating of the battle to 1293, only one year before the commencement of Madog's revolt, can hardly be coincidental however; and regardless of the factual errors and tall stories that pepper the text, there can be no doubt that van Velthem had Madog's revolt in mind when preparing his narrative. His weakness was that he had to rely largely on second-hand reports that came to him only several years after the events which he describes. He certainly had the opportunity to interview former rebels who served with Edward's forces at Ghent in the late 1290s, but the difficulties involved in extracting information from uneducated soldiers through their own second language make it easier to explain van Velthem's frequent confusing of one event with another. For instance, he notes that 'Pierleward' was executed at the end of the revolt, leading one to wonder if he had not inadvertently mixed up an account of Dafydd III's death in 1283 with the events of 1294-5. Given the 1293 date assigned to the battle noted above, it is tempting to suppose that this passage depicts the battle of Maes Moydog; but noting that it is at odds with the depiction of Maes Moydog in Trivet's text, Th. M. Chotzen suggested that van Velthem erroneously attributed an account of the so-called battle of Irfon Bridge from the 1282-3 conflict to the revolt of 1294-5. While it is possible to find fault with this theory, it is equally difficult to find an alternative explanation for this incident's inclusion, except to say that it owes more to the art of story-telling than to the practices of a good historian.[3]

By the end of the fourteenth century, the first of the manuscripts that later became known as *Brut Y Tywysogyon* had been written. Written (at least in part) at the Cistercian abbey of Strata Florida in southern Wales, the accounts of the revolt contained in these manuscripts, while providing a great deal of useful information, are also problematic, contradicting other sources on certain crucial points and omitting others one might have considered worthy of note. By far the fullest account is that contained in *Brenhinedd y Saesson* (The Kings of the Saxons), which notes the death of Sir Roger de Puleston, Cynan's death at Hereford, and an interesting aside on Edward's financial difficulties.

An infuriatingly brief reference to the 1294-5 revolt can also be found in Peniarth MS. 32, also known as the *Llyfr Teg*, a volume written in the late fourteenth and early fifteenth centuries. A short chronicle written in 1404 lists various events in Wales, including the death of Llywelyn II in 1282 and the transfer of the *Croes Naid* into English hands; Dafydd's subsequent continuance of the war and his execution at Shrewsbury; the revolt of Llywelyn Bren in the 1310s; the baronial war of 1321; and various other events such as the coming of plague to Wales. Listed among these is the revolt of 1294-5, described in the bald comment that in 1296 [sic] there occurred the 'war' of Morgan ap Maredudd.[4]

It is worth considering why the revolt should have been deemed worthy of remembrance by a scribe writing over one hundred years after the event, and why he should have described it as the 'war' of Morgan, rather than that of Madog, especially when one considers that Madog had been accredited with leadership of the revolt in the various versions of *Brut Y Tywysogyon* by that time. There can be no firm answers to these questions, but some tentative theories may be advanced. Much of the passage in which the reference is found deals with various aspects of Wales' military history over the one hundred and twenty or so years leading up to 1404: revolts instigated by native leaders are noted, but – what is more interesting – baronial opposition to Edward II's reign in the early 1320s is deemed equally noteworthy. Clearly, keeping a record of military events was important to the writer; and it may not be too misleading to suggest that the fact that he was writing at the height of Owain Glyndŵr's revolt had something to do with it. In the context of an insurrection that had rendered English authority in most of Wales vestigial at best by 1404, the historical precedents for the revolt gained in importance.

Why Morgan was singled out in the entry is more difficult to explain, but geography may have played a part. Identifying the location at which the book was written is impossible, but it may have had its origins in southern Wales. The fact that it is written in large part by a scribe who contributed to the *Llyfr Coch Hergest* (Red Book of Hergest) – largely the responsibility of

Hywel Fychan, a scribe whose patron was Hopcyn ap Tomas ab Einion, a gentleman from Ynysforgan near Ynystawe, Swansea – may allow us to tentatively place its origination in southern Wales, where the exploits of Morgan would have been more readily remembered than those of the revolt's far-off leader. Such mentions in fifteenth-century manuscripts, though brief, show that knowledge of the revolt remained widespread, even if the individual events that constituted it did not.

In later eras, the revolt underwent a period of reconsideration by a new generation of Welsh writers. Foremost among these was Humphrey Llwyd (c. 1527-68), an antiquarian from Denbigh who was educated at Oxford, and whose adaptation of the *Brut Y Tywysogion*, the *Cronica Walliae*, was completed by 1559, but which lay unpublished for centuries afterward. It is here that a curious addendum to the story of Madog's final weeks of liberty first comes to light, for it is in Lluyd's work that we find mention of a great battle fought in the summer of 1295 at 'Kevyn Digolh', or Cefn Digoll (Long Mountain), on the border between Welshpool and Shrewsbury.[5]

It was evidently on this source, and perhaps that of Walter of Guisborough's earlier text, that David Powel based his account of the revolt in his 1584 *Historie of Cambria*. Powel came from Rhiwabon near Wrexham, and was familiar with the writings of those historians such as the Italian Polydore Vergil, who was loathe to ascribe the Welsh victory at Denbigh to any particular military prowess on the rebels' part. Powel was more generous, emphasising the nationwide scope of the revolt, and providing a wealth of detail regarding Madog's alleged raids in the summer. According to Powel, after Edward left Wales Madog reappeared and captured Oswestry, defeated a force led by

Roger Lestrange in a pitched battle near Knockin in Shropshire, won a second battle shortly afterwards, and was marching on Shrewsbury when he was either taken prisoner or pardoned on the condition of travelling to southern Wales to secure the surrender of Morgan ap Maredudd.[6] As Edward was still in Wales as late as the second week of July, all this would have to have taken place in the final two weeks of the month, well after the final submissions are said to have taken place. While the fact that several Welshmen living in the Oswestry area seem to have been implicated in the revolt weigh in favour of Powel's version of events, equally there are other reasons to doubt its truthfulness. R. F. Walker suggests the following: 'It may be strongly suspected that there eventually grew up a Welsh popular demand for a kind of Madoc saga, and that the story preserved by Powel satisfied the demand and gave Madoc a suitably heroic end. [The passage reading] 'Manie adventures and sundrie conflicts' was not specific enough, so Madoc not only compels the submission of Oswestry and defeats the Marchers twice, but is actually threatening Shrewsbury before being finally defeated.'[7]

Walker's theory is also interesting because it implies that Powel's story was derived from an oral tradition of the Welshpool or Oswestry areas. It is made all the more attractive by Richard Morgan's assertion that the place-name 'Llety Fadog' in the hamlet of Hope near Welshpool may well have been the origination of the story that Madog fought a battle in the area. Hope lies only a mile or so to the west of Cefn Digoll, and although the name 'Llety Fadog' first occurs only in 1618, in all probability it was of some antiquity before its first appearance in the historical record.[8] However, while local tradition is one thing, incontrovertible proof is quite another. In the absence of any earlier source for these events it would be wise to regard Powel's story as highly dubious. Still, such speculations, when combined with the aforementioned story concerning Nant y Dwyslyn and John Griffiths' assertion that 'Welsh [oral] tradition' correctly placed the battle of Maes Moydog in the area of Caereinion,[9] strongly suggest that folk memories of Madog's exploits endured there until at least the seventeenth century.

Modern images of Madog

It was from the early chronicle sources that later historians constructed their narratives of Madog's revolt. In the nineteenth century, a spate of history books appeared by Welsh writers that included accounts of the revolt by William Wynne, William Warrington, and also R. W. Morgan, whose *Hanes yr Hen Gymru* (*History of Old Wales*, 1857) was one of the first popular history texts written in Welsh to make reference to Madog.

The nineteenth century was also the time of the romantic ideal, and a great many Welsh and English writers alike found that there was a pretty penny to be made in writing of their adventures in Wales – now reinvented as an exotic and far-flung Celtic country – in the form of travelogues. Such journals could be made more interesting by means of the odd aside on the more melodramatic aspects of Welsh history, as Thomas Pennant found when he came to write his *Tours of Wales* (1781); but it was once again Glyndŵr that received the lion's share of the attention, with Madog mentioned only briefly. George Borrow, whose *Wild Wales* was published in 1860, ignored Madog completely.

Whether or not the decision of these writers to overlook the 1294-5 revolt was a reflection of a lack of oral tradition and popular interest in Madog and his fellow rebel leaders is unclear; as has been noted, the revolt has left precious little in the way of oral history and local legends. A possible tantalising exception is recorded in Edward Jones' *Musical and Poetical Relicks of the Welsh Bards* (1784), which seems to be the first publication to have printed a copy of the tune 'Rhyfelgyrch Cadben Morgan' (Captain Morgan's March). Jones noted:

> Probably, this Morgan was Captain of the Glamorganshire men, about the year 1294; who gallantly defended his Country from the incursions of the Saxons, and who dispossessed the Earl of Gloucester of those lands which had formerly been taken from Morgan's Forefathers.[10]

This story was later reprinted in several volumes including *The Choralist*, which added that the tune 'was probably composed or selected by this prince [sic] to animate the march of his followers'[11] – a charming, if somewhat unlikely, hypothesis. In Jones' 1784 publication, a version of the tune – now well known to Welsh speakers as that played during the Seremoni Cadeirio'r Bardd (Chairing of the Bard Ceremony) at the Eisteddfod Genedlaethol every year – was printed alongside the Welsh text and an English translation. The latter was written by one Mr. Lambert, and was, Jones erroneously claimed, an 'animated and faithful version of the Poem by Meirion Goch of Eryri'.[12] In fact, the English version is very largely independent of the Welsh one, and seems to commemorate actions occurring at Harlech castle during the War of the Roses in the mid-fifteenth century.

The Welsh words, regrettably, shed no light on Morgan's revolt, though the far-fetched story that the tune dated back to Morgan's time died a hard death – the ordinarily sober historian Edgar L. Chappell claimed as late as 1945 that the verses were actually sung by Morgan's men.[13]

Some writers of the period who wrote of Madog's revolt were more given to glorification of the revolt than others. In the popular school text-book *Flame-Bearers of Welsh History* (1905) Owen Rhoscomyl devotes five pages to the revolts of Rhys ap Maredudd, Madog, and Llywelyn Bren, and his depiction of Madog, neatly inserted between two passages bashing the reputation and characters of the two Edwards, is most interesting. Like many earlier writers, he wrongly equated Madog with another man of the same name who died in 1331, and whose tomb lies in Gresford church near Wrexham. Moreover, he takes Powel's doubtful account of the battle at Cefn Digoll at face value, basing his argument that Madog raised an army in northern Powys on the misconception that Madog was descended from the princes of Powys. But the account is also interesting for the emphasis it places on the central role played in the revolt by the people of Wales: 'After the passing of Rhys [ap Maredudd], it is the people who nurse the spark of freedom and keep ready for the struggle, to break out as soon as a leader appears.'[14] It is an interesting account, as it shows that by the end of the Victorian period – a time which in Wales saw the growth of the Cymru Fydd movement, calls for home rule, and a revival of Welsh culture in general – there were authors writing for the popular market supporting the view that the Welsh populace had risen of their own accord and chosen Madog, Morgan, and the other leaders, a view echoed by several contemporary academics, including Thomas Owen Morgan. At the time of the Great Revival and the unbridled growth of Wales' coal industry, this sense of the power of popular will had immense appeal.

Popular accounts of Madog's story were all very well, but, the odd short article in various nineteenth-century antiquarian journals aside, academic study of the revolt was still lacking. The first modern historian to tackle the revolt in detail was J. E. Morris. Fully thirty pages of his 1901 text *The Welsh Wars of Edward I* are devoted to what he described as the rising of 'Madoc, Maelgwn, and Morgan', and it was this work more than any other which brought the revolt to the attention of a wider reading public. Even so, this account, though undoubtedly a massive improvement on what has gone before, was less than perfect. In particular, Morris' decision to rely on the issue of letters of protection to identify the whereabouts of English military commanders during the revolt led to some unfortunate misunderstandings. The mistaken belief that the battle described by Trivet occurred in the vicinity of Conwy instead of near Welshpool caused a great deal of problems in later years that were partly remedied by J. G. Edwards' 1924 essay 'The Battle of Maes Madog and the Welsh Campaign of 1294-5', which appeared in an issue of the academic journal *English Historical Review*. Edwards' expert analysis of financial records of the English armies mustered in 1294 provided a wealth of additional information regarding the strength of English forces, and a subsequent short essay detailing his successful quest to discover the location of the battle of Maes Moydog was published in 1931.

The last sixty years has seen further discoveries, the most

important of which was the analysis of the Hagnaby chronicle, a text found in Lincolnshire and transcribed by Michael Prestwich among others. R. F. Walker's chapter on the revolt in E. B. Fryde's 1962 edition of the *Book of Prests*, a record of financial transactions relating to the provisioning and movements of Edward's forces, expanded knowledge of the English preparations for campaigning in Wales a little further. In the field of archaeology, a number of excavations at Castell Y Bere in the 1950s provided confirmation of the long-held suspicion that the castle had been burnt by the rebels and not merely abandoned by the English after the suppression of the revolt. Doubtless other archaeological discoveries and analyses of documentary evidence will render theories advanced in the present volume obsolete in time.

How, then, should the events of 1294-5 be remembered? Two schools of thought have appeared in recent decades whose readings of the post-invasion era seek to explain its revolts and disturbances in mutually exclusive ways. Firstly, there are those who have developed notions of a relatively smooth transition from the Wales of the native princes to the English-controlled Wales of 1283 onwards. If they are to maintain their coherence, these theories must present the revolts of 1287-8, 1294-5, 1316 – the 1314 revolt and Madog Llwyd's raid in mid-Wales in 1332, referred to by one modern writer as a 'minor uprising',[15] are both frequently overlooked – and the Shaldeford crisis of 1344-5 as minor interruptions in this transitory process. A. D. Carr has recently argued along these lines, presenting Madog's revolt not as a bid for independence, but rather as a 'social protest': 'The revolts in 1287 and 1294-5... were neither popular nor national; the former was a protest by a disappointed Welsh nobleman, and the latter may have been a warning to Edward I by leaders of the native community that his financial demands were excessive.'[16] When applied to certain of the insurrections that swept through Wales in the late thirteenth and early fourteenth centuries, this view is in some respects persuasive. No-one, for example, could argue that the 1316 revolt, which was more or less contained within Morgannwg and Gwent, was meant by its leader Llywelyn Bren to be a serious threat to English authority in the country as a whole (though English confidence in the security of Wales was nevertheless badly shaken by it). Nor could it be seriously claimed that the revolt in the same region in the late summer of 1314 was anything more than an expression of local disgruntlement fuelled only partly by grief and patriotic indignation at the loss of so many Welshmen in the English army on the battlefield at Bannockburn earlier that summer. But it tends to look rather less convincing when applied to the 1294-5 revolt. Here, the role played by the people in bringing about the revolt is frequently exaggerated to the detriment of the examination of the motives of Madog ap Llywelyn, who is often portrayed as something of a anachronism suffering from delusions of grandeur, a relic longing for the return of an earlier age in which the Welsh aristocracy was not shackled by the English administration.

Such readings ought to be treated with care. In *A New History of Wales* (2000), Jeremy Black claims that the 1294-5 revolt can be ascribed to the need of the Welsh to protest against English administrative policy rather than the principle of English control itself. This theory ignores entirely the significance of the evidence contained within the Penmachno document, which reveals much about the substantial political framework which

Madog wished to create to validate his actions, and on which the revolt ultimately rested. A people protesting against 'government policy' does not bear arms and engage in insurrection for upwards of eight months, neglecting their livelihoods and their own well-being; nor do men who are merely unhappy with tax rises and land procurements sanction the request of their leader to be called 'prince of Wales', fight pitched battles, go on long marches, or agree to conduct lengthy, drawn-out sieges.[17] As the attacks on Overton and the murders of English officials suggest, there was certainly a hefty amount of dissatisfaction with English policy in the minds of many of the rebels when they sided with Madog and the other leaders, and scores were undoubtedly settled under the cover of the revolt; but an explanation of its causes cannot end there.

At the other extreme, we have the views of authors such as Peter Berresford Ellis, who, in their desire to redress the historical balance and construct narratives of Welsh history to replace earlier Anglocentric models, claim too much for Madog. In *Wales – A Nation Again* (1968) Ellis wrote that 'in 1294 Madog, another prince, achieved several successes against the English army but was defeated the following year at the Battle of Cefn Digoll'.[18] Here, quite apart from bestowing the status of a battle on an event which is very sketchily attested in the historical record, the use of the phrase 'successes against the English army' is an unintentional but undeniable distortion of the facts, for it implies that Madog's exploits were directed against a single unified force under the leadership of the king of England. The only successes Madog achieved against an English force in battle were at Denbigh, where the rebels defeated a relieving expedition of the earl of Lincoln that was not connected to the royal army in any way, and the successful assault on the supply train on the coast, carried out at a time when Edward was away from the main body of his army and probing westwards with what was likely to have been a reconnaissance force. In neither case could Madog be said to have achieved a success against 'the English army' as such – quite simply, he never faced that army at its full strength. The distinction is a subtle one, but it is easy to see how failing to make it encourages a perception of a revolt whose leaders repeatedly faced down the massed military might of England, rather than scratch forces raised by local landowners and the vanguards of far-off armies.

Should the revolt, therefore, be consigned to history as a foolhardy act, an expression of discontent from a disinherited native aristocracy that counted Maelgwn, Morgan and Cynan among its most intransigent and hot-headed members? And what of Madog himself? Was he an orator of repute, a mere pretender to the Welsh throne, or a dreamer who dreamed of being a statesman at the head of an independent Wales?

There have certainly been few attempts to study his revolt in the context of Welsh constitutional history, in contrast to that of Owain Glyndŵr, whose programme for national revival as recorded in the documents issued by his government was analysed in detail by R. R. Davies. In this light, it seems fitting that historians and public alike should today follow T. Jones-Pierce's lead and accord Madog the status of a native prince of Wales.[19] Like Glyndŵr – whose princely eminence, though short-lived, can hardly be disputed – he established his credentials for the title in writing, and the proof of the fact that his assumption of the title carried weight for a great many people in the revolt's aftermath is in the large number of contemporary or near-contemporary references to him as a prince.

In many respects his story resembles that of another rebel leader, a contemporary who likewise led a nation-wide revolt against English rule, who won victories, stormed castles, and issued charters during his period of supremacy in the name of his nation, but who was ultimately destined to fail in his bid to secure independence. That man was William Wallace of *Braveheart* fame, and seeing as a tale of one man's injustice under the thumb of foreign oppressors seems to translate into good box office receipts, one could be forgiven for assuming that the Welsh public of today would be rather more familiar with Madog's name and his exploits if he had ended his days at the gallows as Wallace did.

In the end, Edward knew better than to make a martyr out of him, and as Madog disappeared from view in his cell in the Tower of London, so too did his revolt. It may not have been the most distinguished of periods in Welsh history, and it would be wise to refrain from glorifying a show of defiance that caused the deaths of thousands of people on both sides; but nor does that mean that the people of today's Wales should forget the vision of freedom that prompted the Welshmen of 1294 to action in the last days of September.

[1] *Nicholae Triveti Annales*, pp. 333-8.
[2] *Flores Historiarum* Vol. III AD. 1265-1326, pp. 91-3.
[3] The section of the *Spiegel Historiael* dealing with the revolt is treated at length in Th. M. Chotzen, 'Welsh History in the Continuation of the 'Spiegel Historiael' by Lodewijk van Velthem', *Bulletin of the Board of Celtic Studies* Vol. 7, pp. 42-54.

[4] The *Llyfr Teg* is noticed in the *Report on Manuscripts in the Welsh Language* Vol. 1 (HMSO, 1898), pp. 363-4.
[5] Humphrey Llwyd (ed. Ieuan M. Williams), *Cronica Walliae* (Cardiff, 2002), p. 224 and note.
[6] David Powel, *A Historie of Cambria* (1584), p. 381.
[7] For the evidence relating to possible Welsh rebels living in Llynclys and other settlements in Shropshire, see R. Morgan, 'The Barony of Powys, 1275-1360', pp. 1-34 of *Welsh History Review* Vol. 10 (1980-1); p. 8, note 37; R. F. Walker, 'The Hagnaby Chronicle and the Battle of Maes Moydog'f, p. 138.
[8] R. Morgan, 'The Barony of Powys, 1275-1360', p. 8, note 37.
[9] John Griffiths, 'The Revolt of 1295 and its effects upon the Edwardian Settlement in the Principality of Wales', p. 59.
[10] Edward Jones, *Musical and Poetical Relicks of the Welsh Bards* (1784), p. 140.
[11] *The Choralist*, No. 191.
[12] Edward Jones, *Musical and Poetical Relicks of the Welsh Bards*, p. 140.
[13] Edgar L. Chappell, *Old Whitchurch: The Story of a Glamorgan Parish*, p. 18. The story is also noticed in Frederic Evans, *Tir Iarll*, p. 59.
[14] Owen Rhoscomyl, *Flame-Bearers of Welsh History* (1905), p. 211.
[15] Paul Remfry, *Castles of Radnorshire*, p. 62.
[16] A. D. Carr, 'Wales: Economy and Society', pp. 125-40 of S. H. Rigby (ed.), *A Companion to Britain in the Later Middle Ages* (Blackwell, 2003); p. 136.
[17] Jeremy Black, *A New History of Wales* (Sutton, 2000), p. 70.
[18] Peter Berresford Ellis, *Wales: A Nation Again* (Tandem, 1968), p. 38.
[19] T. Jones-Pierce, *Medieval Welsh Society: Selected Essays* (ed. J. B. Smith; Cardiff, 1972), p. 437. David Stephenson, *The Governance of Gwynedd*, p. 106, perhaps more accurately refers to Madog as a 'rebel prince'. Pete Brown, Peter King and Paul Remfry, 'Whittington Castle: The Marcher Fortress of the fitz Warin Family', pp. 106-27 of *Shropshire History and Archaeology* Vol. LXXIX (2004), give 'Prince Madog ap Llywelyn' (p. 109).

APPENDIX 1

In addition to the 1308 petition by the burgesses of Harlech, Madog is referred to as being a 'prince' or 'prince of Wales' in the following contemporary or near-contemporary documents and chronicles.

Bartholomew Cotton (*Historia Anglicana*, p. 282): 'Sed Madoke Thlwellyn, qui nominavit se principem North-walliæ, fugit ab exercitu regis'

Trivet (*Nicholae Triveti Annales*, p. 338): 'Circa festum vero S. Laurentii, Madocus, qui se principem Walliæ fecerat, captus et Londonias adductus, perpetuæ custodiæ mancipatur'

Annales de Wigornia (Annals of Worcester), Vol. 4, p. 356: 'Madocus ap Lewelini [c]orum princeps'

Chronica Monasterii de Melsa, Vol. 2, p. 259: 'Tnadem. Castro de Snowdona ab Anglis reaccepto, Wallensibus undique profugatis, rex ipsum Moadocum, qui se fecerat principem Walliæ nuncupari, et Morganum capiebat...'

Annals of Dunstable, p. 387: 'quem Wallenses principem sibi fecerant'

Record of Caernarvon, p. 220: 'Madoc ap Lewelin qui se fecit Principem Walliae in ultima guerra'

John of Sandall's pay roll: 'Maddok ap Thlewelyn, qui se facit principem' (noticed by J. G. Edwards, 'The Battle of Maes Madog and the Welsh Campaign of 1294-5', pp. 1-12 of *English History Review* Vol. 39 (1924); p. 8)

The Hagnaby chronicle: 'principem nomine Madoch' (see Michael Prestwich, 'A new account of the Welsh campaign of 1294-5', pp. 89-92 of *Welsh History Review* Vol. 6 (1972-3)), and on several other occasions

The *Chronicle of Pierre de Langtoft* describes Madog as prince on two occasions, the first of which is quoted below (Vol. II, pp. 216-7):

En la Walesserye un rybald est mountez,
Ke quidayt ke ly rays fust outre mer alez;
Snaudon ad saisy cum ses herytez,
Se fet apeler prynce par noun des parentez.

[In the Welshery [Wales] a ribald is risen,
Who believed that the King was gone beyond sea;
He has seized Snowdon as his heritage,
Caused himself to be entitled prince by name of kindred.]

In addition, E. A. Lewis cites an example in a 1295 letter written in French by Edward I in *The Medieval Boroughs of Snowdonia*, p. 228. It ought to be noted that this is not an exhaustive list of published references; and doubtless there are other references in a similar vein in English administrative documents yet to be calendared or published.

BIBLIOGRAPHY

Michael Altschul, *A Baronial Family in Medieval England: The Clares, 1217-1314* (John Hopkins Press, 1965).
'R. W. B.', 'Caerphilly', pp. 161-74 of *Archaeologia Cambrensis* Vol. 3 (Fifth Series) (1886).
G. W. S. Barrow, *Kingship and Unity: Scotland 1000-1306* (Edward Arnold, 1981).
R. Allen Brown, H. M. Colvin and A. J. Taylor (eds.), *The History of the King's Works Vol. 1: The Middle Ages* (HMSO, 1969).
P. C. Bartrum, *Welsh Genealogies A.D. 300-1400* (8 vols.; Cardiff, 1974).
E. Besly, 'Short Cross and other medieval coins from Llanfaes, Anglesey', pp. 46-82 of *British Numismatic Journal* Vol. 65 (1995).
M. Bevan-Evans, *Mold and Moldsdale* (Flint County Library, 1949).
Jeremy Black, *A New History of Wales* (Sutton, 2000).
Marc Bloch, *Feudal Society* (2 vols.; Routledge and Kegan Paul, 1962).
G. T. O. Bridgeman, *History of the Princes of South Wales* (1876).
– *The Princes of Upper Powys* (1862).
Pete Brown, Peter King and Paul Remfry, 'Whittington Castle: The Marcher Fortress of the fitz Warin Family', pp. 106-27 of *Shropshire History and Archaeology* Vol. LXXIX (2004).
R. Allen Brown, H. M. Colvin and A. J. Taylor (eds.), *The History of the King's Works Vol. 1: The Middle Ages* (HMSO, 1969).
L. A. S. Butler, 'Medieval Finds From Castell-Y-Bere, Merioneth', pp. 78-112 of *Archaeologia Cambrensis* Vol. CXXIII (1974).
Calendar of Inquisitions Post Mortem Edward I Vol. 4 (HMSO, 1913)
Calendar of Patent Rolls 1292-1301.
A. D. Carr, "The last and weakest of his line': Dafydd ap Gruffydd, the last Prince of Wales', pp. 375-99 of *Welsh History Review* Vol. 19 No. 3 (Cardiff, June 1999).
– 'An aristocracy in decline: the native Welsh lords after the Edwardian Conquest', pp. 103-29 of *Welsh History Review* Vol. 5 (1970-1).
– 'Madog ap Llywelyn: The Revolt of 1294-5 in Caernarfonshire', pp. 35-46 of *Caernarfonshire Historical Society Transactions* Vol. 58 (1997).
– 'Wales: Economy and Society', pp. 125-40 of S. H. Rigby (ed.), *A Companion to Britain in the Later Middle Ages* (Blackwell, 2003).
– *Medieval Wales* (Macmillan, 1995).
– *Medieval Anglesey* (Anglesey Antiquarian Society, 1982).
A. D. Carr and Glenda Carr, *Cestyll Gwynedd* (Cadw, 1985).
D. J. Cathcart King and J. Clifford Perks, 'Llangibby Castle', pp. 96-132 of *Archaeologia Cambrensis* Vol. 105 (1956).
Edgar L. Chappell, *Old Whitchurch: The Story of a Glamorgan Parish* (Merton Priory, 1945 (1994)).
T. M. Charles-Edwards, Morfydd E. Owen and Paul Russell (eds.), *The Welsh King and his Court* (Cardiff, 2000).
Theodore M. Chotzen, 'Welsh History in the Continuation of the 'Spiegel Historiael' by Lodewijk van Velthem', pp. 42-54 of the *Bulletin of the Board of Celtic Studies* Vol. 7 (1954).
E. J. L. Cole, 'The Castles of Maelienydd', pp. 3-19 of *The Radnorshire Society Transactions* Vol. 16 (December 1946).
F. G. Cowley, 'Gilbert de Clare, earl of Gloucester (the Red Earl) and the Cistercians of south-eastern Wales', pp. 115-24 of *Archaeologia Cambrensis* Vol. 154 (2005).
H. Helen Davies, *Schedule of the Elwes Collection* (National Library of Wales, 1976).
J. Barry Davies, *The Freemen and Ancient Borough of Llantrisant* (Llantrisant and District Local

History Society, 1989).
James Conway Davies (ed.), *The Welsh Assize Roll 1277-1284* (Cardiff, 1940).
John Davies, *A History of Wales* (Penguin, 1993).
R. R. Davies, *The Age of Conquest: Wales 1063-1415* (Oxford, 2000).
– *The Revolt of Owain Glyndŵr* (Oxford, 1995).
Sean Davies, *Welsh Military Institutions 633-1283* (Cardiff, 2004).
The Dictionary of Welsh Biography down to 1940 (Society of Cymmrodorion, 1959).
Sean Duffy, 'The Bruce Brothers and the Irish Sea World, 1306-29', pp. 55-86 of *Cambridge Medieval Celtic Studies* No. 21 (1991).
Diana Dunn (ed.), *War and Society in Medieval and Early Modern Britain* (Liverpool, 2000).
H. P. Edwards, *A History of Caerphilly* (Cowbridge, 1975).
J. G. Edwards, 'The Battle of Maes Madog and the Welsh Campaign of 1294-5', pp. 1-12 of *English History Review* Vol. 39 (1924).
– 'The Site of the Battle of 'Meismeidoc', 1295', pp. 262-5 of *English History Review* Vol. 46 (1931).
– 'Madog ap Llywelyn, the Welsh leader in 1294-5', pp. 207-10 of the *Bulletin of the Board of Celtic Studies* Vol. XIII Part. 4 (May 1950).
– 'Edward I's Castle Building in Wales' (Proceedings of British Academy, 1944).
– (ed.) *Calendar of Ancient Correspondence concerning Wales* (Cardiff, 1935).
Owen M. Edwards, *Wales* (1907).
Peter Berresford Ellis, *Wales: A Nation Again* (Tandem, 1968).
T. P. Ellis, *The First Extent of Bromfield and Yale* (Society of Cymmrodorion, 1924).
C. J. O. Evans, *Glamorgan: Its History and Topography* (William Lewis, 1938).
– *Monmouthshire: Its History and Topography* (William Lewis, 1953).
E. D. Evans, 'Castell Y Bere', pp.31-44 of *The Journal of the Merioneth Historical and Record Society* Vol. 3 (1957-60).
– 'Was There A Borough of Bere?', pp. 290-5 of the *Journal of the Merioneth Historical and Records Society* Vol. X Part 4 (1989).
Frederic Evans, *Tir Iarll* (Educational Publishing Company, 1912).
Ian Fleming, *Owain's First Victory* (Y Lolfa, 2001).
Robin Frame, *The Political Development of the British Isles 1100-1400* (Clarendon, 1995).
E. B. Fryde (ed.), *Book of Prests of the King's Wardrobe for 1294-5* (Oxford, 1962).
Natalie M. Fryde, 'A Royal Enquiry into Abuses: Queen Eleanor's ministers in north-eastern Wales, 1291-2', pp. 366-76 of *Welsh History Review* Vol. 5 (1970-1).
– *List of Welsh Entries in the Memoranda Rolls 1282-1343* (Cardiff, 1974).
– 'Welsh Troops in the Scottish Campaign of 1322', pp. 82-9 of the *Bulletin of the Board of Celtic Studies* Vol. XXVI (1974-5).
Cledwyn Fychan, 'Bleddyn Fychan a Gwrthryfel Madog ap Llywelyn, 1294-5', pp. 15-22 of *Transactions of the Denbighshire Historical Society* Vol. 49 (2000).
Alexander Grant, *Independence and Nationhood: Scotland 1306-1469* (Edinburgh, 1984).
Thomas Grey, *The Buried City of Kenfig* (T. Fisher Unwin, 1909).
John Griffiths, 'The Revolt of Madog ap Llywelyn, 1294-5', pp. 12-24 of *Transactions of the Caernarvonshire Historical Society* Vol. 16 (1955).
– 'The Revolt of 1295 and its effects upon the Edwardian Settlement in the Principality of Wales', unpublished BA thesis, University of Liverpool, 1932.
R. A. Griffiths, 'Morgan ap Maredudd', p. 95 of *The Oxford Dictionary of National Biography* Vol. 39 (Oxford, 2004).
– (ed.), *Boroughs of Medieval Wales* (Cardiff, 1978).
– *Conquerors and Conquered in Medieval Wales* (Alan Sutton Publishing, 1984).
Ken Lloyd Gruffudd, 'The Development of the coal industry in Flintshire to 1740',

unpublished MA thesis, Prifysgol Cymru Bangor, 1981.
– 'Maritime Wales' import trade during the later Middle Ages Part I', pp. 7-28 of *Cymru a'r Môr/Maritime Wales* No. 27 (2006).
J. S. Hamilton, 'Henry de Lacy', pp. 181-3 of the *Oxford Dictionary of National Biography* Vol. 32 (Oxford, 2004).
Rhŷs W. Hays, *The History of the Abbey of Aberconway* 1186-1537 (Cardiff, 1963).
Raymond Howell, 'Development by Design: An Investigation of Thirteenth-Century Industrialization and Urban Growth at Trelech, Gwent', pp. 211-22 of *Studia Celtica* Vol. XXXIV (2000).
The Rev. Canon C. Z. Hulbert-Powell, 'Allusions to the Isle of Anglesey in the Itinerarium of William Worcester', pp. 25-37 of *Transactions of the Anglesey Antiquarian Society and Field Club* (1949).
R. Ian Jack, 'Records of Denbighshire Lordships II: The Lordship of Dyffryn Clwyd in 1324', pp. 7-53 of *Denbighshire Historical Society Transactions* Vol. 17 (1968).
Brian Ll. James and David J. Francis, *Cowbridge and Llanblethian: Past and Present* (D. Brown and Sons, 1979).
Arthur Jones (ed.), *Flintshire Ministers Accounts 1301-1328* (Flintshire Historical Society, 1913).
Edward Jones, *Musical and Poetical Relicks of the Welsh Bards* (1784).
Francis Jones, 'Welsh bonds for keeping the peace, 1283 and 1295', pp. 142-4 of the *Bulletin of the Board of Celtic Studies* Vol. XIII (1950).
Glanville R. J. Jones, 'The Defences of Gwynedd in the Thirteenth Century', pp. 29-43 of *Transactions of the Caernarvonshire Historical Society* Vol. 30 (1969).
Thomas Jones (ed.), *Brut Y Tywysogyon* (Peniarth Ms. 20 version) (Cardiff, 1952).
T. Jones-Pierce, 'Madog', p. 608 of *The Dictionary of Welsh Biography down to 1940* (Society of Cymmrodorion, 1959).
– 'Morgan ap Maredudd', p. 637 of *The Dictionary of Welsh Biography down to 1940* (Society of Cymmrodorion, 1959).
– 'Maelgwn ap Rhys', pp. 609-10 of *The Dictionary of Welsh Biography down to 1940* (Society of Cymmrodorion, 1959).
– *Medieval Welsh Society: Selected Essays* (ed. J. B. Smith; Cardiff, 1972).
Edward Lewis, *The History of Little England beyond Wales* (1888; Dyfed County Council, 1995).
E. A. Lewis, *The Medieval Boroughs of Wales* (London, 1912).
– 'Industry and Commerce in Medieval Wales', pp. 121-73 of *Transactions of the Royal Historical Society* Vol. XVII (1903).
W. J. Lewis, *Lead Mining in Wales* (Cardiff, 1967).
John E. Lloyd (ed.), *A History of Carmarthenshire* Vol. 1 (London Carmarthenshire Society, 1935).
– *Owen Glendower* (Oxford, 1931).
– *A History of Wales* (2 vols., Longmans, 1912).
Humphrey Llwyd, *Cronica Walliae* (ed. Ieuan M. Williams, Cardiff, 2002).
Henry Richards Luard (ed.), *Bartholomew Cotton, Historia Anglicana* (1859).
– *Annales Monastici* Vol. III: *Annales Prioratus de Dunstapla* (Annals of Dunstable) (1866).
– *Annales Monastici* Vol. IV: *Annales Monasterii de Oseneia* (Osney); *Annales de Wigornia* (Annals of Worcester) (1869).
– *Chronica Monasterii de Melsa* (1867).
– *Flores Historiarum* Vol. III AD. 1265-1326 (1890).
J. D. Mackie, *A History of Scotland* (Penguin, 1964).
Trevor J. Miles, 'Flint: Excavations at the Castle and on the Town Defences, 1971-1974', pp. 67-151 of *Archaeologia Cambrensis* Vol. CXLV (1998).

O. Morien Morgan, *A History of Wales* (Howell, 1911).
Prys Morgan, 'The Welsh At Calais', pp. 181-5 of *Welsh History Review* Vol. 2 (1964).
R. Morgan, 'The Barony of Powys, 1275-1360', pp. 1-34 of *Welsh History Review* Vol. 10 (1980-1).
Thomas Owen Morgan, 'The Insurrection of Maelgwn Fychan', p. 290-300 of *Archaeologia Cambrensis* Vol. 5 (New Series) (1854).
– 'Thesseweit', pp. 87-9 of *Montgomeryshire Collections* Vol. 68 (1980).
J. E. Morris, *The Welsh Wars of Edward I* (Oxford, 1901).
Cynthia J. Neville, *Native Lordship in Medieval Scotland: The Earldoms of Strathearn and Lennox, c. 1140-1365* (Four Courts Press, 2005).
Nicholae Triveti Annales (ed. Thomas Hog; 1845).
B. H. St. J. O'Neil, 'Cricieth Castle, Caernarvonshire', pp. 1-51 of *Archaeologia Cambrensis* Vol. 98 (1944-5).
Aliki Pantos and Sarah Semple (eds.), *Assembly Places and Practices in Medieval Europe* (Four Courts Press, 2004).
Julian Pettifer, *Welsh Castles* (Boydell, 2000).
Neil Phillips, 'Abergavenny Castle 1087-1537', pp. 17-31 of *Gwent Local History* Vol. 88 (Spring 2000).
David Powel, *A Historie of Cambria* (1584).
– (rev. Richard Llwyd) *The History of Wales* (1832).
Hulbert-Powell, 'Allusions to the Isle of Anglesey in the Itinerarium of William Worcester', pp. 25-7 of *Anglesey Antiquarian Society Transactions* (1949)
Maurice Powicke, *The Thirteenth Century: 1216-1307* (Oxford, 1953).
Derrick Pratt, 'Wrexham Militia in the Fourteenth Century', pp. 26-40 of *Denbighshire Historical Society Transactions* Vol. 12 (1963).
– 'The Medieval Borough of Holt', pp. 9-74 of *Denbighshire Historical Society Transactions* Vol. 14 (1965).
Michael Prestwich, 'A new account of the Welsh campaign of 1294-5', pp. 89-92 of *Welsh History Review* Vol. 6 (1972-3).
– *Edward I* (Yale Univ. Press, 1997).
Glanville Price (ed.), *Languages in Britain and Ireland* (Blackwell, 2000).
S. G. Priestley and R. C. Turner, 'Three Castles of the Clare Family in Monmouthshire during the thirteenth and fourteenth centuries', pp. 9-52 of *Archaeologia Cambrensis* Vol. 152 (2003).
Huw Pryce (ed.), *The Acts of Welsh Rulers 1120-1283* (Cardiff, 2004).
– 'Owain Gwynedd and Louis VII: the Franco-Welsh diplomacy of the first Prince of Wales', pp. 1-28 of *Welsh History Review* Vol. 19 No. 1 (June 1998).
– 'Welsh Rulers and the Written Word, 1120-1283', pp. 75-88 of Peter Thorau, Sabine Penth and Rüdiger Fuchs (eds.), *Regionen Europas – Europa der Regionen: Festschrift für Kurt-Ulrich Jäschke zum 65. Geburtstag* (Böhlau Verlag Köln Weimar Wien, 2003).
– (ed.) *Literacy in Medieval Celtic Societies* (Cambridge, 1998).
T. B. Pugh (ed.), *Glamorgan County History Vol. 3: The Middle Ages* (Cardiff, 1971).
The Record of Caernarvon.
Peter Reese, *Wallace: A Biography* (Canongate, 1996).
William Rees, *An Historical Atlas of Wales* (Cardiff, 1951 (Faber and Faber, 1959)).
Paul Remfry, *Castles of Radnorshire* (Logaston, 1995).
Derek Renn and Richard Avent, *Flint Castle and Ewloe Castle* (Cadw, 1995).
Gweirydd ap Rhys, *Hanes y Brytaniaid a'r Cymry* (2 vols., London, 1874).
A. J. Richard, 'Kenfig Castle', pp. 161-216 of *Archaeologia Cambrensis* Vol. 82 (1927).
H. P. Richards, *A History of Caerphilly* (D. Brown and Sons, 1975).

Melville Richards, *Welsh Administrative and Territorial Units: Medieval and Modern* (Cardiff, 1969).
Michael Richter, 'David ap Llywelyn, the first Prince of Wales', pp. 205-19 of *Welsh History Review* Vol. 5 (1970-1).
Owen Rhoscomyl, *Flame-Bearers of Welsh History* (1905).
Glyn Roberts, 'Biographical notes: Madog ap Llywelyn', pp. 41-9 of the *Bulletin of the Board of Celtic Studies* Vol. XVII (1956).
– 'Wales and England: Antipathy and Sympathy, 1282-1485', pp. 375-396 of *Welsh History Review* Vol. 1 (1963).
Richard Arthur Roberts, *The Court Rolls of the Lordship of Ruthin or Dyffryn-Clwyd* (Cymmrodorion Society, 1893).
Rotula Parliamentorum Edward I, Vol. 1.
The Royal Commission on the Ancient and Historic Monuments and Constructions in Wales and Monmouthshire Vol. 1: Montgomery (HMSO, 1911).
The Royal Commission on the Ancient Monuments in Wales and Monmouthshire, Vol. 6: Merioneth (HMSO, 1921).
Mary Salmon, *A Source-Book of Welsh History* (Oxford, 1927).
George Sandford, 'Cefn Digoll', pp. 55-62 of *Montgomeryshire Collections* Vol. 8 (1875).
D. Simon-Evans, *A Mediaeval Prince of Wales: The Life of Gruffudd ap Cynan* (Llanerch, 1990).
J. Beverley Smith, *Llywelyn ap Gruffudd: Prince of Wales* (Cardiff, 1998).
– (ed.) *A History of Merioneth Vol. 2: The Middle Ages* (Cardiff, 2001).
– 'Edward II and the allegiance of Wales', pp. 139-71 of *Welsh History Review* Vol. 8 (1976-7).
Llinos Beverley Smith, 'The Death of Llywelyn ap Gruffudd: The Narratives Reconsidered', *Welsh History Review* Vol. 14 (1982-3), pp. 200-214.
Ian N. Soulsby, 'Trelech: A Decayed Borough of Medieval Gwent', pp. 41-4 of *The Monmouthshire Antiquary: Proceedings of the Monmouthshire Antiquarian Association* Vol. 4, Parts 3 and 4 (1981-2).
– *The Towns of Medieval Wales* (Phillimore, 1983).
C. J. Spurgeon, 'Builth Castle', pp. 47-59 of *Brycheiniog* Vol. XVIII (1978-9) (Brecknock Society).
– 'The Medieval Town Defences of Glamorgan', pp. 161-212 of *Studia Celtica* Vol. XXXV (2001).
David Stephenson, *The Governance of Gwynedd* (Cardiff, 1984).
– '*Fouke Le Fitz Waryn* and Llywelyn ap Gruffydd's claim to Whittington', pp. 26-31 of *Shropshire History and Archaeology: Transactions of the Shropshire Archaeological and Historical Society* Vol. LXXVII (2004).
A. J. Taylor, 'Scorched Earth at Flint in 1294', pp. 89-105 of *The Journal of the Flintshire Historical Society* Vol. 30 (1981-2).
– 'Building at Caernarvon and Beaumaris in 1295-6', pp. 61-6 of *Bulletin of the Board of Celtic Studies* Vol. 15 Part 1 (1952).
– *The King's Works in Wales*, 1277-1330 (London (HMSO), 1974).
Avril Thomas, 'Interconnections between the lands of Edward I: A Welsh-English Mercenary Force in Ireland, 1285-1304', pp. 135-47 of the *Bulletin of the Board of Celtic Studies* Vol. 40 (1993).
R. F. Treharne, *Essays On Thirteenth Century England* (The Historical Association, 1971).
Roger Turvey, *The Lord Rhys: Prince of Deheubarth* (Gomer, 1997).
– *The Welsh Princes: The Native Rulers of Wales 1063-1283* (Pearson Education, 2002).
– *Llywelyn the Great* (Gomer, 2007).
Jean Verdon (transl. George Holoch), *Travel in the Middle Ages* (Notre Dame, 2003).

David Walker, *Medieval Wales* (Cambridge, 1990).
R. F. Walker, 'The Hagnaby Chronicle and the Battle of Maes Moydog', pp. 125-38 of *Welsh History Review* Vol. 8 (1972-3).
– 'The Welsh War of 1294-5', pp. xxvi-liii of *Book of Prests of the King's Wardrobe for 1294-5*, ed. E. B. Fryde (Oxford, 1962).
W. H. Waters, *The Edwardian Settlement of North Wales in its Administrative and Legal Aspects 1284-1343* (Cardiff, 1935).
B. Wilkinson, *The Constitutional History of England 1216-1399* (Longmans, 1948).
David H. Williams, *Atlas of Cistercian Lands in Wales* (Cardiff, 1990).
Gwyn A. Williams, *When Was Wales?* (Penguin, 1985).
Keith Williams-Jones, *The Merioneth Lay Subsidy Roll 1292-3* (Cardiff, 1976).
John Wynne, *Hanes Sir a Thre Caernarfon* (1861).
W. W. E. Wynne, 'Harlech Castle', pp. 21-31 of *Archaeologia Cambrensis* Vol. 6 (Fourth Series) (1875).
Philip Ziegler, *The Black Death* (Collins, 1969).

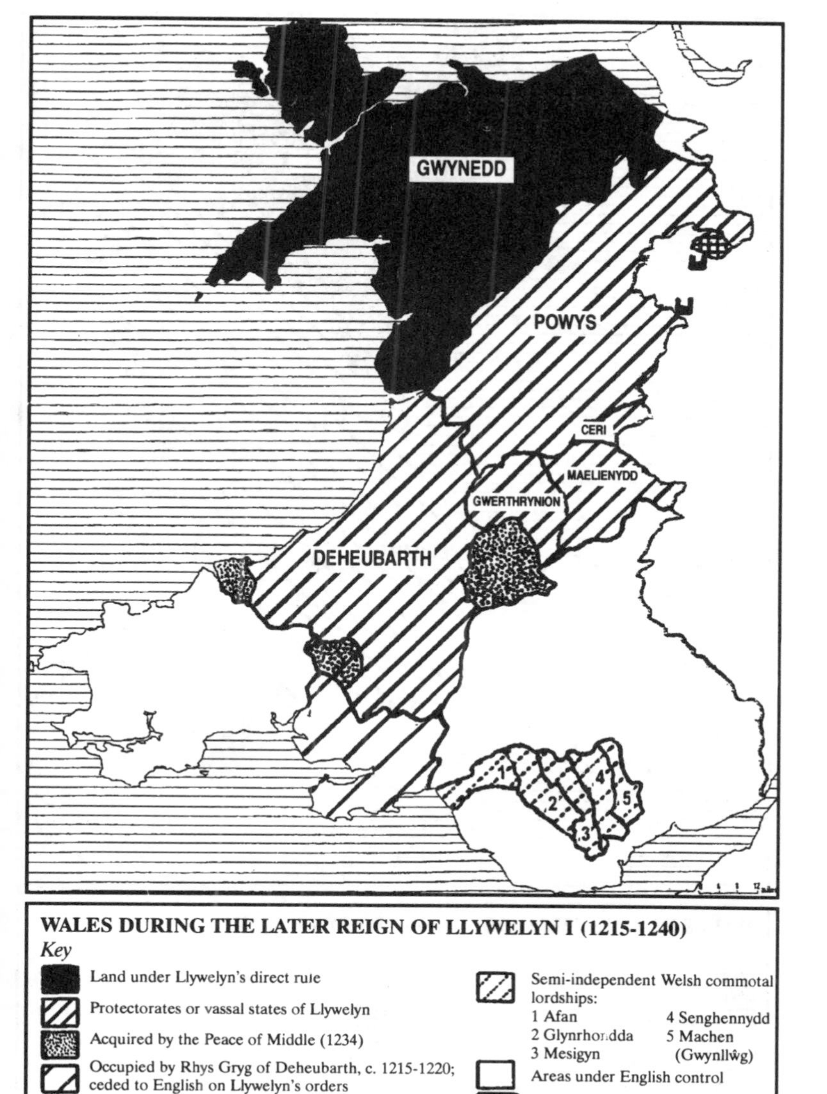

WALES DURING THE LATER REIGN OF LLYWELYN I (1215-1240)

Key

- Land under Llywelyn's direct rule
- Protectorates or vassal states of Llywelyn
- Acquired by the Peace of Middle (1234)
- Occupied by Rhys Gryg of Deheubarth, c. 1215-1220; ceded to English on Llywelyn's orders
- English castles temporarily occupied by Llywelyn in 1223
- Semi-independent Welsh commotal lordships:
  1 Afan
  2 Glynrhondda
  3 Mesigyn
  4 Senghennydd
  5 Machen (Gwynllŵg)
- Areas under English control
- Effectively under Welsh control

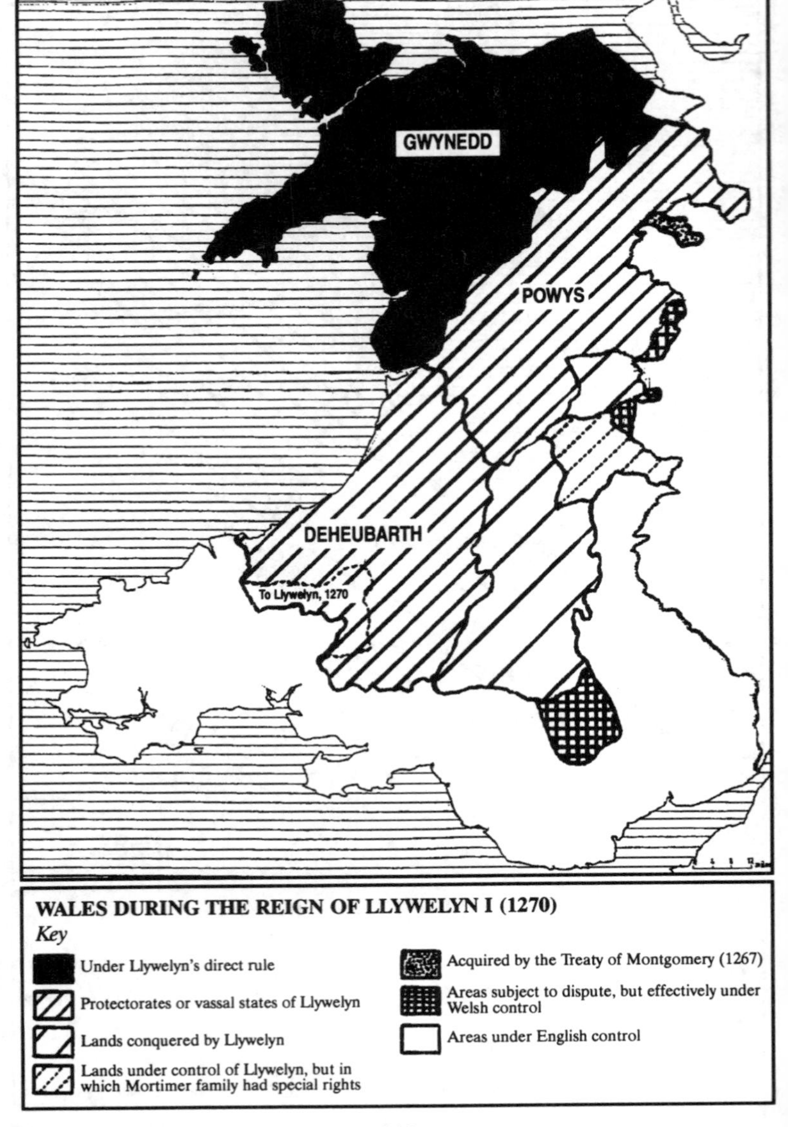

WALES DURING THE REIGN OF LLYWELYN I (1270)

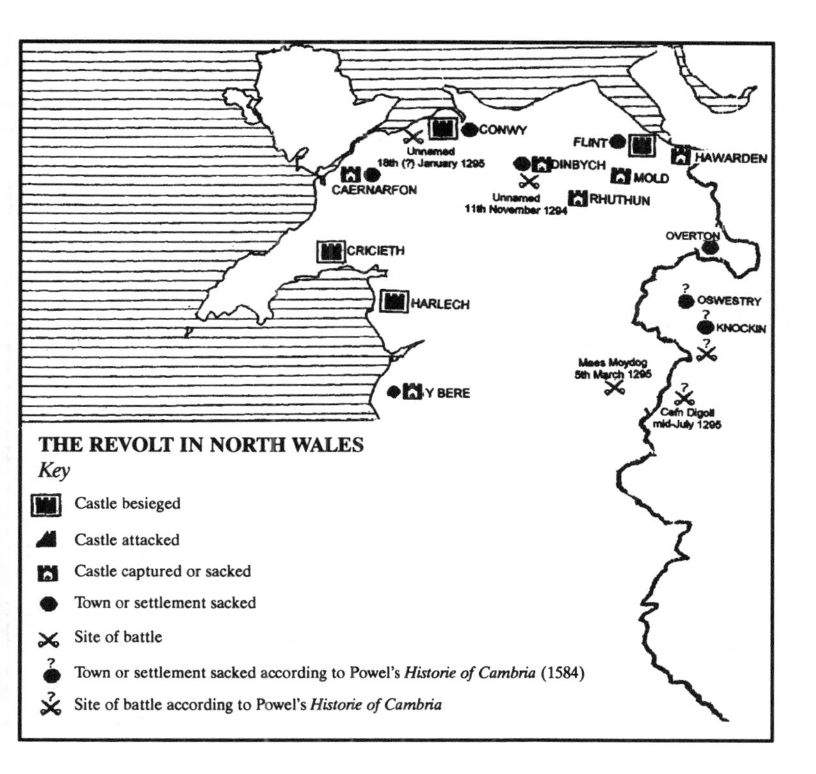
CONWY
Unnamed
18th (?) January 1295
CAERNARFON
FLINT
HAWARDEN
DINBYCH
MOLD
Unnamed
11th November 1294
RHUTHUN
OVERTON
CRICIETH
HARLECH
OSWESTRY
KNOCKIN
Maes Moydog
5th March 1295
Y BERE
Cefn Digoll
mid-July 1295
THE REVOLT IN NORTH WALES
Key
Castle besieged
Castle attacked
Castle captured or sacked
Town or settlement sacked
Site of battle
Town or settlement sacked according to Powel's Historie of Cambria (1584)
Site of battle according to Powel's Historie of Cambria

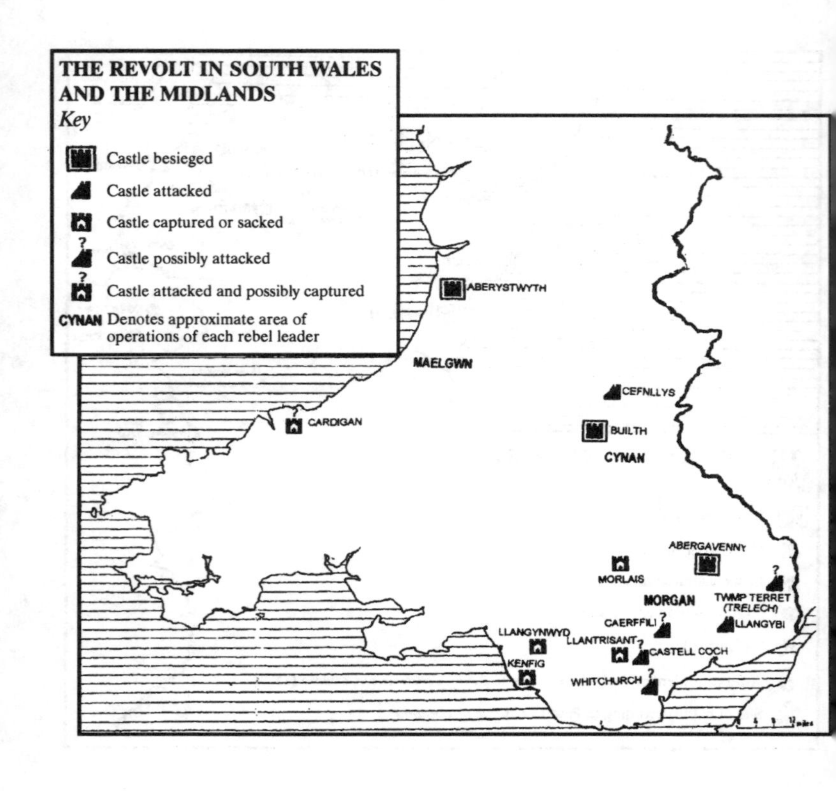
THE REVOLT IN SOUTH WALES AND THE MIDLANDS
Key
Castle besieged
Castle attacked
Castle captured or sacked
Castle possibly attacked
Castle attacked and possibly captured
CYNAN Denotes approximate area of operations of each rebel leader
ABERYSTWYTH
MAELGWN
CARDIGAN
CEFNLLYS
BUILTH
CYNAN
ABERGAVENNY
MORLAIS
MORGAN
TWMP TERRET
(TRELECH)
CAERFFILI
LLANGYBI
LLANGYNWYD
LLANTRISANT
CASTELL COCH
KENFIG
WHITCHURCH

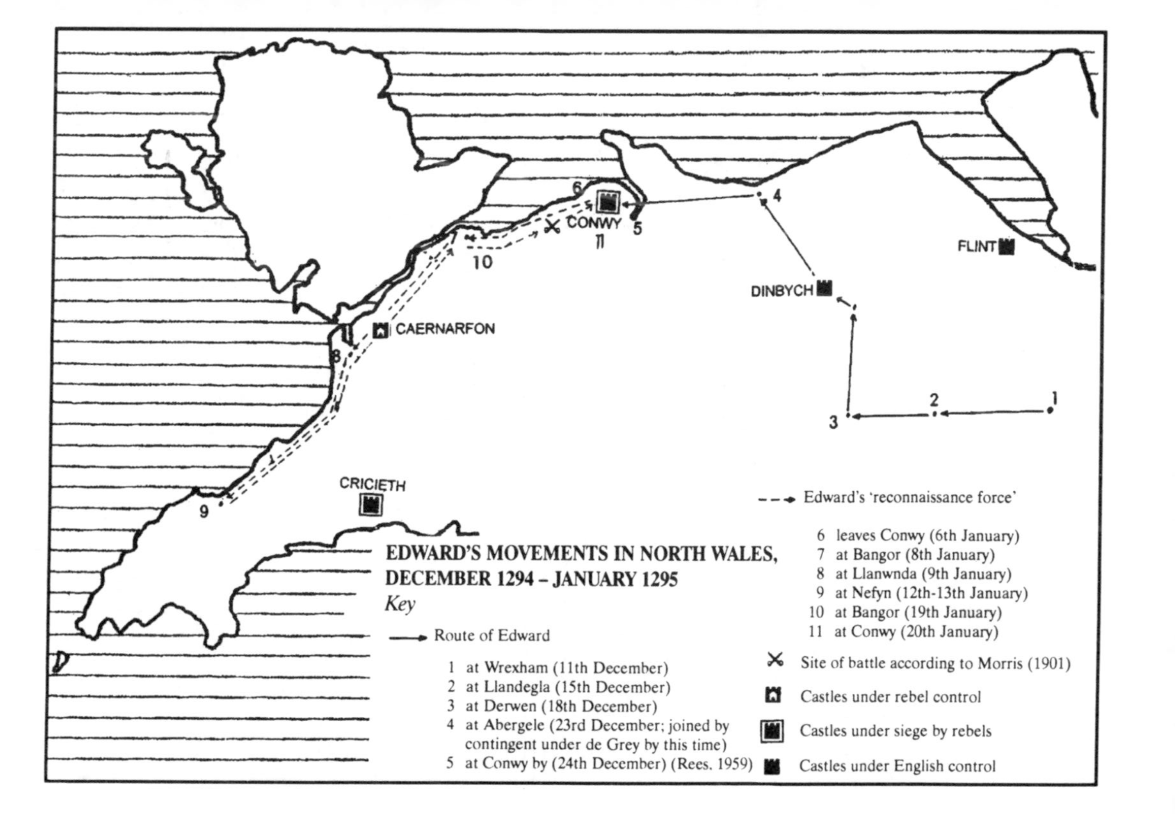

CONWY
CAERNARFON
DINBYCH
FLINT
CRICIETH
EDWARD'S MOVEMENTS IN NORTH WALES,
DECEMBER 1294 – JANUARY 1295
Key
Route of Edward
1 at Wrexham (11th December)
2 at Llandegla (15th December)
3 at Derwen (18th December)
4 at Abergele (23rd December; joined by contingent under de Grey by this time)
5 at Conwy by (24th December) (Rees, 1959)
Edward's 'reconnaissance force'
6 leaves Conwy (6th January)
7 at Bangor (8th January)
8 at Llanwnda (9th January)
9 at Nefyn (12th-13th January)
10 at Bangor (19th January)
11 at Conwy (20th January)
Site of battle according to Morris (1901)
Castles under rebel control
Castles under siege by rebels
Castles under English control

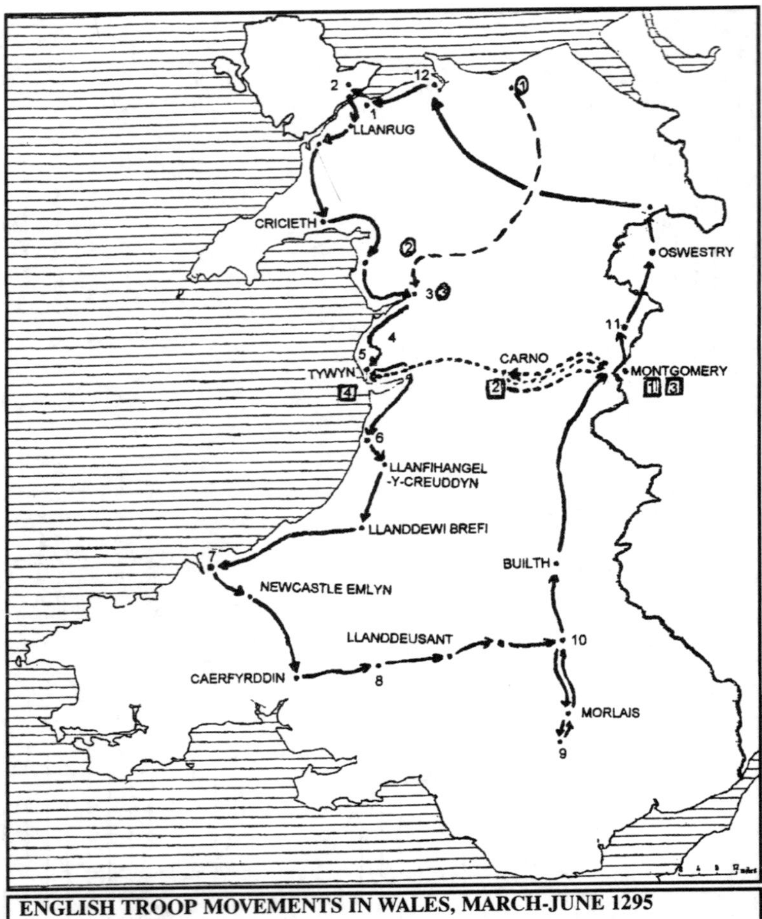

ENGLISH TROOP MOVEMENTS IN WALES, MARCH-JUNE 1295

Key

Route of Edward's army after leaving Conwy:
1 at Bangor (8th-9th April)
2 at Llanfaes (10th April – 6th May)
3 at Dolgellau (11th-12th May)
4 at Talybont (15th May)
5 at Tywyn (16th-18th May)
6 at Aberystwyth (20th-24th May)
7 at Cardigan (1st June)
8 at Dryslwyn (6th June)
9 at Merthyr Tudful (13th-15th June)
10 at Brecon (16th June)
11 at Welshpool (21st-24th June)
12 at Conwy (30th June)

Route of de Grey's army:
①– leaves Rhuddlan (6th March)
②– at 'Ketthlieconham' (April?)
③– joins Edward's army probably at Dolgellau (11th May)

Route of earl of Warwick's army:
1 – leaves Montgomery for operations in upper Severn valley (probably 16th-28th April)
2 – at Carno (25th April)
3 – at Montgomery (30th April–13th May)
4 – joins Edward's army either at Talybont or Tywyn (15th-16th May)

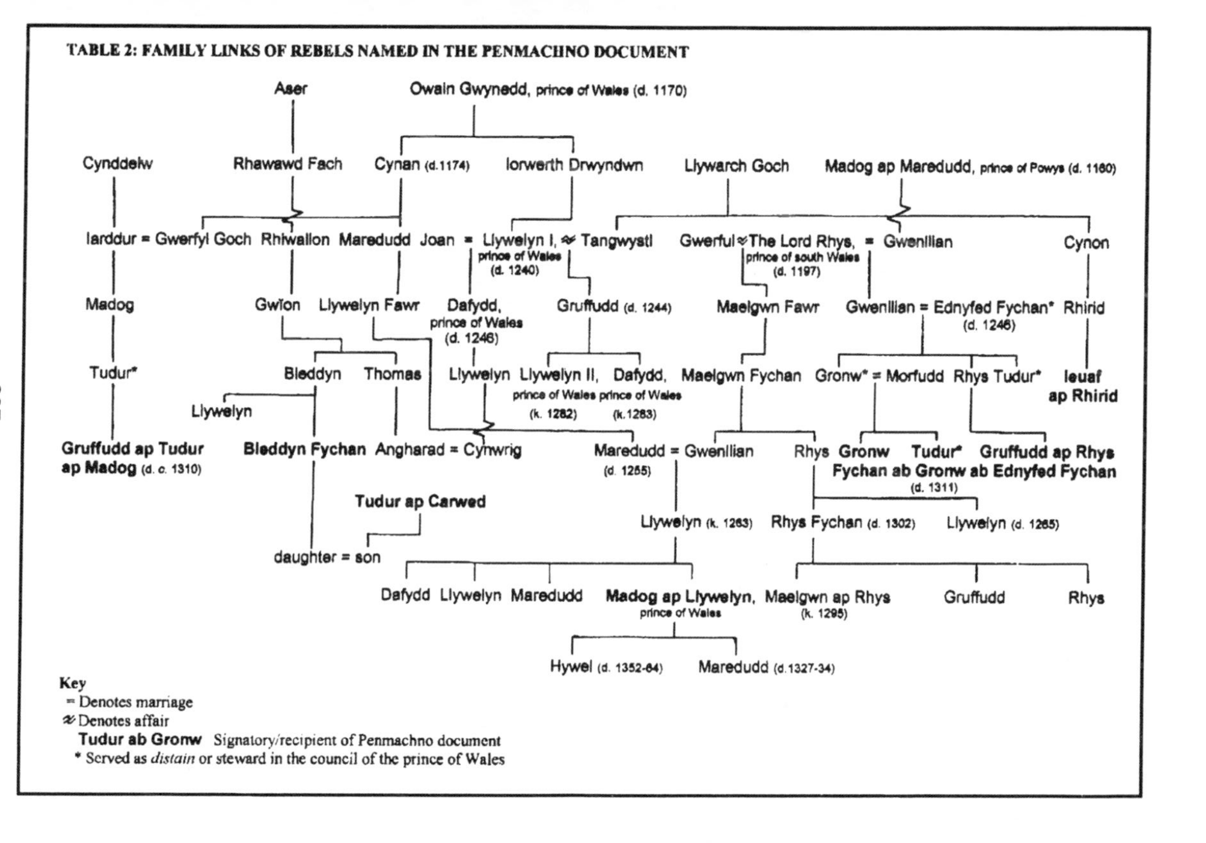
TABLE 2: FAMILY LINKS OF REBELS NAMED IN THE PENMACHNO DOCUMENT
Aser
Owain Gwynedd, prince of Wales (d. 1170)
Cynddelw
Rhawawd Fach
Cynan (d.1174)
Iorwerth Drwyndwn
Llywarch Goch
Madog ap Maredudd, prince of Powys (d. 1160)
Iarddur = Gwerfyl Goch
Rhiwallon
Maredudd
Joan = Llywelyn I, prince of Wales (d. 1240)
Tangwystl
Gwerful
The Lord Rhys, prince of south Wales (d. 1197)
Gwenllian
Cynon
Madog
Gwion
Llywelyn Fawr
Dafydd, prince of Wales (d. 1246)
Gruffudd (d. 1244)
Maelgwn Fawr
Gwenllian = Ednyfed Fychan* (d. 1246)
Rhirid
Tudur*
Bleddyn
Thomas
Llywelyn
Llywelyn II, prince of Wales (k. 1282)
Dafydd, prince of Wales (k.1283)
Maelgwn Fychan
Gronw* = Morfudd
Rhys
Tudur*
Ieuaf ap Rhirid
Llywelyn
Gruffudd ap Tudur ap Madog (d. c. 1310)
Bleddyn Fychan
Angharad = Cynwrig
Maredudd = Gwenllian (d. 1255)
Rhys
Gronw Fychan
Tudur* ab Gronw (d. 1311)
Gruffudd ap Rhys ab Ednyfed Fychan
Tudur ap Carwed
Llywelyn (k. 1263)
Rhys Fychan (d. 1302)
Llywelyn (d. 1265)
daughter = son
Dafydd
Llywelyn
Maredudd
Madog ap Llywelyn, prince of Wales
Maelgwn ap Rhys (k. 1295)
Gruffudd
Rhys
Hywel (d. 1352-64)
Maredudd (d.1327-34)
Key
= Denotes marriage
≉ Denotes affair
Tudur ab Gronw Signatory/recipient of Penmachno document
* Served as distain or steward in the council of the prince of Wales

INDEX